W9-CWE-690

Second Edition

The
Personnel
Evaluation
Standards

The 27 standard statements presented inside the back cover of this book have been approved and declared as an American National Standard by the American National Standards Institute (ANSI/JCSEE 1-2008). *The Personnel Evaluation Standards* describes and elaborates these statements to guide sound evaluations of educators in prekindergarten through graduate schools. This supporting information has not been processed in accordance with ANSI's requirements for an ANS. As such, this supporting information may contain material that has not been subjected to public review or a consensus process. In addition, it does not contain requirements necessary for conformance to the standard.

THE PERSONNEL EVALUATION STANDARDS

How to Assess Systems for Evaluating Educators
Second Edition

THE JOINT COMMITTEE ON STANDARDS
FOR EDUCATIONAL EVALUATION

Arlen R. Gullickson, Chair

Sponsored by

American Association of School Administrators
American Counseling Association
American Educational Research Association
American Evaluation Association
American Indian Higher Education Consortium
American Psychological Association
Association for Supervision and Curriculum Development
Canadian Evaluation Society
Canadian Society for the Study of Education
Consortium for Research on Educational Accountability and Teacher
    Evaluation
Council of Chief State School Officers
National Association of Elementary School Principals
National Association of School Psychologists
National Association of Secondary School Principals
National Council on Measurement in Education
National Education Association
National Legislative Program Evaluation Society

http://jc.wmich.edu/

Second Edition

The
Personnel
Evaluation
Standards

How to Assess Systems
for Evaluating Educators

The Joint Committee on Standards
for Educational Evaluation
Arlen R. Gullickson, Chair
Barbara B. Howard, Task Force Chair

CORWIN PRESS
A SAGE Company

For information:

Corwin Press
A SAGE Company
2455 Teller Road
Thousand Oaks, California 91320
www.corwinpress.com

SAGE Ltd.
1 Oliver's Yard
55 City Road
London EC1Y 1SP
United Kingdom

SAGE Pvt. Ltd.
B 1/I 1 Mohan Cooperative Industrial Area
Mathura Road, New Delhi 110 044
India

SAGE Asia-Pacific Pte. Ltd.
33 Pekin Street #02-01
Far East Square
Singapore 048763

Printed in the United States of America

Library of Congress Cataloging-in-Publication Data

Joint Committee on Standards for Educational Evaluation.
The personnel evaluation standards : how to assess systems for evaluating educators.—2nd ed.
    p. cm.
Prepared under the leadership of Barbara B. Howard and Arlen R. Gullickson.
Includes bibliographical references and index.

ISBN 978-0-7619-7508-3 (cloth)
ISBN 978-0-7619-7509-0 (pbk.)
    1. School personnel management—United States. 2. Education—Standards—United States—Evaluation. 3. Educators—Rating of—Standards—United States—Evaluation.
I. Howard, Barbara B., 1955— II. Gullickson, Arlen R. III. Title.

LB2831.5.J65 2009
371.2'01—dc22   2008022888

This book is printed on acid-free paper.

08   09   10   11   12   10 9 8 7 6 5 4 3 2 1

Senior Acquisitions Editor:	Debra Stollenwerk
Editorial Assistant:	Allison Scott
Production Editor:	Veronica Stapleton
Copy Editor:	Tina Hardy
Typesetter:	C&M Digitals (P) Ltd.
Proofreader:	Dennis W. Webb
Indexer:	Sheila Bodell
Cover Designer:	Lisa Miller

Authors

A task force appointed by the Joint Committee on Standards for Educational Evaluation revised *The Personnel Evaluation Standards.*

Chair

Barbara B. Howard, Appalachian State University, Boone, North Carolina

Members

Peter Airasian, Boston College

Joyce Annuniziata, Miami-Dade County Schools, Florida

Jane Davidson, Western Michigan University

Janet Henderson, Starkville School District, Starkville, Mississippi

Don Klinger, Queen's University, Kingston, Ontario

Jean Miller, Council of Chief State School Officers

Tarrell Awe Agahe Portman, University of Iowa

W. Todd Rogers, University of Alberta

Ann-Marie Ryan, Michigan State University

Other individuals participated in drafting the standards and conducting a literature review.

Jerry Horn, Western Michigan University

Diana Pullin, Boston College

James Sanders, Western Michigan University

Daniel L. Stufflebeam, Western Michigan University

Patricia Wheeler, EREAPA Associates

Pamela Zeller, Western Michigan University

Table of Contents

Functional
Table of Contents

The Functional Table of Contents is intended to provide the user with those standards that are most applicable to the more common situations involving personnel evaluations and, as such, should be considered first before continuing on to other standards. It is not to imply that any standard is of any greater importance or that personnel evaluations should not meet all standards to ensure a sound evaluation.

Training for Evaluators

Most Applicable Standards

Developing a Personnel Evaluation System

Most Applicable Standards

Using Evaluation Results for Staff Development

Most Applicable Standards

Merit Awards, Tenure, or Promotion Decisions

Most Applicable Standards

Evaluating Individuals From Diverse Backgrounds

Most Applicable Standards

Termination Decisions

Most Applicable Standards

The Joint Committee

Ronald Fuller, Terri Duggan Schwartzbeck, and Gary Wegenke, representing the American Association of School Administrators (AASA)

Stephan Henry, Raymond Pecheone, and Mark Wilson, representing the American Educational Research Association (AERA)

Jerry Horn, at-large member

Elmima Johnson, Dianna Newman, and Wendy Tackett, representing the American Evaluation Association (AEA)

Mary Beth Klotz and William Strein, representing the National Association of School Psychologists (NASP)

Brigitte Maicher, James Cullen, and Joan Kruger, representing the Canadian Evaluation Society (CES)

Patricia McDivitt, representing the American Counseling Association (ACA)

Charles Moore, representing the National Association of Secondary School Principals (NASSP)

Michael Resnick, Kevin Hollenbeck, and Darrell Drury, representing the National School Boards Association (NSBA)

Todd Rogers, at-large member

Lyn Shulha and Robert Wilson, representing the Canadian Society for the Study of Education (CSSE)

Donald Yarbrough, representing the National Council on Measurement in Education (NCME)

Pamela Zeller, at-large member

Staff

Dale Farland, Western Michigan University

Mary Ramlow, Western Michigan University

Sally Veeder, Western Michigan University

Acknowledgments

Work on revising these standards began with a grant from the W. K. Kellogg Foundation. Additional financial and in-kind support was provided by the National Science Foundation, the Western Michigan University Evaluation Center, and the organizations that appointed members to the Joint Committee: American Association of School Administrators (AASA), American Counseling Association (ACA), American Educational Research Association (AERA), American Evaluation Association (AEA), American Indian Higher Education Consortium (AIHEC), American Psychological Association (APA), Association for Supervision and Curriculum Development (ASCD), Canadian Evaluation Society (CES), Canadian Society for the Study of Education (CSSE), Consortium for Research on Educational Accountability and Teacher Evaluation (CREATE), Council of Chief State School Officers (CCSSO), Educational Testing Service (ETS), National Association of Elementary School Principals (NAESP), National Association of Secondary School Principals (NASSP), National Association of School Psychologists (NASP), National Council on Measurement in Education (NCME), National Education Association (NEA), National Legislative Program Evaluation Society (NLPES).

Many people assisted the Joint Committee in developing this document, especially the personnel evaluation standards task force led by Barbara B. Howard. The task force surveyed educators to assess needs to be addressed by the revision, incorporated work from previous revision efforts, drafted the revised document, and then improved the document through iterative processes of panel reviews, field tests, and national hearings. Members of the various support groups are listed in Resource C. The Joint Committee thanks those individuals and organizations that helped develop this document. However, the Joint Committee is solely responsible for its contents. The formal endorsement of the sponsoring groups has not been sought or given.

> **Royalties from the sales of the published version of this document will be used to promote effective use of *The Personnel Evaluation Standards* and to support ongoing review and revision activities.**

Invitation to Users

The Personnel Evaluation Standards: How to Assess Systems for Evaluating Educators is the product of a collaborative effort to provide personnel evaluators within the field of education and users of their evaluations with standards and guidelines to improve personnel evaluations and personnel evaluation systems. Our goal is to produce standards to help ensure ethical, useful, feasible, and accurate evaluations of employees.

The Joint Committee on Standards for Educational Evaluation (Joint Committee} requires that consideration be given to revising its standards every five years. We invite you to share your experience in using *The Personnel Evaluation Standards* with the Joint Committee. To help in this process, the Joint Committee has prepared a package containing a letter of acknowledgment, information about the review and revision process, and a supply of feedback forms with directions for their use. The feedback forms request two types of feedback. First, to help us understand the context in which the evaluations were conducted, we would like you to do the following:

- Describe roles and responsibilities of the people—personnel evaluators, evaluatees, supervisors, management, and in-service personnel—involved in the evaluation or evaluation system being examined.
- Provide a summary of the evaluation or evaluation system, including how you applied the standards.
- Describe the data collection methods used and, if possible, provide copies of the instruments that were used.

Within the context, we would like you to do the following:

- Describe any problems you had in applying individual standards.
- Describe any conflicts you found among the standards and how you resolved them.
- Identify terms or terminology that was not clear to you.
- Identify important topics or areas that you think should be covered by the standards.

You may obtain a copy of the package from the Internet at http://jc.wmich.edu/or by contacting the Joint Committee at

The Joint Committee on Standards for Educational Evaluation
The Evaluation Center
Western Michigan University
1903 W. Michigan Avenue
Kalamazoo, MI 49008-5237

The Joint Committee also has developed the form, Checklist for Applying the Standards, that you may wish to attach to evaluation plans, contracts, reports, or other personnel evaluation materials that you reviewed using *The Personnel Evaluation Standards.* The checklist also may be useful when evaluating proposals submitted to develop or conduct personnel evaluations. A copy of the checklist is provided on pages 17–19. You may make as many copies of this form as needed.

Preface

The Personnel Evaluation Standards have now been in print for nearly two decades. During that time, there has been a great deal of work and pressure surrounding schools, administrators, teachers, and student learning. This revision reflects both the changing educational climate and the strong effects of national policy decisions. In particular, the No Child Left Behind Act has pushed accountability of schools and teachers to extremes not seen before in American education. At every turn, educators are beset by calls to improve the quality of teachers and administrators and the processes used to evaluate them. These standards provide strong guidance for such improvement efforts.

When the first edition was published in 1988, it stood alone as an acceptable national guide to evaluating educators. Ensuing years have provided important supporting materials to be used in tandem with these standards. Joint Committee sponsors have prepared two of the best known documents:

The *Interstate School Leaders Licensure Consortium* (ISLLC): *Standards for School Leaders* was developed and published in 1996 by the Council of Chief State School Officers as "common standards for school leaders."

Leading Learning Communities: Standards for What Principals Should Know and Be Able to Do was published by the National Association of Elementary School Principals (NAESP) in 2001.

Alone, *The Personnel Evaluation Standards* provides substantial guidance for educators in how to build and improve their systems for evaluating the qualifications and performance of educators. But we believe standards used in combination with ISLLC and NAESP standards or similar standards will provide stronger, better guidance for education professionals. This book, *The Personnel Evaluation Standards,* provides guidance for how evaluations are to be conducted, while both the ISLLC and NAESP standards provide direction as to what their respective organizations value in the qualities of school leaders and expect in terms of productivity. As such, the ISLLC and NAESP materials describe and set standards for what professionals are to achieve. *The Personnel Evaluation Standards* calls for the use of such parameters and enjoins evaluators to address such matters with careful attention to the propriety, utility, feasibility, and accuracy of their evaluations. Above all, by following the standards set forward in this book, school leaders can be assured that they are conducting themselves in ways that are productive, valued by the profession, and that produce sound evaluative findings for serving student learning in schools.

Personnel evaluation is by its very nature a difficult task—too often it is done poorly with detrimental outcomes; too seldom it is done well with positive results. Use of these standards can make the difference by providing evaluations that uplift our education systems. Teachers who have been "mis-evaluated" will appreciate this book because it provides strong guidance for what should be done as well as common errors in evaluation. Teachers who find themselves in difficulty because of a poorly constructed or conducted evaluation will find that these standards, which carry the weight of the profession, can be a powerful advocate and defense. Importantly, principals and teachers who use these standards as guides to help build sound personnel evaluation systems and practices will enjoy improved evaluations and much greater satisfaction with the fruits of the evaluation process.

Many stories surround the use of these standards. My favorite stems from a colleague whose daughter received poor guidance and evaluation from her supervising professor in an internship teaching situation. With the standards in hand, this young intern confronted the supervision situation, obtained strong positive results for herself, and turned a very negative evaluation into a strong learning situation for all involved. While improving bad situations can be a substantial benefit of the standards, we much prefer that these evaluation standards be used from the outset to guide evaluations and yield positive results from the beginning.

The task force that prepared this revision worked carefully and extensively, not just with the original text, but also with input from educators in the field and with materials gathered and organized over a 10-year period. As is the case with all standards prepared by this Joint Committee, the revision included direct input from practitioners and researchers in the field, drafts and reviews of drafts, field trials of standards, national hearings on the standards, and reviews of the development process by an external validation panel. As the book cover notes, these standards are certified as American National Standards by the American National Standards Institute. That certification provides quality assurance to you, the user.

New to the 2nd Edition

Every standard in this second edition was revised in substantive ways. Long-time users of these standards will first note that the "so that" portion of the standard statements is no longer included. While widely appreciated for focusing the standards on use, there was a consensus that the "so that" terminology too often focused use narrowly and did not include important attributes. Attempts to list all pertinent "so that" outcomes yielded lengthy and cumbersome statements.

This edition retained the first edition's organization of standard-level information—explanation, rationale, guidelines, common errors, case examples, and references. However, each section of every standard was reviewed and updated. The case studies were rewritten with new cases to make them more interesting and to provide more extensive coverage of important facets, such as attention to cultural diversity and use of computer technology in obtaining, storing, and applying evaluation data.

Several standards changes occurred in each of the propriety, utility, and accuracy sections; standards were retitled and reordered within these sections. In the propriety section, two new standards, one focusing on comprehensive evaluation and a second addressing the legal viability of personnel evaluations, were created. In the utility section, two new standards that focus on professional development and use of explicit criteria were added. One utility standard, U6 Follow-Up and Impact, was revised extensively, and some of its main ideas were merged into the U5 Functional Reporting standard. In the accuracy section, two new standards, A5 Defensible Information and A9 Analysis of Information, were added. No new standards were drafted for the Feasibility section, but one standard was retitled. In general, the addition of new standards closed what were viewed as significant gaps in the previous standards.

The chapter on applying the standards was extensively revised and moved ahead of the standards statements to give readers foreknowledge about applying evaluation standards before they are presented individually. The new case example included in this chapter describes an extensive application. The case began within the confines of a one-day workshop in which a school team conducted an overall analysis of a school district's personnel evaluation system. Preliminary findings from that analysis led to a partitioned and more in-depth analysis of selected parts of the evaluation system. We think readers will appreciate the approach employed by that district.

The Audience for This Book

If you teach or provide professional development instruction, this book provides a wealth of information and materials for your use. The book is a must for teacher and administrator preparation. The case examples describe real situations, not made up or hypothetical possibilities. They convey what has been done and what can be done in actual school and university settings. Individual workshops and even full courses can be constructed from these examples. As a getting-started tool, individual standards and case examples can be discussed as part of instruction or evaluation development efforts. Certainly, the situations described, the guidelines, common errors, and case examples bring attention to major issues in a direct and interesting way.

Thank you for selecting this book and for using it to improve your education personnel evaluation practices. Please use it regularly as a working tool. Reference it, mark it up, dog-ear it, and make it your own. As you see ways in which these standards can serve you better, please bring your ideas and suggestions to the attention of the Joint Committee. We continually seek to improve these standards. We need input from you and your colleagues in the field to help us build improvements into our next edition confidently and competently.

Arlen R. Gullickson, Chair
Joint Committee on Standards for Educational Evaluation

About the Author

Arlen R. Gullickson, PhD, is professor emeritus at Western Michigan University where he served as director of The Evaluation Center and professor in the College of Education. Since 1998, he has served as chair of the Joint Committee on Standards for Educational Evaluation. His and the Center's work focuses on improving the theory and practice of evaluation. Much of his writing has focused on the practical aspects of program evaluation, on practices for evaluating teachers and students, and on improving teachers' assessment practices. He is the 2007 recipient of the American Evaluation Association's Myrdal Practice Award for outstanding evaluation practitioners who have made substantial cumulative contributions to the professional practice of evaluation.

CORWIN
PRESS

The Corwin Press logo—a raven striding across an open book—represents the union of courage and learning. Corwin Press is committed to improving education for all learners by publishing books and other professional development resources for those serving the field of PreK–12 education. By providing practical, hands-on materials, Corwin Press continues to carry out the promise of its motto: **"Helping Educators Do Their Work Better."**

Introduction

The fundamental purpose of personnel evaluation in education settings is to help provide effective services to students. Personnel evaluations in the public and private sectors allow educators to determine the quality of how they perform the responsibilities of their work and to gain direction for improving their performance. The second edition of *The Personnel Evaluation Standards* expands knowledge about personnel evaluation based on information gained from professional literature and years of experience conducting personnel evaluations since the first edition of this book was published in 1988. The 27[1] standards presented in this book represent a national and international consensus of what is most important to sound personnel evaluations and personnel evaluation systems. These standards require that personnel evaluations be ethical, fair, useful, feasible, and accurate. The Joint Committee recommends that education and training institutions adopt this book as their primary reference for developing, assessing, upgrading, and implementing institutional policies and procedures for evaluating education personnel.

The Personnel Evaluation Standards provides a guide for developing and assessing personnel evaluations and systems in a variety of education and training settings. They are intended for the *evaluatees* (teachers, instructors, administrators, and other staff members who are evaluated), the *personnel evaluators* (people who conduct the evaluations), and the *users* (employers and others who have a legitimate need for access to the evaluation results).

People who commission or conduct personnel evaluations or who use their results to improve performance of their employees in schools, colleges, universities, technical programs, and training institutes will find this book useful. When making hiring decisions, *The Personnel Evaluation Standards* helps faculty committees, administrators, supervisors, managers, and human resource officials conduct rigorous evaluations to identify promising candidates and assess their qualifications. Following hiring decisions, this book guides peer review committees, administrators, supervisors, managers, and human resource officials in periodically assessing the performance of individual evaluatees for key purposes including, but not confined to, the following:

- Guiding promotion and tenure decisions
- Recognizing and rewarding meritorious contributions
- Assessing the quality of service and production
- Identifying evaluatees' strengths and weaknesses to help them discover where they need improvement
- Prescribing remediation goals and in-service education and training
- Developing a fair, valid, and effective case for terminating those whose performance after remediation efforts is ineffective and does not contribute to the effectiveness of the education system and the well-being of its students
- Providing feedback to administrators, faculty committees, and human resource officials to plan meaningful staff development activities

Resource B, Personnel Evaluations to Which the Standards Apply, provides a table titled "Types of Evaluations and Decisions Involved in Preparing, Deploying, and Developing Professional Educators," which readers are encouraged to use in evaluation planning and professional development settings. This table sets forward a variety of personnel practice and decision situations in which the standards are known to be useful.

The need for personnel evaluations is pervasive and multifaceted. Experience, however, indicates that different groups will find different uses for the standards. The Joint Committee encourages innovative applications of *The Personnel Evaluation Standards,* such as in teaching others about personnel evaluation and personnel evaluation systems. The Joint Committee would appreciate learning about such applications as part of its ongoing work.

The 27 standards in this book are intended to facilitate thoughtful dialogue about the appropriate practice of personnel evaluation. The standards can help users confront the political and practical realities of the evaluation process by raising such questions as who establishes the criteria for judging the evaluatee and who mediates when charges of an unfair or unsound personnel evaluation are made. The standards address such issues as evaluator bias, conflict of interest, and diversity in the workplace. They stimulate thought about issues such as how often and for what purposes evaluatees should be evaluated, the qualifications required to be a fair and effective evaluator, the control of access to information, legal viability, follow-up remediation, and professional development.

The task force charged with revising the first edition of *The Personnel Evaluation Standards* developed the principles set forth in this book for the Joint Committee. The principles have been reviewed and agreed to by the Joint Committee, whose members represent 17 major education organizations. Members of these organizations and members in the field of education personnel evaluation have reviewed and field-tested these standards. These activities were monitored by a six-member validation panel, with representatives from education, business, and law. A detailed description of the project's participants and the process followed is provided in Resource C.

These standards are certified as American National Standards for the evaluation of personnel and personnel systems.

The standards in this book do not apply to the evaluation of programs or of individual students of the evaluatees. For more information regarding the evaluation of programs and students, the reader is encouraged to refer to *The Program Evaluation Standards* (2nd ed., 1994) and *The Student Evaluation Standards* (2003).

Definitions

The Joint Committee defines personnel evaluation as the systematic assessment of a person's performance and/or qualifications in relation to a professional role and some specified and defensible institutional purpose. It defines a standard as a principle mutually agreed to by people engaged in the professional practice that, if met, will enhance the quality and fairness of that professional practice, which in the present case is personnel evaluation.

Guiding Assumptions

Six major assumptions guided the development of *The Personnel Evaluation Standards:*

1. The fundamental purpose of personnel evaluation must be to help provide effective services to students. This book is dedicated to the proposition that personnel evaluation can and must be designed and conducted to encourage and guide evaluatees to perform more effectively in providing this service.
2. Personnel evaluation practices should be constructive and free of unnecessarily threatening or demoralizing characteristics. When individuals have confidence in the evaluation criteria and process, when they experience clear communication and fair treatment, and when they see evaluation contributing to their success, they are more likely to be enthusiastic in their work and receptive to evaluation.
3. Personnel evaluations should be conducted with an understanding that the evaluation system adheres to culturally competent practice. Cultural competence requires that attention be paid to factors such as age, gender, ethnicity, disability, religion, nation of origin, socioeconomic status, and sexual orientation (see Resource A). Therefore, the guiding principle set forth by the American Evaluation Association (2004) should be considered in all evaluations:

    > Evaluators provide competent performance to stakeholders . . . to ensure recognition, accurate interpretation and respect for diversity, evaluators should ensure that the members of the evaluation team collectively demonstrate cultural competence. Cultural competence would be reflected in evaluators seeking awareness of their own culturally-based assumptions, their understanding of the worldviews of culturally-different participants and stakeholders in

the evaluation, and the use of appropriate evaluation strategies and skills in working with culturally different groups. Diversity may be in terms of race, ethnicity, gender, religion, socio-economics, or other factors pertinent to the evaluation context. (p. 2)

4. Personnel evaluations are vital for planning sound professional development and training experiences. It is, for example, demeaning and wasteful to ask or require all staff members to take particular courses or training when some already possess the necessary knowledge and skills. Evaluation should point the way to new learning that is directly related to the needs, interests, and job responsibilities of evaluatees.

5. Disagreements about what constitutes good teaching, good administration, or good research may complicate personnel evaluations, but such disagreements are warranted. Job descriptions and educational approaches vary legitimately because of different philosophies of and approaches to education, different state or institutional policies, and different local needs and orientations. In addition, there may be lack of agreement about what conditions, qualifications, and performances are necessary and sufficient for achieving defined educational expectations in a particular context. Depending on the circumstances, different approaches may be more or less effective in various situations. For these reasons, the Joint Committee has adopted a pluralistic view regarding the application of these standards. Users of *The Personnel Evaluation Standards* must define their own expectations, approaches, and role definitions, and then apply the standards accordingly.

6. As reflected by the Functional Table of Contents, personnel evaluations vary in complexity and importance. Consequently, applications of some standards may be crucial in some circumstances but not needed in others. In general, more time and effort should be devoted to applying standards when personnel actions are uncertain or potentially controversial. In those cases, the standards can contribute most by promoting sound evaluations and by assuring all interested parties of the rationality, fairness, and defensibility of the decisions.

Nature of the Standards

This book contains a set of 27 standards that speak to the responsible conduct and use of personnel evaluations in a variety of settings. These standards provide a framework for designing, conducting, and judging personnel evaluations and evaluation systems. These standards do not specify either (a) the criteria for personnel evaluations (knowledge and performance expectations of personnel) or (b) evaluation procedures, such as specific assessment methods, data processing, and data analyses, to be used in personnel evaluation. *The Personnel Evaluation Standards* is not intended to replace textbooks, manuals, and handbooks concerned with personnel evaluation. Instead, it should be used in tandem with such materials, helping, for example, to identify what evaluation techniques and skills should be learned and employed.

The Joint Committee cautions that the individual standards are not equally applicable in all evaluations. Users of *The Personnel Evaluation Standards* should weigh the relevance of each standard in context and use professional judgment to identify which standards are most appropriate in each situation, and then decide which should be accorded the most importance. These decisions should be documented for later reference.

To assist in identifying the most important standards for a given situation, a Functional Table of Contents is provided at the beginning of this book. This table is organized into sections that correspond to major decisions, such as certification, licensure, selection of an existing system of personnel evaluation, merit awards, tenure, promotion decisions, and termination decisions. It also addresses issues in personnel evaluations, such as developing a personnel evaluation system, training evaluators, defining roles within an evaluation system, using evaluation results for staff development, and evaluating individuals from diverse backgrounds. This table will help evaluators and those who commission or use evaluation results to gain a comprehensive understanding of the many facets of personnel evaluation.

The Joint Committee recognizes that there are overlaps among the different standards. These result from the complexity of personnel evaluations and the strong relationships among the various evaluation issues addressed. These overlaps describe the many and varied relationships and nuances important to understanding and resolving personnel evaluation problems. Further, the overlaps help address the omission of possible relevant material when only some, and not all, of the standards are used (see Functional Table of Contents).

The second edition of *The Personnel Evaluation Standards,* like the first edition, was developed for use in the United States. The standards may or may not apply or be appropriate for use in international settings. The Joint Committee has based its work on American ideals, laws, and education and occupation systems and has used examples that are familiar in the United States. We appreciate the useful reviews and suggestions from colleagues in other countries. We intend to contribute to continued international exchange in personnel evaluation. However, we have not tried to develop standards that fit the laws, systems, and circumstances of other countries.

Organization and Substance of the Standards

The 27 standards contained in the second edition of *The Personnel Evaluation Standards* are organized around four essential attributes of sound evaluation practice: *propriety, utility, feasibility,* and *accuracy.* The Joint Committee believes that these four attributes are necessary and sufficient for sound and fair evaluations. Although individual standards may strengthen more than one attribute, each has been placed in the group that reflects its principal emphasis in promoting sound evaluations. The issue of diversity is such that it cannot be separated into its own set of standards but should permeate all areas of personnel evaluation (see Resource A). For this reason, diversity issues related to personnel evaluation have been integrated into the guidelines of individual standards and, when appropriate, into the case illustrations.

PROPRIETY STANDARDS

The Propriety Standards are intended to ensure that a personnel evaluation will be conducted legally, ethically, and with due regard for the welfare of the evaluatee and those involved in the evaluation. The seven Propriety Standards reflect the fact that personnel evaluations may violate or fail to address certain ethical and legal principles. The primary principle is that schools, colleges, universities, and training institutes exist to serve students. Therefore, personnel evaluations should concentrate on determining whether educators and trainers are effectively meeting the needs of their students. In general, the Propriety Standards are aimed at protecting the rights of persons affected by an evaluation. These include students, instructors, counselors, administrators, and evaluators.

Propriety Standards promote sensitivity to and warn against unlawful, unscrupulous, unethical, and inept actions by those who conduct evaluations. Overall, the Propriety Standards require that evaluators understand and obey laws concerning such matters as privacy, access to information, diversity, and the protection of human subjects. They charge those who conduct evaluations to respect the rights of others.

The seven Propriety Standards are as follows: Service Orientation, Appropriate Policies and Procedures, Access to Evaluation Information, Interactions with Evaluatees, Comprehensive Evaluation, Conflict of Interest, and Legal Viability.

UTILITY STANDARDS

The six Utility Standards are intended to guide evaluations so that they will be informative, timely, and influential. The primary principle is that schools, colleges, universities, training institutes, and other professional developers serve students. Therefore, personnel evaluations should concentrate on determining whether the providers of these services are meeting the needs of those they serve effectively.

Above all, Utility Standards require that evaluations have a constructive orientation and provide information useful to individuals and to groups of educators for improving their performance. These standards also require that persons with appropriate expertise and credibility conduct the evaluations. The Utility Standards emphasize that evaluations should be focused on predetermined users and uses, for example, informing selection, promotion, and tenure decisions or providing direction for staff development. The topics of the Utility Standards are Constructive Orientation, Defined Uses, Evaluator Qualifications, Explicit Criteria, Functional Reporting, and Follow-Up and Professional Development. In general, Utility Standards view personnel evaluation as an integral part of an institution's ongoing effort to recruit outstanding staff members, provide them with timely and relevant evaluative feedback, and encourage and guide them to deliver high quality service.

FEASIBILITY STANDARDS

The Feasibility Standards are intended to guide personnel evaluation systems so that they are as easy to implement as possible, efficient in their use of time and resources, adequately funded, and viable from a political standpoint. These standards recognize that personnel evaluations are conducted in a dynamic, real-world setting and are affected by multiple factors, such as the choice of evaluation method or procedures, political pressures, and resource constraints, any of which can affect the quality of evaluations. Personnel evaluations should be conducted in efficient and easy to use ways: viable in the face of social, political, and governmental forces and constraints and adequately funded.

The three Feasibility Standards are Practical Procedures, Political Viability, and Fiscal Viability.

ACCURACY STANDARDS

The Accuracy Standards determine whether an evaluation has produced sound information. Personnel evaluations must be technically adequate and as complete as possible to allow sound judgments and decisions to be made. The evaluation methodology should be appropriate for the purpose of the evaluation, the evaluees being evaluated, and the context in which they work.

The 11 Accuracy Standards are Valid Judgments, Defined Expectations, Analysis of Context, Documented Purposes and Procedures, Defensible Information, Reliable Information, Systematic Data Control, Bias Identification and Management, Analysis of Information, Justified Conclusions, and Metaevaluation. The overall rating of a personnel evaluation against the accuracy standards gives a good assessment of the evaluation's validity.

FORMAT

The Personnel Evaluation Standards follows a format intended to elaborate on each standard and to facilitate understanding of the principle involved. The following content describes and elaborates each standard:

Descriptor: A number and descriptive title for each standard: for example, Utility 1 (U1), Constructive Orientation.

Standard: A definition expressed in a sentence that describes what the evaluator or evaluation system should do. In some instances, the standard includes information as to what is to be accomplished through this action. For example, the Constructive Orientation standard (U1) is stated as follows: "Personnel evaluations should help institutions develop human resources and encourage and assist evaluatees to perform in accordance with the institution's mission and goals."

Explanation: A conceptual introduction that defines key terms in the standard and describes the essence of the requirements embodied in the standard.

Rationale: A generalized argument for the inclusion of the standards within the full set of standards.

Guidelines: A list of procedural suggestions intended to help evaluators and their audiences meet the requirements of the standard. The guidelines are strategies for avoiding mistakes in applying the standard. They should not be considered exhaustive or mandatory, but rather as procedures to be followed when they are judged potentially helpful and feasible.

Common Errors: A list of errors associated with the standard. These errors may occur under many circumstances and, if not addressed, may compromise the evaluation.

Illustrative Case: One or more cases based on actual personnel evaluations illustrate how the standard might be applied. Each case includes a description of a setting, a situation in which the standard is or is not met, an analysis of attending problems, and, if needed, a discussion of corrective actions that should lead to compliance with the standard. The corrective actions discussed are only illustrative and are not intended to encompass all possible corrections.

Supporting Documentation: Selected references provided to assist the reader in further study of the principle stated in the standard.

Uses of the Standards

The function of these standards is to correct deficiencies in current practice and present evaluatees, personnel evaluators, and users with a widely shared view of general principles for developing and assessing sound, satisfactory personnel evaluations and personnel evaluation systems, along with practical advice for implementing them. The following list, while not intended to be exhaustive or complete, provides an indication of the variety of uses of the standards.

Faculty committees, administrators, supervisors, managers, and human resource officials can use the standards to do the following:

- Provide the primary reference document for developing and applying a board policy on personnel evaluation.
- Foster due process in evaluation practices, thereby providing fair treatment and reducing legal vulnerability in personnel evaluation cases.
- Assess and improve institutional evaluation systems used in certification, selection, assignment, reassignment, promotion, tenure, and other types of recognition and decisions.
- Strengthen the role of personnel evaluation by ensuring high standards of teaching, administration, research, curriculum development, and service.
- Help establish new policy initiatives (e.g., incentive pay, career ladders, and mentoring programs) and ensure the policy objectives are accomplished and assessed appropriately.
- Help clarify the rights and responsibilities of professionals in the institution who are involved in a personnel evaluation.
- Help assure that personnel evaluations hold educators, instructors, and trainers accountable for the delivery of high quality services.
- Promote personnel evaluation practices that help the institution attract, develop, and retain qualified employees.

- Promote personnel evaluation practices that reinforce positive behaviors as well as identify areas for improvement and thereby foster greater job satisfaction and performance.
- Obtain personnel evaluations that provide a just and defensible basis for terminating employees who persist, after remediation activities, in providing unacceptable services.
- Promote and provide quality assurance for diversity in the workplace (e.g., hiring and retention policies).

Personnel evaluators can use the standards to do the following:

- Train those who are to serve in the role of personnel evaluator.
- Examine alternative personnel evaluation approaches and systems.
- Plan particular personnel evaluations and overall personnel evaluation systems.
- Guide and monitor particular personnel evaluations.
- Assess (metaevaluate) particular personnel evaluations.
- Help avoid or settle disputes in the evaluation of personnel.
- Provide direction for addressing a specific issue in a particular evaluation.

Evaluatees can use the standards to do the following:

- Improve their understanding of and skills in personnel evaluation.
- Promote or demand personnel evaluations that lead to increased professional development.
- Identify and resolve possible due process issues before mistakes occur in a personnel evaluation.
- Investigate whether given personnel evaluations are fair, valid, practical, and professionally useful.

In addition, *The Personnel Evaluation Standards* can be used to do the following:

- Act as a supplementary resource for courses on personnel evaluation.
- Develop a set of criteria against which to evaluate alternative models for personnel evaluation.
- Provide a framework for use in developing evaluation systems and better models for personnel evaluation.
- Give logical structure to deriving and investigating questions and hypotheses about personnel evaluation.

Organization of the Publication

A discussion of how to apply the standards to real-life situations follows this introduction. The main part of the book consists of a full explication of the 27 standards grouped according to emphasis on propriety, utility, feasibility, and accuracy. The book ends with a list of individuals who participated in the development of *The Personnel Evaluation Standards* (2nd ed.), including those who offered reviews or conducted field trials of the revised standards. A glossary provides definitions and guidance in the use of terminology specifically related to the field of personnel evaluation.

Applying the Standards

Personnel evaluations and the standards that guide them affect every professional employee within an education organization, whether in the role of evaluatee, evaluator, or user of the information. Consultants, researchers, and developers in the field of personnel evaluation also should be cognizant of these standards. Regardless of role, the Joint Committee suggests five steps in applying these standards:

1. Become very familiar with the standards.
2. Clarify your purpose for applying the standards.
3. Review and select one or more appropriate standards.
4. Apply the standards you have selected.
5. Based on your application of the standards, decide on and implement a course of action.

The following sections present each of these five steps in greater detail, illustrated by an extended case study example.

Step 1: Become Very Familiar With the Standards

The first recommendation is to become very familiar with all the standards to develop an overall understanding of their interconnectedness and direct relationship to the various attributes of sound evaluation. While the standards do not attempt to recognize or recommend any specific design of personnel evaluation (e.g., observation/checklist, rubric/evidence, performance-based, summative/formative, etc.), they most appropriately are used to guide the sound development and implementation of any system. Each standard addresses areas most applicable to specific concerns or issues related to either development or implementation. Understanding the overall function of each standard will help the user target those most useful to a particular application.

Reading the book may be the most effective means of establishing familiarity with all the standards. This book is organized conveniently to lead the reader in a number of different approaches. You may wish to begin with reading only the explanation and rationale in the overview section of each standard chapter. An examination of the guidelines and common errors for each standard also may prove useful as a first step in understanding each standard. Illustrative cases provide examples of actual practice directly related to each standard. Just reading the standard statements without examining at least some part of the supporting sections may be misleading.

Another way to become familiar with the standards and their application is to read supporting literature (suggestions can be found at the end of each chapter and in the References) or attend workshops and conference presentations. Such annual conferences as those for the CREATE National Evaluation Institute, the American Evaluation Association, and the American Educational Research Association generally offer papers and presentations directly related to this field of work.

Step 1: Specific Case Application

A preconference workshop offered at the CREATE National Evaluation Institute provided the opportunity for teams of educators from districts around the country to come together to examine and apply *The Personnel Evaluation Standards.* Each participating district had teams composed of district-level administrators, building-level administrators, and, in two cases, teachers. The first step of the process was to review the entire set of standards as a team. The workshop facilitators provided an overview of the standards, their development, and their potential uses.

Step 2: Clarify Your Purpose for Applying the Standards

The second step, once you have become familiar with the standards, is to decide your primary purpose for applying them. Do you want to develop a new model of personnel evaluation? Does your district need to select from among several existing models? Does your university or college department need to revise an existing system of awarding tenure? Do you simply want to ensure that the current procedures and policies of your district personnel system are fair, appropriate, and effective?

An assessment of your current system of personnel evaluation is usually an excellent beginning for clarifying your purpose. The Key Question resource starting on page 20 provides additional guidance in examining current practice. For example, if the standards of performance for teachers have changed significantly since the development of your current process, then a revision of the process to better address these new performance standards would be in order. It also may be that you would need to adopt an entirely new process or develop one on your own.

Unfortunately, school districts often wait until personnel evaluations result in grievances and lawsuits to evaluate their current system for flaws such as lack of training for evaluators, improper storage of personnel records, missed deadlines, and so forth that may have contributed to grievance incidents. While it is never possible to

---

Step 2: Specific Case Application

After examining the standards during the preconference workshop, District A determined that its current process of teacher evaluation and the Key Questions for each standard needed to be adjusted, as did several procedures in its current system. Of primary concern was the lack of training for new administrators. Several years prior to this workshop, the district had adopted a new model of teacher evaluation that required extensive training and expense. An outside consultant worked with the district for two years to develop the evaluation skills of all principals and assistant principals. The staff developer for the district assumed training duties once the contract with the consultant expired. The staff developer, however, was no longer in that position, and her replacement had not placed teacher evaluation training as a high priority. This resulted in new administrators beginning to evaluate with little or no training.

This seemed like an easy deficiency to fix by arranging for two or three days of training for all administrators; however, as the team began delving further into the Key Questions, it discovered that personnel records also were being managed inappropriately. Since there was no real oversight of the evaluators other than checking off completed evaluations at the end of each school year, the reports often were not filed properly and might sit stacked on a desk at the central office for several weeks. The district team was not sure whether anyone checked for proper signatures and dates.

In addition to these concerns, the district team began questioning whether the issue of diversity among the teaching staff was addressed appropriately. While this would certainly overlap with the training of evaluators, the team thought that with a growing population of immigrants in their district, the personnel evaluation system should provide safeguards against unfair treatment due to cultural, racial, or other differences.

---

totally avoid human error in judgment, a sound system of personnel evaluation will greatly reduce the risk of errors caused by improper procedures or policies.

Step 3: Review and Select One or More Appropriate Standards

Once the purpose has been defined, the Functional Table of Contents is an excellent resource to identify the most pertinent standards applicable to most uses of the standards. If your purpose is not found there, a quick review of the standards and their explanations may help focus your application. Each set of standards is organized into four attributes of sound evaluation: *Propriety, Utility, Feasibility, and Accuracy.* If, for example, the question arises concerning the practicality of your process in terms of resources available, you may wish to begin with the Feasibility standards. Cross-references to other standards within the contents of each standard chapter may lead you to other pertinent standards in other attributes.

Step 3: Specific Case Application

The team from District A reviewed the Functional Table of Contents and the Key Questions to select specific standards applicable to the issues raised by the examination of its current system. To work more efficiently in the time allotted for the workshop, the six-member team divided into three pairs, each of which examined specific standards relevant to one issue.

The first pair of teammates examined the issue of lack of consistent training for evaluators. Of the 22 standards listed, they used the standards' explanations to focus on those most pertinent to their district's concerns, which included the following: P4, P5, P6, U3, U5, A5, A6, A7, A8, A9, and A10.

The second pair of teammates examined the issues surrounding the team's concerns regarding lack of oversight of personnel records. While there did not seem to be a specific category for this in the Functional Table of Contents, the pair decided to use the overview of the standards provided in the morning session and the Key Questions to select the most relevant standards to consider. They decided to target the following: P2, P3, P7, U5, F1, F3, A4, and A7. This pair decided to examine these standards to create a chart of appropriate application, the existing deficits within their current system, and possible remedies.

The final team pair was charged to look at issues of diversity among the population of teachers and the fairness of the current policies and procedures of the existing system. The Functional Table of Contents provided an entire section of suggested standards for evaluating individuals from diverse backgrounds. The third pair decided to examine their current system in light of all these standards.

Step 4: Apply the Standards You Have Selected

How you go about using the standards once they have been selected depends on your purpose. If your purpose is to ensure that your current system of teacher evaluation is being used appropriately, you might want to review the Utility Standards and reflect on practices as suggested by specific standards to adjust practice as necessary.

If you are engaged in developing a personnel evaluation system, this would require a much more extensive application of the standards. You might choose to develop a checklist of your own or use the one on page 17 to determine whether your system meets, partially meets, or does not meet each standard. You could then make adjustments as required to meet the standards.

Another purpose for an extensive application of the standards involves a metaevaluation of a current system. Metaevaluation requires an accurate and complete examination of all current policies, procedures, documents, uses, and other aspects of a personnel evaluation system against the practices outlined by the standards. This may involve examining a large selection of completed personnel records to check signatures, dates, comments, ratings, and so forth. It also may involve interviews or focus groups of evaluatees and evaluators to determine appropriateness of such activities as interactions, balance of comments, extent of follow-up, and professional development. A careful reading of all pertinent policies and laws is essential to determine the system's legal and political viability, appropriateness of policies and procedures, and orientation.

This level of examination may be viewed as too time consuming and demanding for school district administrators and staff who have many other pressing duties and responsibilities. Nevertheless, a sound personnel evaluation system is essential to a district's ability to meet expected goals. A district may conduct a metaevaluation in stages based on level of concern. For example, the district may schedule the metaevaluation extending over a period of time to focus on specific aspects such as storage of personnel information and appropriate procedures for conducting evaluations. Such a systematic approach will alleviate undue burden on district staff. Another approach would be to hire an outside consultant with expertise in this type of evaluation. In either case, knowledge of the standards by district administrators who will oversee the project will ensure more useful outcomes.

Step 4: Specific Case Application

The District A teammates reviewed their selected standards. Then they used the form on pages 18–19 to rate the current level of application for each of the selected standards based on the review of their system. Each pair was able to determine which of the selected standards were met, partially met, or not met at all. They also were able to eliminate some of the standards as not being applicable to their situation once they had reviewed them. By completing this checklist based on the evidence provided by examining their current practices and their understanding of the standards, the teammates were able to develop a list of recommendations for improvement.

Step 5: Decide On and Implement a Course of Action

Just knowing that your personnel evaluation system does not fully meet certain standards is an appropriate start, but inadequate for providing your organization with a sound system. Action must be taken to correct any deficiencies that prevent fair and useful evaluations of personnel. This action may range from putting appropriate training and support in place for evaluators to more extensive revision or replacement of the current system. The development of a plan for improving a system of personnel evaluation is essential to correcting such deficiencies. Such a plan should be based on the standards and best practices.

Applying the standards to personnel evaluation systems can result in effective management of human resources, which is necessary to attain organizational goals. A great deal of money, energy, and manpower can be expended in correcting errors made as a result of poor personnel evaluation. Good teachers may be lost to the system.

Step 5: Specific Case Application

District A teammates came back together as a group to compare their lists of the standards not met or only partially met within their current teacher evaluation system with respect to the issues each pair examined. Where they found overlap among the findings of the different pairs, they eliminated duplication to make a more concise list.

As a group, they developed a list of recommendations for correcting deficiencies between actual practice and that recommended by the standards to take back to their district for discussion with a broader range of stakeholders. The team then agreed on a plan of action that included steps to introduce the standards to the district, solicit suggestions, and offer recommendations for improvement within a specific timeline.

Other, poor performing teachers may be allowed to continue, resulting in lower student achievement gains if appropriate procedures are not in place to set explicit criteria for necessary follow-up and professional development. Unfair evaluations may occur if evaluators are not trained adequately to guard against bias or to analyze the context of the performance correctly. In some cases, effective teachers may be evaluated unfairly, resulting in their loss to the district or university simply due to poor procedures.

Checklist for Applying the Standards

The Personnel Evaluation Standards guided the following activities (check one):

_____   Development of a personnel evaluation system
_____   Review and revision of existing personnel evaluation system
_____   Training of evaluators
_____   Selection of a personnel evaluation system
_____   Other: _____

Check the roles of all involved in the activity selected above:

_____   Consultant
_____   State department level administrators or staff
_____   Superintendent
_____   Assistant/associate/deputy superintendent
_____   District level director
_____   Building level administrator
_____   Teacher
_____   Parent
_____   School board member
_____   Union representative
_____   Other(s): _____

Check the type of organization for which the personnel evaluation system was intended:

_____   State
_____   University department
_____   College
_____   Graduate school
_____   Community college
_____   Regional education services
_____   Public school district (pre-K–12)
_____   Independent school
Grade level configuration: _____
_____   Charter school
Grade level configuration: _____

> To interpret the information provided on this form, the reader needs to refer to the full text of *The Personnel Evaluation Standards.* Following the review (either by an individual or committee) of the personnel evaluation system in question against these standards, please rate the appropriate level of implementation for each standard using the scale below.

The standard was Met   M   The standard was Not Met   NM
The standard was Partially Met   PM   The standard was Not Applicable NA

Standard	Rating	Comments
P *Propriety Standards*		
P1 Service Orientation		
P2 Appropriate Policies and Procedures		
P3 Access to Evaluation Information		
P4 Interactions With Evaluatees		
P5 Comprehensive Evaluation		
P6 Conflict of Interest		
P7 Legal Viability		
U *Utility Standards*		
U1 Constructive Orientation		
U2 Defined Uses		
U3 Evaluator Qualifications		
U4 Explicit Criteria		
U5 Functional Reporting		
U6 Follow-Up and Professional Development		
F *Feasibility Standards*		
F1 Practical Procedures		
F2 Political Viability		
F3 Fiscal Viability		

Standard	Rating	Comments
A *Accuracy Standards*		
A1 Valid Judgments		
A2 Defined Expectations		
A3 Analysis of Context		
A4 Documented Purposes and Procedures		
A5 Defensible Information		
A6 Reliable Information		
A7 Systematic Data Control		
A8 Bias Identification and Management		
A9 Analysis of Information		
A10 Justified Conclusions		
A11 Metaevaluation		

Linking Standard Statements to Key Questions
of Evaluatee Evaluations

Attribute	Standard Statement	Key Questions
PROPRIETY	**P1—Service Orientation**	Are job descriptions clearly written and understood by both evaluatees and evaluators? Are these job expectations aligned with district goals and sound educational practice?
	P2—Appropriate Policies and Procedures	Are policies regarding all aspects of evaluatee evaluation written, adopted by governing boards, and available to all evaluatees and evaluators as well as other stakeholders? Is there oversight of the process to ensure consistency and the evaluator's fairness of judgment?
	P3—Access to Evaluation Information	Is the information gathered during an evaluation protected and held confidential? Is a process in place to ensure that only those with a legitimate purpose have access to personnel evaluations?
	P4—Interactions With Evaluatees	Are safeguards and oversights in place to ensure that evaluators conduct all interactions (both written and verbal) in a professional, constructive manner? Is a process in place to address incidences of unprofessional interactions with evaluatees?
	P5—Comprehensive Evaluation	Do procedures and expectations allow both strengths and weaknesses to be identified rather than focusing solely on the deficits of performance? Are the ratings conducive to differentiating among levels of performance?
	P6—Conflict of Interest	Are safeguards and oversights in place to ensure that preexisting conditions or events would not compromise the evaluator's ability to be fair and unbiased?

Attribute	Standard Statement	Key Questions
PROPRIETY	**P7—Legal Viability**	Does the evaluation process meet all federal, state, and local laws and guidelines, including those established through collective bargaining? Do those involved generally agree that the evaluations are fair and efficient?
UTILITY	**U1—Constructive Orientation**	Does the evaluation process reflect the institution's goals and mission? Is a process in place that aligns feedback and professional development based on evaluation with the institution's goals and mission?
	U2—Defined Uses	Have all users (evaluatee, administrators, school board members, etc.) of the evaluation process been clearly identified from the beginning of the evaluation cycle? Have the uses for the information (dismissal, tenure, merit pay, etc.) been clearly identified?
	U3—Evaluator Qualifications	Have all the evaluators received appropriate training in the evaluation process? Have those who manage the records received appropriate training, and do they hold appropriate credentials?
	U4—Explicit Criteria	Do the criteria reflect only the job expectations of those evaluated? Are criteria for one group used for another group with unrelated job expectations (i.e., an evaluation form for teachers used for guidance counselors)?
	U5—Functional Reporting	Is there a system of oversight to ensure that all reports generated by the evaluator meet deadlines and provide useful, accurate information?

(Continued)

(Continued)

Attribute	Standard Statement	Key Questions
UTILITY	**U6—Follow-Up and Professional Development**	Is a structure in place to allow the data generated by evaluations to be used in developing professional development plans? Are procedures in place that allow oversight to ensure appropriate follow-up of evaluation results?
FEASIBILITY	**F1—Practical Procedures**	Are procedures for collecting data as simple and job-embedded as possible to prevent undue overburdening of either the evaluatee or the evaluator?
	F2—Political Viability	Is a process in place that allows all stakeholders the opportunity to question the procedures or results of an evaluation? Is there a process to determine the outcome of questions asked concerning an evaluation?
	F3—Fiscal Viability	Can the district afford the resources to conduct evaluatee evaluation in the way that will maximize its effect?
ACCURACY	**A1—Valid Judgments**	Is there an adequate number of data sources to provide a comprehensive view of performance? Is there a system of oversight in place to ensure that the evaluators follow procedures, analyze all appropriate data, and report judgments based only on the criteria set forth in the system?
	A2—Defined Expectations	Are the expectations and scope of work for the evaluatee clearly defined and understood by both the evaluatee and evaluator?

Attribute	Standard Statement	Key Questions
ACCURACY		Have these expectations been provided to all evaluatees in both written and verbal formats? Are these expectations reasonable and directly related to stated job descriptions?
	A3—Analysis of Context	Whenever data are collected, is there a structure or expectation in place that the details regarding the circumstances also be recorded (i.e., notation on observation forms)?
	A4—Documented Purposes and Procedures	Is a structure in place for ensuring that all evaluators and evaluatees clearly understand the purposes and procedures to be followed?
	A5—Defensible Information	Is oversight in place to ensure that the results of any given evaluation would be the same regardless of evaluator?
	A6—Reliable Information	Is there oversight to ensure that the evaluation procedures are the same for all evaluatees regardless of the evaluator?
	A7—Systematic Data Control	Is a structure in place that ensures that all evaluative information is held in a secure location (e.g., locked file cabinets, secure server, etc.)? Is a system in place to record person, time, date, and purpose of access to records?
	A8—Bias Identification and Management	Is there oversight to ensure that the results of any evaluation are not influenced by preconceived ideas of the evaluator that may be unrelated to the actual job performance of the evaluatee? Does evaluator training include bias control and diversity awareness training? Is there a grievance process in place to offer protection to evaluatees?

(Continued)

(Continued)

Attribute	Standard Statement	Key Questions
ACCURACY	**A9—Analysis of Information**	Is there oversight of the evaluator's final reports and disposition to ensure continued accuracy and use of data? Are conclusions drawn consistent with the data gathered?
	A10—Justified Conclusions	Is a structure in place that requires the evaluator to justify the disposition of an evaluation based on documentation of performance?
	A11—Metaevaluation	Is a system in place to allow the periodic review of the personnel evaluation system to ensure its continued usefulness?

Adapted from Howard, B. B., & Sanders, J. R. (2006). Applying the personnel evaluation standards to evaluatee evaluation. In J. H. Stronge (Ed.), *Evaluating teaching: A guide to current thinking and best practice.* Thousand Oaks, CA: Corwin Press.

THE STANDARDS

P PROPRIETY STANDARDS

Summary of the Standards

Propriety Standards   Intended to ensure that a personnel evaluation will be conducted legally, ethically, and with due regard for the welfare of the evaluatee and those involved in the evaluation.

> **P1**   **Service Orientation**   Personnel evaluations should promote sound education of all students, fulfillment of institutional missions, and effective performance of job responsibilities of educators.
>
> **P2**   **Appropriate Policies and Procedures**   Guidelines for personnel evaluations should be recorded and provided to the evaluatee in policy statements, negotiated agreements, or personnel evaluation manuals.
>
> **P3**   **Access to Evaluation Information**   To maintain confidentiality, access to evaluation information should be limited to the people with established, legitimate permission to review and use the information.
>
> **P4**   **Interactions With Evaluatees**   The evaluator should respect human dignity and act in a professional, considerate, and courteous manner.
>
> **P5**   **Comprehensive Evaluation**   Personnel evaluations should identify strengths and areas for growth.
>
> **P6**   **Conflict of Interest**   Existing and potential conflicts of interest should be identified and dealt with openly and honestly.
>
> **P7**   **Legal Viability**   Personnel evaluations should meet the requirements of applicable laws, contracts, collective bargaining agreements, affirmative action policies, and local board or institutional policies.

P1   Service Orientation

STANDARD   Personnel evaluations should promote sound
education of all students, fulfillment of institutional missions, and
effective performance of job responsibilities of educators.

Explanation.   Students and the community have the right to receive sound
educational services, which should be supported by a sound system of personnel
evaluation. The primary purpose of personnel evaluation in education is to guide
and support educators in delivering high quality services in whatever role they serve:
pre-K–12 teacher, university professor, instructor, or administrator. Personnel
evaluations should help ensure that educators understand and pursue their
organization's mission and goals. To support this, responsibilities should be specified,
promised services delivered, and professional capabilities advanced to meet the needs
of students.

Personnel evaluation must reflect an organization's goals. The institution's staff
and constituents should be informed that the results of a personnel evaluation will
be used to recognize and encourage excellent service, motivate and assist evaluatees to
improve, and, when needed, document just cause for dismissing evaluatees who are
performing in an unacceptable manner (see U6, Follow-Up and Professional
Development; P7, Legal Viability).

Rationale.   Education institutions exist to meet the needs of students, the
community, and society. Personnel evaluations should be directed toward achieving
that purpose. To encourage the beneficial aspects and avoid the detrimental aspects
of personnel evaluations, evaluators should employ practices that provide useful
information about the performance of the evaluatee. With this information, teachers,
instructors, administrators, and others who work with students are better able to
provide superior, pertinent services to their students and to maintain and encourage
their own professional development.

GUIDELINES

    A. Determine purposes and uses of the evaluation that reflect the needs of the
students and community and the roles and responsibilities of the evaluatee,

then plan and conduct the evaluation to serve those needs (see U2, Defined Uses; A2, Defined Expectations).

B. Ensure that evaluations serve to protect the rights of students for adequate instruction, service, and equal educational opportunity.

C. Include all potential stakeholders, such as faculty, administrators, board members, students, and union officials, when determining the purpose(s) and procedures of an evaluation, and check their level of understanding.

D. Inform the institution's staff and constituents that personnel evaluation will be directed to encourage excellent service, motivate and assist all personnel to improve and, if needed, document just cause for dismissing those whose performance is unacceptable (see U6, Follow-Up and Professional Development; P7, Legal Viability).

E. Set and maintain high standards for granting tenure, making sure that the standards are responsive to the needs of stakeholders and understood by the evaluatee.

F. Implement a thorough screening process at the time of hiring, followed by one to three years of comprehensive evaluation to assure sound decisions regarding retention of personnel. Ensure that appropriate professional development opportunities are available when needed (see U6, Follow-Up and Professional Development).

G. Subject all personnel in the institution to a consistent and procedurally fair process of evaluation aligned with organizational goals.

H. Inform the public periodically about how personnel evaluation is promoting the best interests of the students and the community (e.g., describe and discuss the system at meetings of the school board and the parent-teacher organization, provide information in school newsletters to parents; see U5, Functional Reporting.)

COMMON ERRORS

A. Failing to base criteria and performance standards on job roles and responsibilities and on legal requirements (see P7, Legal Viability; U4, Explicit Criteria).

B. Failing to align evaluation criteria with institutional goals and mission (see U4, Explicit Criteria).

C. Failing to invest adequate resources in the development and implementation of evaluation procedures, including the training of evaluators (see F3, Fiscal Viability).

D. Failing to recognize and encourage excellent performance.

E. Seeking to remove an evaluatee whose performance was judged unacceptable before attempting to improve that person's performance.

F. Failing to appropriately address unsatisfactory performance in a timely manner.

G. Failing to invest in and to provide employee development plans and professional growth opportunities while expecting improvement in performance.

Illustrative Case 1: Inheriting an Underperforming Principal
Description

As one of her first tasks, Dr. Ferguson, the new superintendent in a small school district, reviewed the personnel files of the three elementary school principals and found that one principal had been performing poorly for years. The information in his file included data from teachers' surveys over the years in which teachers tended to view his leadership unfavorably. It also contained several memoranda to him from previous superintendents "reminding him of the need to be on campus before the students arrived." Several parent complaints appeared unresolved. Dr. Ferguson noted that on several visits to the school, she always found this principal in his office. During one recent walk-through of the school, in which she was accompanied by the principal, several students recognized and spoke to her, but did not know their principal. Information in his file also showed that the majority of teachers in this school were seasoned veterans who tended to function independently.

There was evidence of only perfunctory compliance with district initiatives, such as the new reading program. Dr. Ferguson thought this lack of leadership resulted in lower accountability for teachers' performance. As a consequence of poor implementation of the reading program, the students in this school were steadily underperforming their peers in other schools in reading. She feared this decline in scores would adversely affect these students even more as they moved forward to middle school and high school.

Many parents were aware of the situation and routinely requested that their children be placed in other schools. Complaints by parents and teachers to the school board had apparently fallen on deaf ears, perhaps because the principal was a close friend of several board members and the brother of the mayor. Board members were appointed in this district, not elected.

This principal had been in the school district for more than 20 years. Rather than build a case and fire him, the previous superintendents had chosen not to make waves, opting instead for damage control by letting experienced teachers cover many of the principal's responsibilities. Dr. Ferguson knew she would have a difficult task removing this principal. As a new superintendent, she would most likely follow the lead of her predecessors. She desperately hoped the principal would retire soon.

Illustrative Case 1: Inheriting an Underperforming Principal
Analysis

Dr. Ferguson, the new superintendent, recognized that the principal was not performing in accordance with his defined job responsibilities. While she had documentation of his inadequate performance across several superintendents and her own observations, there was no plan for improvement or any indication of attempts at the district level to address or remediate his inadequacies. It appeared that the previous superintendents and board members found their own self-interests in job security more important than service to the students and the interests of their parents.

No sound evaluation system was in place before Dr. Ferguson's arrival, a deficiency for which the entire school and community paid. The attempts at damage control, along with unprincipled and uncritical loyalty to senior employees and avoidance of controversy, are unacceptable practices when student welfare and the public good are at stake.

Dr. Ferguson failed to serve the students of her district by accepting less than adequate performance from the principal and teachers at this elementary school. She recognized that lack of leadership resulted in poor implementation of effective teaching strategies, which led to long-term negative consequences for students. Perhaps she feared the perceived political connections of the principal or lack of support for her position, but she became part of the continued dysfunction of the school when she did not attempt to remedy the situation through sound personnel evaluation.

Fair and accurate personnel evaluation, coupled with appropriate actions based on the evaluation results, serve a school superintendent well in building staff morale, increasing student learning, and establishing credibility with the parents and the community. The absence of such a system or its misuse invariably harms all of a school's constituencies.

Illustrative Case 2: Dismissing an Unsatisfactory Instructor
Description

Dr. Alverez, a newly hired department chair in a large university, found herself in the uncomfortable position of being required to respond to several student complaints regarding an instructor on her staff. The class in question was a third-year class with 384 students. The students alleged that the lecturer could not maintain appropriate classroom control. They also charged that he was not prepared adequately for each class, indicating that he often got lost while he was lecturing and at times contradicted himself from one class session to the next.

Dr. Alverez reviewed the instructor's file and found detailed evidence of previous similar shortcomings. She confirmed these deficiencies by observing him several times, informed him in writing of her concerns about his teaching competency, and finally awarded him a zero merit increment for the year. She next informed him in writing that, as outlined in the university faculty agreement, instructors are evaluated only on teaching. Therefore, should he receive a zero merit increment the following year, she would have to recommend his dismissal to the dean. At the same time, she advised him to seek assistance with his teaching and directed him to the teaching services on campus.

In accordance with the university faculty agreement, Dr. Alverez and three other faculty members observed the instructor periodically during the following year. They met to compare their findings and found that they all agreed that the instructor's performance was unsatisfactory, citing a lack of classroom control, apparent lack of understanding of subject matter, and confused classroom presentations.

Based on these findings, the department chair awarded a zero merit increment for the second time and recommended to the dean that this instructor be released. The dean accepted the recommendation, and the Faculty Evaluation Committee (FEC) upheld the action. The FEC noted that the department chair had provided adequate notice of deficiency as well as the opportunity to correct it and assistance to do so and that the four evaluators, observing separately, all had found that the instructor's teaching performance was unsatisfactory. The instructor did not appeal the case, recognizing that due process had been followed.

Illustrative Case 2: Dismissing an Unsatisfactory Instructor
Analysis

Dr. Alverez considered the students' complaints as worthy of attention. She investigated the situation on her own, checking the instructor's file and making personal classroom observations. She followed the procedures outlined in the university faculty agreement.

The rights of the instructor were safeguarded by the faculty agreement. During the first of the two years, he was observed on multiple occasions. At the end of the year, he was given specific written feedback and provided with information as to where he could get help on campus. He was observed on multiple occasions by multiple observers in the second year. Dr. Alverez's involvement and her adherence to the faculty agreement demonstrated her commitment to safeguarding the rights of students to appropriate and adequate instruction and to the instructor for appropriate evaluation.

Charges of unsatisfactory or incompetent instruction should be addressed as early as possible. If they are not confirmed and dealt with before the tenure or retention decision, they cannot be part of that crucial judgment. After tenure is granted, dismissal becomes difficult. If the previous chairs had instituted the aforementioned procedure before granting tenure to this instructor, they would have had more options and would have shortened the time that students were exposed to inadequate instruction. Even after the instructor had passed the tenure review, if incompetence subsequently was identified, a detailed investigation and appropriate actions should have been pursued immediately since institutions can dismiss staff to protect the interests of students.

Supporting Documentation

Andrews, H. A. (1995). *Teachers can be fired.* Peru, IL: Catfeet Press.

Bridges, E. M. (1992). *The incompetent teacher: Managerial responses.* Washington, DC: Falmer Press.

Haertel, G. D. (1994). *Qualification, roles, and responsibilities of assessors, evaluators, and mentors in teacher evaluation.* Livermore, CA: EREAPA Associates.

Haertel, G. D., & Wheeler, P. H. (1994). *Rater effects when judging performance.* Livermore, CA: EREAPA Associates.

McConney, A., Wheeler, P. H., Wiersma, W., Millman, J., Stufflebeam, D., Gullickson, A., et al. (1996). *Teacher evaluation kit and data base of CREATE products* [CD-ROM]. Kalamazoo: Western Michigan University, Center for Research on Educational Accountability and Teacher Evaluation.

Scriven, M. (1988a). Duty-based teacher evaluation. *Journal of Personnel Evaluation in Education, 1,* 319–334.

Scriven, M. (1988b). Evaluating teachers as professionals: The duties-based approach. In S. J. Stanley & W. J. Popham (Eds.), *Teacher evaluation: Six prescriptions for success* (pp. 110–142). Alexandria, VA: Association for Supervision and Curriculum Development.

Stanley, S. J., & Popham, J. W. (Eds.). (1988). *Teacher evaluation: Six prescriptions for success.* Alexandria, VA: Association for Supervision and Curriculum Development.

Strike, K. A. (1990). The ethics of educational evaluation. In J. Millman & L. Darling-Hammond (Eds.), *The new handbook of teacher evaluation: Assessing elementary and secondary school teachers* (pp. 356–373). Newbury Park, CA: Sage.

Stronge, J. H., & Helm, V. M. (1991). *Evaluating professional support personnel in education.* Newbury Park, CA: Sage.

Wheeler, P. H., & Scriven, M. (1997). Building the foundation: Teacher roles and responsibilities. In J. H. Stronge (Ed.), *Evaluating teaching: A guide to current thinking and best practice* (pp. 27–58). Thousand Oaks, CA: Corwin Press.

P2 Appropriate Policies and Procedures

> **STANDARD** Guidelines for personnel evaluations should be recorded and provided to the evaluatee in policy statements, negotiated agreements, or personnel evaluation manuals.

Explanation. Formal evaluation guidelines are written statements that define the purpose and uses of the personnel evaluation system, outline the data collection and reporting procedures to be followed, identify the persons who will have access to the evaluation data and information, and describe how the data will be stored and for how long (see U2, Defined Uses; U5, Functional Reporting; A2, Defined Expectations; P3, Access to Evaluation Information). The development of policy guidelines should take into consideration relevant laws and ethical codes and should include contractual, administrative, statutory, and constitutional provisions pertinent to the school district or state (see P7, Legal Viability). The guidelines should be written and presented in a way that is easily understood and applicable to all engaged in or affected by the evaluation. It is important for all evaluatees and users to have a common understanding of the purposes, uses, and procedures of the evaluation to help ensure that evaluations are conducted consistently in a respectful, fair, and equitable manner.

The governing board of the institution should adopt formal written policies to set parameters for fair and effective personnel evaluations. Written policy guidelines should address the following key issues:

- Purposes and uses of the evaluation (see U2, Defined Uses).
- Specific performance expectations for each job or level of certification (see A2, Defined Expectations).
- Diversity, including experience, qualifications, race, culture, gender, sexual orientation, and disabilities in the workplace (see A8, Bias Identification and Management).
- Access to and security of personnel evaluation files (see P3, Access to Evaluation Information; A7, Systematic Data Control).

- Local, state, and federal requirements concerning employment practices and decisions (see P7, Legal Viability).
- Criteria for dismissal and mandated professional development (see U6, Follow-Up and Professional Development).
- Appeal and grievance procedures.
- Evaluation schedule.
- Data collection, analysis, and reporting procedure.
- Skills, training, and qualifications of evaluators (see U3, Evaluator Qualifications).

Rationale.   A clear understanding of the policies and procedures guiding evaluations is needed to support the goals of the institution and promote professional development and growth of all personnel. Personnel evaluations must be carried out in a consistent, equitable, and legal manner. Formal written guidelines provide a foundation for the understanding necessary to conduct sound and effective evaluations. In addition, written policies reduce the likelihood of litigation and promote trust in and support of the personnel evaluation.

Clearly written purposes, criteria, and procedures that are outlined in formal policy statements, collective bargaining agreements, and procedural handbooks should be shared and discussed with stakeholders in the evaluation process. This will increase the likelihood that performance expectations are understood, a uniform standard of judgment is applied, diversity is appropriately and consistently addressed, and evaluation results are respected and used. Importantly, this will give evaluatees and other legitimate users of the evaluations greater confidence in both the evaluations and the evaluators.

GUIDELINES

A. Require formal written policies stating that all employees are subject to systematic evaluation.
B. Include written policies in all appropriate and accessible documents such as employee handbooks, memos of understanding, faculty agreements, and so forth.
C. Ensure that policies address all the elements for effective personnel evaluation set forth in these standards and are aligned with the goals and mission of the organization (e.g., school, school district, college, university, training institute).
D. Clarify in writing the differences in performance expectations associated with identified personnel classification levels (e.g., by certification level, job assignment), so that evaluations are performed in accordance with the specific job expectations (see A2, Defined Expectations).
E. Ensure that all written policies respect and take account of the diversity found in the workplace (e.g., experience, qualifications, race, culture, gender, sexual orientation, and disabilities; see U1, Constructive Orientation).
F. Ensure that all written policies regarding personnel evaluations meet local, state, and federal legal requirements for employment decisions such as state teacher certification and federal antidiscrimination protections and are consistent with basic principles of fairness and human rights (see P7, Legal Viability).

    G. Make guidelines sufficiently specific and clear to enhance common Understanding.

    H. Ensure that all employees are provided with copies of personnel evaluation policies and are given an opportunity to review and discuss policies on an annual basis, at minimum.

    I. Provide for a systematic review of policies by a governing board of stakeholder groups (see A11, Metaevaluation).

    J. Change evaluation guidelines when evaluation practices are changed, when guidelines are in conflict with applicable law, or when role definitions change.

COMMON ERRORS

    A. Writing or adopting policy guidelines that are vague or unrealistic to implement (see F1, Practical Procedures).

    B. Failing to provide adequate oversight so that all evaluators correctly and consistently adhere to policies (see A11, Metaevaluation).

    C. Failing to provide written policies that include all levels of certification or jobs so that some employees are not evaluated or not evaluated using a valid process.

    D. Failing to provide written policies that adequately adhere to the legal and ethical requirements governing personnel evaluations (see P7, Legal Viability; U1, Constructive Orientation).

    E. Failing to provide all employees with written guidelines in an appropriate medium (e.g., employee handbooks) or to provide an opportunity for review and discussion on a regular basis.

    F. Making policy changes without changing written guidelines.

    G. Making changes in job roles and responsibilities without making necessary changes in written policy.

Illustrative Case 1: Changing an Entrenced Evaluation System
Description

The Springdale Unified School District school board adopted a new teacher evaluation system following the recommendation of the superintendent, Dr. Alducente. Before selecting the new system, Dr. Alducente appointed a committee representing elementary and secondary school teachers and administrators to meet throughout the school year and review various plans of evaluation. The existing evaluation model had been in place for the past 15 years. It required only two classroom observations by the principal, and Dr. Alducente thought the practice was too narrow. The new model added parent and student surveys, peer evaluation by other teachers, and self-evaluation against goals set by each teacher and agreed to by the principal at the beginning of the school year.

    Once school board members had reviewed an outline of the new evaluation model, Dr. Alducente formed a second committee, again representing teachers and administrators at the elementary and secondary school levels, to develop guidelines for collecting, compiling, and analyzing evaluation data. A detailed timeline also was established to guide the correct implementation of the system.

Once the new evaluation policies were written, the school board's attorney reviewed them to ensure their compatibility with all local, state, and federal legal requirements. A series of meetings then provided opportunities for all teachers, principals, supervisors, senior administrators, and parents in the Springdale Unified School District to review and discuss the new policies, evaluation components, and procedures. The school board formally adopted the new policies governing the personnel evaluation system after these reviews and discussions, which revealed a high level of acceptance. The employee handbooks for the district and the school board policy manual were updated to reflect the new policies. Resources were then provided to train teachers and staff to gather and use the needed data and information in a constructive manner.

Illustrative Case 1: Changing an Entrenched Evaluation System
Analysis

The school board and Dr. Alducente acted correctly in reviewing and making changes in the personnel evaluation procedures and policies to accommodate the new model. Often policies are not considered and revised when a new system is adopted. Failure to do so endangers proper implementation of the new model. The evaluation model and the policies that govern it must reflect the actual current methods of evaluation. It is equally important to ensure a common understanding of new policies through a series of reviews and opportunities for discussion.

Whenever a new system of personnel evaluation is adopted, new written policies must be developed to ensure effective implementation. These guidelines also must be reviewed to ensure compliance with local, state, and federal legal requirements. Encouraging participation by stakeholders through committee work or review increases common understanding and ownership of the process.

By involving a wide group of stakeholders and including a training component in the new system, the Springdale Unified School District avoided issues that may have emerged over time through a lack of understanding or support. Ongoing reviews, discussions, and training, however, should be built into the policies to ensure continued awareness and understanding.

Illustrative Case 2: Gradual Development of Inequities in Evaluation
Description

A university required that all departments evaluate faculty performance on an annual basis. The written policies, however, did not specify the criteria to be used across departments. Instead, department chairs were instructed to determine criteria appropriate to their discipline. The policies did, however, provide specific guidelines on the uses of the evaluations in terms of faculty promotions and salary levels.

When the university first adopted the evaluation policy calling for annual evaluations to be conducted within departments, the department chairs met regularly to review and align their evaluation criteria and procedures to ensure a uniform system. This process evolved informally rather than being specified by written policy. Over time, department chairs were replaced, and the informal process gradually diminished. As a result, each department ultimately developed its own set of criteria and procedures for evaluation. The rigor of the evaluations varied widely among the departments. Different departments used varying combinations of student feedback, peer evaluations of classroom instruction, and current scholarly activities, such as publications and professional involvement in departmental activities. This resulted in a general sense of inequitable treatment, lowered morale, and an increase in the number of grievances filed by faculty members.

Illustrative Case 2: Gradual Development of Inequities in Evaluation
Analysis

In this case, lack of a clearly written policy resulted in inconsistencies across departments within the university. The original intention may have been to allow maximum freedom to the departments, but the outcome led to inequities in evaluation results. The lack of procedural guidelines jeopardized the evaluation process and greatly diminished its usefulness as seen in the decline in morale and the increase in grievances.

The lack of formal written policies could lead to cases in which bias could not be identified and managed, resulting in unfair treatment of evaluatees on the basis of race, gender, age, national origin, and so forth. Written policies can specify practices that would discourage consideration of such factors in conducting evaluations and raise the awareness of bias among evaluators. Ordinarily, university-level policies address overarching issues such as cultural diversity, with departments assuring compliance with that policy.

This university could have avoided many of these concerns about the inequity of evaluations had it first examined whether a uniform evaluation system across all departments was appropriate or whether establishing evaluation criteria and procedures should be the responsibility of each department. After responsibility for these elements was defined, the university should have presented its decision in a written document made available to all faculty members through the university's Web site.

Based on its initial action, the senior officials of the university appeared to believe that each department should be responsible for developing its own evaluation criteria. However, the department chairs initially believed that a uniform set of criteria and a unified approach to evaluation were needed. Over time this view changed, perhaps due to failure to agree on uniform criteria or a common approach to evaluation procedures. Given the present variety of departmental practices, the written policy should require that the faculty members in each department discuss and agree on the criteria to be used in their department, with these criteria reflecting the expectations of the department's discipline. Likewise, procedures for collecting information and data used in evaluations should be discussed and agreed to within each department. The agreements should then be written and published in a departmental handbook. A common understanding by all faculty members would increase the likelihood of equitable and fair treatment. Faculty members would know the expectations for their job performance and could work to meet these clearly defined expectations (see A2, Defined Expectations). Such policies would lead to greater understanding of the purpose and uses of the evaluation process, thus creating a sense of fairness.

Supporting Documentation

Airasian, P. W., & Gullickson, A. (1997). Teacher self-evaluation. In J. H. Stronge (Ed.), *Evaluating teaching: A guide to current thinking and best practice* (pp. 215–247). Thousand Oaks, CA: Corwin Press.

American Association of School Administrators. (1978). *Standards for school personnel administration* (3rd ed.). Seven Hills, OH: Author.

American Federation of Teachers. (2003). *Where we stand: Teacher quality.* Washington, DC: Author.

American Psychological Association, Division 14. (1980). *Principles for the validation and use of personnel selection procedures.* Washington, DC: Author.

Andrews, H. A. (1985). *Evaluating for excellence.* Stillwater, OK: New Forums Press.

Cooper, B. S., Ehrensal, P. A., & Bromme, M. (2005). School-level politics and professional development: Traps in evaluating the quality of practicing teachers. *Educational Policy, 19*(1), 112–125.

Costa, E. W., II. (2004). Performance-based evaluation for superintendents. *School Administrator, 61*(9), 14–16, 18.

Elmore, R. F. (2005). Accountable leadership. *The Educational Forum, 69*(2), 134–142.

Fenstermacher, G. D., & Richardson, V. (2005). On making determinations of quality in teaching. *Teachers College Record, 107*(1), 186–212.

French-Lazovik, G. (Ed.). (1982). *Practices that improve teaching evaluation.* San Francisco: Jossey-Bass.

Grossman, P., & Thompson, C. (2004). District policy and beginning teachers: A lens on teacher learning. *Educational Evaluation and Policy Analysis, 26*(4), 281–301.

Koppich, J. (2005). Addressing teacher quality through induction, professional compensation, and evaluation: The effects of labor-management relations. *Educational Policy, 19*(1), 90–111.

Landy, F. J., & Farr, J. L. (1983). *The measurement of work performance: Methods, theory, and applications.* New York: Academic Press.

Lingenfelter, P. E. (2003). Educational accountability: Setting standards, improving performance. *Change, 35*(2), 18–23.

National Association of Elementary School Principals. (2001). *Leading learning communities: Standards for what principals should know and be able to do.* Alexandria, VA: Author.

Reeves, D. R. (2004). Evaluating administrators. *Educational Leadership, 61*(7), 52–58.

P3　Access to Evaluation Information

> **STANDARD**　**To maintain confidentiality, access to evaluation information should be limited to the people with established legitimate permission to review and use the information.**

Explanation.　Access to personnel evaluation information must be limited to those who have a professional need and authorization to view these records. This includes the evaluatee, evaluator, supervisors of the evaluator and evaluatee, and others who have established a legitimate use of the records (see U2, Defined Uses).

No records should be included in the formal personnel folder without the knowledge of the evaluatee. To ensure this, all documents, such as data reports and evaluation summaries, must be signed and dated by the evaluatee and the evaluator to indicate that a review of the document has taken place, regardless of whether or not there was agreement concerning the data contained in the report. All written records submitted by the evaluatee, such as those pertaining to a grievance or other documentation pertinent to the evaluation process, must be included in the personnel evaluation folder.

Confidentiality of personnel records must be strictly maintained. Anyone who meets the criteria for legitimate access may not discuss anything contained in the records outside the context of professional review or with others not privy to the information. Appropriate measures must be maintained by the institution to ensure compliance with this standard. Access should be granted only to those who can display legitimate purpose and provide the necessary credentials and written authorization to view such records.

Rationale.　Personnel records necessarily contain sensitive materials pertaining to an individual's job performance. In most cases, use of these records affects the livelihood of the individual. While it is necessary to have full knowledge and use of this type of record when making personnel decisions, such as granting tenure, dismissal, or promotion, other uses of records should be scrutinized carefully for legitimate justification.

All uses of personnel records should be defined in written policies (see P2, Appropriate Policies and Procedures). Only those individuals who can establish a legitimate use of the records in accordance with written policies should be granted access. Even then, a procedure should be in place for recording who accessed each personnel file and for what purpose (e.g., review, modification, etc.).

The use of electronic records and databases for warehousing school records, including personnel records, has become increasingly common. It is especially important that any electronic system of data management have safeguards that prevent unauthorized access to these records.

GUIDELINES

A. Specify within written policies the uses and users of personnel evaluation records (see U2, Defined Uses).

B. Maintain a system within the institution or organization to safeguard personnel records (e.g., locked filing cabinets kept in a central location) against casual or illegal access by individuals who do not have a legitimate purpose (see A7, Systematic Data Control).

C. Provide a means for maintaining written documentation including signature, purpose, file name, and date of those who access records.

D. Establish a written policy for all documents required to be included in the personnel records.

E. Establish a written policy for accurate dating and signing of all documentation and records to be included in a personnel folder.

F. Review records periodically and systematically to provide oversight and to ensure that these policies are followed consistently; immediately address any oversights or misuse of personnel records.

G. Establish firewalls and secure passwords to prevent unauthorized access to electronically stored records.

COMMON ERRORS

A. Failing to provide a written policy to address issues of maintaining restricted access to personnel evaluation records.

B. Failing to maintain a system to prevent unauthorized access to personnel records.

C. Failing to provide written documentation of dates and users of personnel records.

D. Carelessly handling records or allowing unauthorized personnel, such as secretaries or school volunteers, to have easy access to records.

E. Granting access to personnel records by individuals who have no legitimate need or purpose.

F. Storing personnel files and documents in an unsupervised area, in unlocked file cabinets, or in poorly secured electronic databases.

G. Failing to include issues of confidentiality and access in evaluator training (see U3, Evaluator Qualifications).

Illustrative Case 1: The Sneak-a-Peek Principal
Description

Mr. Beck, a middle school principal, and Ms. Manganaro, a high school assistant principal, worked in the Hallowell School District. Along with several candidates from outside the district, Mr. Beck and Ms. Manganaro applied for the job of principal at the new high school. Following a round of intense interviews with staff, parents, students, and central office administrators, the choice came down to one of the two internal candidates, Mr. Beck or Ms. Manganaro.

Mr. Beck was worried that a review of personnel records might show that Ms. Manganaro had received superior ratings over the past three years, and his own evaluation records might not be as favorable in comparison. He also wondered if there was anything in Ms. Manganaro's records that might "give him an edge" in the final stage of interviews.

On a visit to the central office, Mr. Beck stopped by the unlocked records room that housed all student files and staff personnel evaluation records. The records were stored alphabetically in unlocked file cabinets. Anyone who used the back hallway to the board room had easy access to the unlocked room and the records.

Mr. Beck easily found Ms. Manganaro's personnel file and while reviewing it found an unfavorable report based on an evaluation completed several years earlier. The deficiency in performance had been addressed satisfactorily through professional development. Nevertheless, hoping to discredit Ms. Manganaro, Mr. Beck made several comments at strategic times about this report, ensuring that the issue would be raised during the final stage of interviews.

Illustrative Case 1: The Sneak-a-Peek Principal
Analysis

While nothing can absolutely prevent unethical, illegal, or immoral actions on the part of individuals, steps can be taken to safeguard the rights of those persons who might otherwise be harmed. In this case, the school district did not have *any* safeguards in place to protect the confidentiality of the personnel records of its employees. Files were kept in an area where they were easily accessible by anyone using the hallway to the boardroom. This included all employees of the district as well as the public.

Neither the room nor the files were locked or monitored. This careless maintenance of sensitive records invited misuse. No system was in place to document access or require users to show justification for access to the records. Mr. Beck felt perfectly safe in breaching the confidentiality of the files without worrying about discovery. Had he been required to sign out the file, document his purpose, and show justification for access, he may have been prevented from seeing Ms. Manganaro's file. As it was, he was able to find damaging information and use it outside its intended context to further his own career.

All personnel evaluation records should be maintained under a strict monitoring system that prevents unauthorized use (see A7, Systematic Data Control). No one should be able to access personnel records without documentation and without providing a legitimate purpose. Every precaution should be taken to maintain the integrity of such files.

Mr. Beck's lack of ethics may not have been solved through a system to protect confidentiality of files, but the reputation and fair treatment of Ms. Manganaro would have been safeguarded.

Illustrative Case 2: Breaching Confidentiality by Transferring Work Assignments
Description

Ms. Bawa, a department chair at a community college, was charged with completing the personnel evaluation summary records for each faculty member within her department. The community college was in the planning stage for a much needed expansion program that involved a great deal of time and effort on the part of all department chairs. Because of this unusual demand on her time, Ms. Bawa had fallen behind in completing the write-ups of her faculty evaluations. She had always taken this task very seriously, but this year she felt overwhelmed with other obligations. Although she had completed the tasks associated with the evaluations and had already held the required conferences, she had not yet written the final reports.

Feeling the pressure of deadlines, Ms. Bawa called in her secretary, Mrs. Rosales, who also was overburdened with end of term obligations. Ms. Bawa handed Mrs. Rosales her handwritten evaluation notes and other documentation and instructed her to type the formal evaluation reports. Mrs. Rosales was to use her own computer. Ms. Bawa reminded her that the reports were confidential and should be handled as such.

Mrs. Rosales intended to maintain the confidentiality of the reports, and her own past performance and her professional attitude had inspired confidence by the department chair. Other job requirements, however, demanded an unusually large amount of her time, had more pressing deadlines, and were more directly related to her own job. Therefore, Mrs. Rosales allowed a particularly mature student worker to complete the task of typing the evaluation reports. She thought that it was just a matter of entering and, when necessary, arranging Ms. Bawa's handwritten text and that the student worker was capable of doing this task. The student, however, discovered a low evaluation of a particularly popular instructor. In an effort of support for this instructor, he rallied several classmates and began a campaign to change the evaluation. Once the source of the personnel information was revealed, this action caused a great deal of embarrassment, not only to the instructor, but also to Ms. Bawa.

Illustrative Case 2: Breaching Confidentiality by Transferring Work Assignments
Analysis

Ms. Bawa began the chain of breaking confidentiality when she transferred her duties to Mrs. Rosales. While her trust in Mrs. Rosales may have been well placed, Mrs. Rosales was not identified as a legitimate user of evaluation information and should not have been assigned the task of writing up the reports.

Mrs. Rosales further violated confidentiality of evaluation reports by giving them to a student to complete. The task was more than simply entering text, because the information needed to be reorganized. Handing off work to other employees may be a common practice among administrators faced with deadlines and other pressing commitments, but in this case, Ms. Bawa allowed unauthorized access to records. Personnel evaluation was not within the scope of work for either Mrs. Rosales or the student worker, so neither of them had a legitimate purpose for access to what could be sensitive documentation. Neither Mrs. Rosales nor the student had any expectation of confidentiality in performing this task. Ms. Bawa seriously violated procedures by not ensuring confidentiality of the records.

While time constraints and other demands may be a realistic part of any administrative job, the department chair could have delegated less sensitive tasks to her secretary if needed. By prioritizing job requirements and duties, Ms. Bawa could have completed the evaluation reports herself, thus maintaining the integrity of the process.

The community college might also explore whether a less time-consuming and cumbersome method of maintaining and writing up evaluation reports could be developed to ensure feasibility of the process (see F1, Practical Procedures). This would alleviate the temptation to involve others who do not have authorization to view sensitive records.

Supporting Documentation

Avraamidou, L. (2003). Exploring the influence of web-based portfolio development on learning to teach elementary science. *Journal of Technology and Teacher Education, 11*(3), 415–442.

Bennett, D. E. (2000/2001). Electronic educational data security; system analysis and teacher training. *Journal of Educational Technology Systems, 29*(1), 3–20.

Olsen, F. (2001, July 6). Hacker attack strikes Indiana U. for second time in 4 months. *The Chronicle of Higher Education,* p. A30.

Remington, L. R. (2002). School internal investigations of employees, open records law, and the prying press. *Journal of Law & Education, 31*(4) 459–468.

Revell, P. (2004). Why big brother must be right. *The Times Educational Supplement, 4576,* 9.

Smith, P. L. (2001). Using multimedia portfolios to assess preservice teacher and P–12 student learning. *Action in Teacher Education, 22*(4), 28–39.

Zembal-Saul, C. (2002). Web-based portfolios: A vehicle for examining prospective elementary teachers' developing understandings of teaching science. *Journal of Science Teacher Education, 13*(4), 283–302.

P4   Interactions
With Evaluatees

STANDARD   The evaluator should respect human dignity and
act in a professional, considerate, and courteous manner.

Explanation.   Evaluators must recognize and take into account evaluatees' personal and professional needs as well as the context within which the evaluatees work (see A3, Analysis of Context). When evaluatees are treated with respect, they are more likely to respond to fair and equitable evaluations, regardless of their cultural and ethnic background and experience. It is important to develop rapport, be professional, and follow institutional protocol. An evaluator must demonstrate a genuine interest in the evaluatee as a person who can gain competence from valid evaluative feedback and who, in turn, can provide improved professional service.

Rationale.   The benefits of acting in a professional, considerate, and courteous manner are pervasive throughout the evaluation process. Evaluatees are less likely to feel anxious when the evaluator and evaluatee share a sense of professionalism and basic human dignity. Evaluation findings are more likely to be presented and received as constructive (see U1, Constructive Orientation) and oriented to professional growth (see U6, Follow-Up and Professional Development). The morale of the evaluatee and the credibility of the evaluation process likely will be enhanced. When positive and negative findings and the accompanying evidence are presented clearly, objectively, and privately, the evaluatee is more likely to judge the process as fair and the evaluator as credible. Overall, the exercise of good human relations can support the evaluatee's sense of worth and professionalism, foster better service, and strengthen the credibility of personnel evaluation.

Evaluators who neither understand nor respect the feelings of evaluatees may needlessly offend them or provoke hostility toward personnel evaluation. Such offense violates the moral imperative that a person's dignity be respected. Such behavior on the part of an evaluator also can lead to lawsuits and grievances.

GUIDELINES

A. Inform evaluatees about all aspects of the evaluation process. The information provided should include the following:

- Criteria to be used to judge performance (see A2, Defined Expectations).
- Assessment methods and procedures (see A4, Documented Purposes and Procedures).
- Information on how the results and collected information will be reported and used (see U2, Defined Uses).
- Process for evaluatees to appeal an evaluation finding or the decision.

B. Require evaluators and evaluatees to seek mutually acceptable goals and time lines, and encourage them to establish a productive, cooperative relationship.

C. Before formal assessment, ensure adequate time for early interaction among all participants in an evaluation to develop mutual trust and understanding (see F2, Political Viability).

D. Schedule and publish evaluation activities before beginning the evaluation and maintain the schedule as published.

E. Communicate results and supporting documentation clearly, objectively, privately, and sensitively in a way that helps evaluatees see the value of the evaluation in relation to the expectations held and the uses made of the evaluation (see U1, Constructive Orientation; A2, Defined Expectations; and U2, Defined Uses).

F. Provide suggestions that will inform future professional development in areas that need improvement and that will enhance the evaluatee's performance in terms of the defined expectations for the position held (see U6, Follow-Up and Professional Development).

G. Provide evaluators with periodic training in human relations procedures and sensitivity to diversity (see A8, Bias Identification and Management).

H. Monitor the conduct of the evaluation to determine if it has been conducted fairly and respectfully (see A11, Metaevaluation).

I. Ensure that all employees are evaluated using standardized procedures and policies (see P2, Appropriate Policies and Procedures).

J. Ensure that balanced reporting of performance is presented in all conferences and written or verbal communication (see P5, Comprehensive Evaluation).

COMMON ERRORS

A. Failing to create the conditions for timely and constructive interactions between evaluatees and evaluators.

B. Failing to consider the context in which the evaluatee works (see A3, Analysis of Context).

C. Allowing too much time to elapse between data collection (e.g., classroom observation) and conferencing.

D. Showing a general lack of respect for an employee whose work is unsatisfactory.

E. Engaging in public disparagement of an employee.

F. Using evaluation punitively by such practices as increasing the number of observations unnecessarily, changing job expectations without due notice, disregarding issues of cultural diversity, or providing exceptionally harsh criticism beyond the scope of the evaluation.

Illustrative Case 1: Evaluation Feedback Helps a New Teacher
Description

Ms. Mak, a new teacher in a middle school, possessed an initial teaching certificate. She asked her principal if she could be evaluated during her first year of teaching, even though such evaluations were required only in the first half of the second year of teaching. The purpose of the second year evaluation was to determine if a teacher should be awarded a permanent teaching certificate. Ms. Mak pointed out that she did not want the first year evaluation to take the place of the second year evaluation and recognized that she would be evaluated in two consecutive years. She indicated that she wanted feedback on how well she was doing now and what she needed to do to improve prior to the critical second year evaluation. The principal agreed with her request. Working together, Ms. Mak and the principal agreed that the evaluation process regularly used in the second year would be used without change for the first year evaluation.

The evaluation process involved two scheduled and two unscheduled classroom observations by the principal, a review of sample lessons by the department head for the content area taught by Ms. Mak, and a review of the teacher's assessment methods and reporting procedures by the department head and the assessment specialist in the district office.

The evaluation findings revealed that Ms. Mak's instructional methods and the activities she assigned her students to complete were more than adequate for a beginning teacher. It also was apparent that she was well liked and respected by her students. Her one area of weakness appeared to be her assessments and reporting. After presenting these finding to Ms. Mak, the principal asked her why she thought her instruction was stronger than her assessments. She indicated that she understood the results and explained that her teacher preparation program included courses on learning and development, cross-culture psychology, the foundations of education, and curriculum and instruction, but not a course in student assessment. The principal then showed her *The Student Evaluation Standards'* (Joint Committee on Standards for Educational Evaluation, 2003) list of evaluator qualifications for evaluating student work (U3, Evaluator Qualifications) and suggested that she take a six-week summer course in assessment and evaluation as a way of improving her qualifications in this area. Ms. Mak accepted the principal's recommendation. She also began work on a master's degree in education.

Illustrative Case 1: Evaluation Feedback Helps a New Teacher
Analysis

The principal's attitude was one of interest, respect, and support. Quite obviously, Ms. Mak was comfortable in approaching the principal with a request for additional evaluations. The principal accepted Ms. Mak's request and worked collaboratively with her to plan and implement a sound and credible evaluation. She sought Ms. Mak's explanation concerning why assessment and evaluation practices were weaker than her instructional practices. The principal then introduced Ms. Mak to *The Student Evaluation Standards* (Joint Committee on Standards for Educational Evaluation, 2003) and provided relevant suggestions for follow-up (see U6, Follow-Up and Professional Development). The principal's willingness to conduct a comprehensive, balanced evaluation and the way the evaluation results were reported and discussed allowed strengths to be identified and reinforced and a problem area to be addressed in a meaningful way (see P5, Comprehensive Evaluation; U6, Follow-Up and Professional Development).

Illustrative Case 2: Devaluing an Employee and His Job
Description

Mr. Sharma, the director of admissions at a small liberal arts college, was due for an annual evaluation. The evaluator was an administrator who had responsibility for all student records and services. Because of their busy schedules, Mr. Sharma and the administrator responsible for the evaluation did not see each other except for the occasional staff meeting, even though admissions was an area that the college needed to improve. The administrator perceived admissions as a necessary, but nonacademic, salesmanship function. Her perception was well known among the senior administrators of the college.

When Mr. Sharma arrived for his evaluation, the administrator invited him into her office, but continued to work on other papers on her desk. Without referring to any formal, written evaluation, she stated that she "supposed" Mr. Sharma had done "as good a job as could be expected, considering the nature of the student pool" and that "at least the admissions office had managed to maintain the entering class sizes at nearly the same level as the prior year." She commented that Mr. Sharma had at least found some warm bodies to fill the student places.

The administrator failed to give Mr. Sharma any opportunity to ask questions or present evidence of his job performance. She also did not offer any feedback on specific performance expectations. Mr. Sharma left the meeting feeling confused about the outcomes of his performance review. He was not aware of any changes that he needed to make, and he did not have any indication from the administrator's tone of voice and attention to him that she valued either him or his job.

Illustrative Case 2: Devaluing an Employee and His Job
Analysis

The administrator in this case failed to communicate the results of her evaluation clearly, objectively, or with sensitivity. Her attitude toward Mr. Sharma lacked professionalism and collegiality, and it strongly conveyed her lack of respect for both Mr. Sharma and his work. There also could have been bias on the part of the administrator if Mr. Sharma's race, gender, or national origin played any role in the administrator's treatment of him. The administrator missed an opportunity to build a solid professional relationship that would help create a stronger admissions program, thus furthering the goals and mission of their institution.

The administrator's overtly negative attitude toward Mr. Sharma and the admissions office was another issue. Knowing how this particular administrator felt about the admissions function, the college president should have appointed another administrator to evaluate Mr. Sharma's performance (see A8, Bias Identification and Management). The administrator, knowing her own attitude, could have asked to be replaced. Once she had agreed to undertake the role of evaluator, however, she should have accepted the marketing-oriented admissions program as a bona fide method of recruitment and approached the task of evaluating Mr. Sharma's performance on that basis (see A2, Defined Expectations), according him the respect and consideration she would have given a teaching member of the faculty. The college administrator should stress the need for professional courtesy in all personnel evaluations conducted in the college.

Supporting Documentation

Burmeister, L., & Hensley, P. A. (2004). It's all about relationships. *Leadership, 34*(1), 30–31.

Cooper, B. S., Ehrensal, P. A., & Bromme, M. (2005). School-level politics and professional development: Traps in evaluating the quality of practicing teachers. *Educational Policy, 19*(1), 112–125.

Fredricks, J. G. (2001). Why teachers leave. *The Education Digest, 66*(8), 46–48.

Heller, D. A. (2002). The power of gentleness. *Educational Leadership, 59*(8), 76–79.

Honaker, C. J. (2004). How leaders can enrich the school environment. *Kappa Delta Pi Record, 40*(3), 116–118.

Joint Committee on Standards for Educational Evaluation. (2003). *The student evaluation standards.* Thousand Oaks, CA: Corwin Press.

Regan, S. D. (1998). Becoming a dean: The impact of humanistic counselor training on a career in academic administration. *Journal of Humanistic Education and Development, 37*(1), 21–26.

Weber, M. R. (2003). Coping with malcontents. *School Administrator, 60*(2), 6–10.

Whitaker, T. (2003). Power plays of difficult employees. *School Administrator, 60*(2), 12–14, 16.

P5 Comprehensive Evaluation

> **STANDARD** Personnel evaluations should identify strengths and areas for growth.

Explanation. Comprehensive evaluations involve identifying both an evaluatee's strengths and the areas for growth to provide a fair and balanced evaluation. Acknowledgment of strengths (e.g., mastery of information, skills, positive interest, enthusiasm for the job, etc.) provides a basis for reinforcing job performance and building on existing talents. Areas in need of improvement include any skills related to job performance that need to be addressed to ensure that each employee is performing to maximum potential. Educators, regardless of level of competence and effectiveness, always should engage in learning and improvement in their knowledge and skills because education is a constantly changing and dynamic field.

Balancing an evaluation does not mean generating equal numbers of strengths and areas for growth. A balanced and comprehensive evaluation results in thorough and fair assessment and reporting both positive and negative aspects. It also means addressing deficiencies in performance when they occur. In the case of the marginal employee, where the evaluation identifies serious deficiencies, it is particularly important to also recognize identified areas of strength. Recognizing those strengths helps to prevent unnecessary harm to the employee's dignity and self-worth (see P4, Interactions With Evaluatees) and provides a basis for professional development (see U6, Follow-Up and Professional Development).

Rationale. Personnel evaluations should help evaluatees improve their job performance. The failure to address both strengths and weaknesses accurately will result in bias. This bias reduces validity (see A1, Valid Judgments) and utility (see U2, Defined Uses; U3, Evaluator Qualifications) of the evaluation findings. When positive and negative findings, accompanied by relevant and representative evidence, are presented clearly, objectively, and privately, the evaluatee is more likely to judge the process as fair, accept the evaluation findings and decisions made, and engage in an ongoing process of professional development.

GUIDELINES

A. Ensure that the evaluation procedures allow for comprehensive and accurate indications of evaluatees' strengths and weaknesses.
B. Ensure that evaluatees know what will be assessed, how evaluation data will be collected, how evaluation information will be used to identify strengths and weaknesses, and how the evaluation results can be used to design appropriate follow-up actions (see U6, Follow-Up and Professional Development).
C. Take into account the evaluatees' backgrounds, including factors such as race, culture, gender, sexual orientation, and disabilities, that might prejudice an evaluation and prevent a balanced view of performance (see A8, Bias Identification and Management).
D. Describe and justify the basis for interpreting both positive and negative assessment information and results.
E. Fully report both strengths and weaknesses with supporting evidence (see A10, Justified Conclusions; U5, Functional Reporting).
F. Record incidents outside the evaluatee's control that might account for inadequate performance (see A3, Analysis of Context).

COMMON ERRORS

A. Focusing the evaluation and data gathering in ways that will cause the findings to be inappropriately weighted positively or negatively.
B. Discontinuing a personnel evaluation that may prove embarrassing to please individuals (e.g., evaluatee, supervisor, evaluator) with a vested interest in the evaluation.
C. Reporting only positive findings and ignoring negative findings or reporting only negative findings and ignoring positive findings.
D. Failing to consider alternative perspectives that might change the interpretation of an evaluation result.
E. Reporting speculative or tentative findings to achieve a balance of strengths and weaknesses.
F. Relying on biased or limited data sources for data collection.
G. Failing to provide a clear outcome or report of the evaluation so that the evaluatee remains uncertain about results.

Illustrative Case 1: Looking at All Sides
Description

In September, the school board of a large school district asked Ms. Levine, a personnel evaluation consultant from another state, to evaluate the district's school superintendent. The board wanted the review completed in time to make a decision about whether to reappoint the superintendent at the end of his current contract. While there appeared to be no serious questions about the superintendent's performance, board policy called for a mandatory evaluation in the last year of a superintendent's contract. The district's director of human resources was responsible for Ms. Levine's contract and seeing that the contracted work was done. He told Ms. Levine that using out-of-state external evaluators was part of the district's overall evaluation system and that the out-of-state evaluators were expected to complete a site visit as part of their evaluations.

Ms. Levine decided to use the 360-degree personnel evaluation approach and conveyed this to the director of human resources. She pointed out that the decision was one of high stakes for the superintendent as the evaluatee, the board as his employer, the district and school staff as employees, and the students, their parents, and the taxpayers in the city as his clients. She then stated that she would prepare a proposal for the evaluation, including a budget, for his and the board's consideration and that the proposal would be based on the new edition of *The Personnel Evaluation Standards.*

The director approved this procedure and asked that the proposal be submitted within 20 days so that it could be considered for approval at the next board meeting. Ms. Levine complied with this request in 15 days and asked that the proposal be shared with the superintendent during the next five days. She stated that if the superintendent had any questions or suggestions, he should not hesitate to discuss his questions with her. Both the director and the superintendent contacted her separately to say that they appreciated the opportunity to comment on the proposal prior to its submission to the board and that they found the evaluation plan to be relevant and comprehensive. The board accepted the proposal without change and awarded the contract at its next meeting.

Ms. Levine spent one week in the district gathering data on two different occasions during November. With the assistance of the human resources director and a group of graduate students from a nearby university who helped conduct the evaluation as part of a class assignment involving application of *The Personnel Evaluation Standards,* she selected and surveyed samples of high school students, parents or guardians of elementary and secondary students, teachers, assistant principals, principals, support staff, district office administrators, members of the public, and board members. This was in accordance with the 360-degree personnel evaluation approach.

Each respondent group received a questionnaire that contained questions common to all participants and unique questions relevant to that group. The questions, which were related to the defined expectations for the superintendent as set out in his contract and job description, asked the respondents to indicate how well they thought the superintendent was performing and their level of satisfaction with that performance. Five-point Likert-type scale items were used with provision for additional comments. Confidentiality was assured in the cover letters sent to stakeholders. Separate focus groups comprised of high school junior council members, parents or guardians, teachers, assistant principals, and principals were conducted to clarify the information gleaned from the questionnaires for these groups. Individual interviews were conducted with the superintendent, representatives of the local teacher association, the senior administrators, and members of the local chamber of commerce. Each board member was interviewed separately. The response rates were high; all individuals selected for the focus groups and interviews cooperated.

Statistical analyses of the questionnaires and content analysis of the information recorded from the focus groups and interviews revealed that the superintendent's performance was strong in all areas except communication with teachers, parents or guardians, and the public. These three groups noted the following positive attributes: the superintendent was managing the school district well; the district performed well on state-mandated tests; a good variety of course options, sports, and fine arts programs were available for middle and senior high school students; and children were satisfied with their schools. The respondents thought, however, that the superintendent was not visible enough. Ms. Levine noted that visibility was not an activity that was explicitly listed in the defined expectations of the superintendent's position, although it seemed apparent that this expectation was valued.

Ms. Levine submitted the draft of her final report, which contained an executive summary followed by the complete report containing a presentation and discussion of the full set of results and documentation of the evaluation procedures, to the human resources director, superintendent, and the board chair to check for factual accuracy and clarity. She noted the issue of visibility and suggested that the superintendent visit the schools in the district on a scheduled basis and meet more frequently with teachers and the parent-teacher associations. The final copy of the report was submitted to the board before its January meeting. Ms. Levine then met with the board during the first part of the January meeting to answer any questions board members might have. Both the board and the superintendent accepted the report. The decision was made to renew the superintendent's contract, and the set of defined expectations was changed to call explicitly for greater visibility and communication with teachers, parents, and the public. Following the board meeting, Ms. Levine met with the superintendent to further discuss the evaluation results and findings.

Illustrative Case 1: Looking at All Sides
Analysis

Use of the 360-degree personnel evaluation approach in conjunction with *The Personnel Evaluation Standards* led to an evaluation that was comprehensive, complete, and balanced in scope. The evaluator, Ms. Levine, generally held a service and constructive orientation (see P1, Service Orientation; U1, Constructive Orientation). She attended to the defined expectations of the superintendent (see A2, Defined Expectations) and submitted a proposal that clearly was acceptable to the director of human resources, the superintendent, and the board (see U2, Defined Uses). She employed graduate students studying personnel evaluation and *The Personnel Evaluation Standards* to assist her in conducting the evaluation, so that it was completed as proposed in a confidential, efficient, nondisruptive, and timely way (see F1, Practical Procedures). Not only did the evaluation provide graduate students with hands-on experience in an actual evaluation and the need to maintain confidentiality, it also helped reduce Ms. Levine's costs (see F3, Fiscal Viability).

Ms. Levine involved the superintendent early and appropriately, so that he was informed of the evaluation plan and given the opportunity to comment on his own performance (see P4, Interactions With Evaluatees). Similarly, she shared the final report with the board chair, director of human resources, and the superintendent to ensure factual accuracy and clarity, and she met with the superintendent following the January board meeting (see U5, Functional Reporting). All the stakeholder groups contributed information, and the results provided an opportunity to compare and validate responses across groups (see P1, Service Orientation). Likewise, the mixed design and analyses produced results that were used to explain each other (see A9, Analysis of Information). Taken together, all the steps taken in the evaluation of the superintendent resulted in a balanced personnel evaluation in which strengths and areas in need of improvement emerged.

Illustrative Case 2: Diversity in the Classroom
Description

School had been in session for approximately six weeks when Mr. Stolfutz, an elementary principal, began receiving phone calls and visits from parents and guardians of third graders about a newly hired teacher, Ms. Doumbia, a recent immigrant to the United States. The adults expressed mild to moderate concerns that Ms. Doumbia was "difficult for my child to understand" and wore "clothes that were different." Others raised questions about some of the classroom decorations, which reflected a culture foreign to their children. They questioned why their children should be "exposed" to many things they might not understand and thus adopt as their own culture. Mr. Stolfutz responded politely to each question and comment. He openly supported the teacher and indicated that he would monitor the situation.

After Mr. Stolfutz received the first calls, he started frequent classroom walk-throughs followed by more formal classroom observations. During these observations, he noted two areas closely related to district goals that needed improvement. These areas related to the implementation of the district's reading program. These could be addressed effectively through professional development activities offered at the district office. He also noted, as he had during the informal walk-throughs, that Ms. Doumbia's students were highly motivated and engaged in learning. Further, district benchmark test scores and quality of the class project recently completed were quite satisfactory.

At the conference following the observation, Mr. Stolfutz addressed each area in which Ms. Doumbia performed well and the two areas that needed improvement. He then made suggestions for improvement and gave her information from the district professional development coordinator on relevant upcoming training sessions and teacher study groups.

At the end of the conference, when asked if there were any questions, Ms. Doumbia brought up the concerns of some parents. She had received several comments about the artifacts and wall coverings decorating her class that she thought were unreasonably critical of her culture. She asked Mr. Stolfutz if she should simply remove them. She explained to him that she liked to use the artifacts as prompts for writing assignments and to help her illustrate stories. Relatives had made the wall coverings for her to reflect important events in her life, and she used them to create a more inviting classroom environment. She planned to help her students create their own wall coverings later in the year.

Mr. Stolfutz, aware of the teacher's cultural background, assured her that he did not see her artifacts and wall coverings as adversely affecting the performance of her job and that other teachers and some parents or guardians had spoken positively about her classroom. Further, he told her that during the last week, two parents who initially raised concerns had called to say that they were too hasty in making their judgments. He did not mention Ms. Doumbia's accent or the clothes she wore as being an impediment to her teaching because during his observations, he had not noted that any students had trouble following directions, responding to her questions, or otherwise communicating with her. He also did not think her style of dress interfered at all with student learning and, in fact, perhaps added to their understanding of diverse cultures.

Illustrative Case 2: Diversity in the Classroom
Analysis

The principal, Mr. Stolfutz, responded quickly to the concerns of the parents and guardians by conducting more frequent walk-throughs to observe for himself the practice of the teacher. He focused primarily on her teaching strategies and job performance as related to district initiatives. While the parents' concerns centered on negatively perceived differences in the teacher's culture, the principal dismissed this once he observed the effectiveness of the teaching and the lack of evidence that the accent, dress, and artifacts inhibited student learning. The principal correctly provided a balanced and fair assessment of this teacher's practice.

Supporting Documentation

American Federation of Teachers. (2003). *Where we stand: Teacher quality.* Washington, DC: Author.

Kleinfeld, J., & McDiarmid, G. W. (1986). Living to tell the tale: Researching politically controversial topics and communicating the findings. *Educational Evaluation and Policy Analysis, 8*(4), 393–401.

Manatt, R. P. (1988). Teacher performance evaluation: A total systems approach. In S. J. Stanley & W. J. Popham (Eds.), *Teacher evaluation: Six prescriptions for success* (pp. 79–108). Alexandria, VA: Association for Supervision and Curriculum Development.

National Association of Elementary School Principals. (2001). *Leading learning communities: Standards for what principals should know and be able to do.* Alexandria, VA: Author.

P6   Conflict of Interest

> **STANDARD**   **Existing and potential conflicts of interest should be identified and dealt with openly and honestly.**

Explanation.   Conflicts of interest arise when an evaluator's personal situation, goals, or biases inappropriately influence a judgment or decision. Conflicts of interest can intrude at key points in the personnel evaluation process, such as planning and designing the evaluation, selecting members for an evaluation team, obtaining data, analyzing and interpreting information and data, writing the evaluation report, and making decisions based on results. By assessing an evaluatee's performance more positively or negatively than warranted, the evaluator might obtain an advantage or disadvantage of position, realize better or poorer professional or personal relationships, or become vulnerable to retaliation.

Sources of conflict of interest are many and varied. Conflicts can arise from differing philosophies of education, preferences for certain styles of teaching or leadership, political preferences, racial and cultural backgrounds, sexual orientations, familial relationships, and moral codes (see A8, Bias Identification and Management). For example, the reputation, status, or political influence of the evaluatee or pressure by leaders in the organization of which the evaluator is a member can influence the planning and implementation of a system of personnel evaluation. Moreover, personnel evaluation results may reflect on the performance of the evaluator as well as the evaluatee. Cases in which a supervisor is the sole evaluator are particularly subject to this form of conflict.

Often conflicts of interest and their sources are hard to detect or address and can persist to the detriment of sound evaluations. For example, the conflict may not occur directly between the evaluator and the evaluatee but at higher levels of authority (e.g., superintendent or school board). Those conflicts in turn produce a conflict of interest for those involved in evaluative situations. The case example for standard P1, *Inheriting an Underperforming Principal,* describes such a situation and shows how self-interest can seep in and for years improperly influence individuals who are well meaning but reluctant to properly evaluate when the results may place them at risk.

Conflicts of interest are prevalent in cases where close friendships, family ties, and personal working relationships exist and may influence the outcomes of the personnel evaluations. Decisions about evaluatees are placed in disrepute if the belief exists that any of the evaluation results are influenced or determined by personal self-interest rather than organizational or professionally shared goals. At the same time, evaluators need to recognize that everyone carries bias in some form; it is how biases are acted on that matters, since the total removal of bias is difficult to do and rarely achieved. To help protect adverse outcomes for the evaluator or the process itself, procedures for filing grievances if an evaluatee believes a conflict of interest existed and adversely influenced the evaluation process need to be included in personnel evaluations (see P2, Appropriate Policies and Procedures).

Rationale.   Conflicts of interest can undermine and compromise the integrity of judgments made in personnel evaluations. Conflicts may exert such a powerful and negative influence on evaluations and evaluatees that even the appearance of an impropriety can reduce the intended impact of an evaluation. Potential conflicts must be identified, acknowledged, and dealt with in an open and honest manner if the evaluation is to be constructive (see U1, Constructive Orientation).

GUIDELINES

A. Establish evaluation guidelines for providing remedies for potential conflicts of interest (see P2, Appropriate Policies and Procedures).
B. Ensure that evaluators are not in the position of supervising or evaluating close relatives, life partners, or spouses.
C. Ensure that evaluators are not in the position of supervising or evaluating those who have an established conflict of interest (e.g., competitors for the same job, opponents in a court case, etc.)
D. Train evaluation personnel to identify and avoid conflicts of interest (see U3, Evaluator Qualifications).
E. Take proactive steps in the planning and implementation of the evaluation to remove or reduce the effects of conflict of interest:
   - Identify potential conflicts of interest and how they have been or will be addressed prior to beginning the evaluation (this includes conflicts of interest for those in charge of the evaluators and supervisors).
   - Develop clear criteria and performance standards (see A2, Defined Expectations).
   - Define the range of evidence to be admitted into the evaluation.
   - Develop data collection and analysis procedures.
   - Prepare guidelines for the content and organization of evaluation reports (see A4, Documented Purposes and Procedures).
F. Employ evaluation procedures requiring comparison of multiple sources of information to discover any tainted evidence.
G. Discuss in the evaluation report how the data used in judging the performance of individuals are related to the evaluation's purposes and criteria (see A6, Reliable Information; A10, Justified Conclusions).

H. Involve the evaluatee in the review process before finalizing the evaluation report (see P4, Interactions With Evaluatees).

I. Provide appeal procedures so that alleged conflicts of interest can be investigated and addressed (see P2, Appropriate Policies and Procedures).

J. Provide protection against unwarranted actions by the evaluatee or employer during a rebuttal or appeal.

K. Give priority to using another evaluator, more than one evaluator, or a third-party evaluator if a conflict of interest exists.

L. Mutually define, in writing, the conditions of the evaluation, so that role-specific behaviors are assessed under defined conditions if a conflict of interest exists and it is not possible to appoint another evaluator.

M. Ensure the security of all materials and findings that could be used to resolve a conflict of interest situation (see P7, Legal Viability; P3, Access to Evaluation Information; A7, Systematic Data Control).

COMMON ERRORS

A. Failing to anticipate and control subjectivity (e.g., evaluating without specifically defined criteria, not collecting objective evidence, ignoring objective evidence from other sources).

B. Failing to provide, in writing, an explanation of a decision that runs counter to the evaluation results and findings.

C. Making assessment and evaluation the sole responsibility of one individual, without the possibility of appeal.

D. Relying on evaluatees' self-evaluation and not verifying their judgments about their own performance.

E. Ignoring obvious sources of conflict of interest (e.g., life partner, relative, prior opponent in a grievance) when assigning evaluators.

Illustrative Case 1: Hidden Conflict of Interest Taints an Evaluation
Description

Mr. Vlahov, a secondary science head interested in an administrative position that was at another, more desirable high school, received a poor evaluation from his school principal. Since he had received very positive evaluations from the principal in previous years, he was puzzled by the negative review and confused by the ambiguity of its contents. Mr. Vlahov tried unsuccessfully to obtain a clear, satisfactory explanation from his principal, who denied that his review was biased in any way. Given his interest in the administrative position and following board policy, Mr. Vlahov asked the principal for a third-party review of the evaluation. His request was denied.

Mr. Vlahov and the principal generally were considered by others both within and outside the school to be two of the district's outstanding employees. Mr. Vlahov was unaware that both he and his principal were competing for the same administrative position and that a negative review at this time would adversely affect his opportunity for this promotion. Only later, when his principal was selected for the new administrative position, did Mr. Vlahov fully understand his negative evaluation.

Illustrative Case 1: Hidden Conflict of Interest Taints an Evaluation
Analysis

Mr. Vlahov was unaware of the conflict of interest existing between him and his principal and that the conflict had affected his assessment. When confronted, the principal denied that there was any conflict of interest affecting his review. Nevertheless, he could not justify his negative judgments stated on the evaluation (see A10, Justified Conclusions). The competition seemed to have made the principal far more critical than in the past, which seriously affected Mr. Vlahov's career opportunities. The evaluator and the evaluation process were compromised.

The principal should have removed himself from the role of evaluator to avoid the compromising situation, or he should have been removed by a superior. He should have demonstrated greater regard for a fair process and for the rights of Mr. Vlahov (see P4, Interactions With Evaluatees), and he should have recognized that the circumstances would, at best, create the appearance of a conflict of interest. The system should have assured that judgments of Mr. Vlahov's performance were based on accepted administrative practice and defensible criteria. It should have included safeguards for the integrity of the evaluation and provided an appeal process guaranteeing the right to an impartial investigation of conflict of interest charges.

Illustrative Case 2: Avoiding the Appearance of Conflict of Interest
Description

Mrs. Bookman, a classroom teacher, was promoted to assistant principal of the elementary school where she had taught for six years. During those years, she had become good friends with another member of the staff whom she, along with the principal, would now have the responsibility of evaluating. With the agreement of the principal and her friend on staff, Mrs. Bookman asked one of the central office personnel to take her place on the evaluation team. The resulting evaluation was completed, Mrs. Bookman was informed of the results, and the teacher was then directed to her for help in improving the areas of weakness that were identified correctly in the teacher's evaluation report.

Illustrative Case 2: Avoiding the Appearance of Conflict of Interest
Analysis

The steps taken by Mrs. Bookman avoided the potential conflict of interest that would have been created if she had evaluated her friend. Although the principal also evaluated her friend and the results of the two evaluations could be compared, by removing herself,

Mrs. Bookman also removed the appearance of a potential conflict. Mrs. Bookman still could function as an instructional leader and work with the teacher to foster improvements, but the burden of judgment about the teacher's performance had been shifted to an objective colleague.

Supervisors can help subordinates examine and address their performance deficiencies, even when the subordinates are friends or relatives. Nevertheless, to provide such assistance effectively, the supervisor must address the potential conflicts of interest squarely. To ameliorate these possible conflicts, the supervisor could take such steps as the following:

- Replace herself with a disinterested, but otherwise qualified evaluator when judging an employee's performance, which Mrs. Bookman did.
- Meet with the evaluatee and the replacement evaluator before the evaluation to clarify and examine the evaluation questions and procedures, such as who would be performing the different evaluation tasks and their qualifications.
- Provide guidance for staff development based on the written evaluation report.

Supporting Documentation

Airasian, P. W., & Gullickson, A. (1994). Teacher self-assessment: Potential and barriers. *Kappa Delta Pi Record, 31*(1), 6–9.

Airasian, P. W., & Gullickson, A. (1997). Teacher self-evaluation. In J. H. Stronge (Ed.), *Evaluating teaching: A guide to current thinking and best practice* (pp. 215–247). Thousand Oaks, CA: Corwin Press.

Haertel, G. D. (1994). *Qualification, roles, and responsibilities of assessors, evaluators, and mentors in teacher evaluation.* Livermore, CA: EREAPA Associates.

Landy, F. J., Barnes, J. L., & Murphy, K. R. (1978). Correlates of perceived fairness and accuracy of performance evaluation. *Journal of Applied Psychology, 63,* 751–754.

Millman, J. (Ed.). (1981). *Handbook of teacher evaluation.* Beverly Hills, CA: Sage.

Millman, J., & Darling-Hammond, L. (Eds.). (1990). *The new handbook of teacher evaluation: Assessing elementary and secondary teachers.* Newbury Park, CA: Sage.

Scriven, M. (1990). Can research-based teacher evaluation be saved? *Journal of Personnel Evaluation in Education, 4*(1), 19–32.

Scriven, M. (1997). Due process in adverse personnel action. *Journal of Personnel Evaluation in Education, 11*(2), 127–137.

Sweeney, J. (1992). The effects of evaluator training on teacher evaluation. *Journal of Personnel Evaluation in Education, 6*(1), 7–14.

P7 Legal Viability

STANDARD **Personnel evaluations should meet the requirements of applicable laws, contracts, collective bargaining agreements, affirmative action policies, and local board or institutional policies.**

Explanation. Evaluatees have specific rights. When evaluating employees, evaluators always must take into account the legal provisions that pertain to the local context in which the personnel evaluation takes place. In almost every instance, particular federal, state, or local legal provisions and affirmative action policies will impose specific requirements governing the evaluation situation. Legally viable evaluations will address pertinent legal issues successfully and avoid debilitating legal difficulties that may arise in the course of carrying out evaluations and making decisions about evaluatees, such as whether to recommend further professional development, training, or termination of employment.

Evaluations must follow substantive and procedural due processes that comply with federal, state, and local laws. Substantive due process prohibits actions against an individual based on unfair, arbitrary, or unreasonable practices. Procedural due process requires that evaluatees have fair opportunities to know the performance standards against which they will be judged and to respond to the evaluation information and results. Procedural due process also requires that mechanisms be in place for fair and impartial review of personnel actions with major consequences, such as termination of employment. In addition to defining the evaluatee's role and expectations, the employer ordinarily must give the evaluatee reasonable advance notice of a need to show improvement, a timeline, and steps required to correct deficient performance.

To ensure that evaluatees who consistently receive poor evaluations are asked either to participate in professional development or training programs as a condition of continuing employment or be dismissed as an employee, personnel evaluations and systems must be both ethically and legally sound. Moreover, evaluations and dismissal processes must be fiscally responsible and accountable; it is a violation of public trust to use taxpayer funds longer than necessary to support employees who are not meeting their job responsibilities.

Rationale. The vast body of legal mandates contained in the Constitution and laws of the United States, the constitution and statutes of each state, local and case laws, and the provisions and interpretations of employment contracts, collective bargaining agreements, and affirmative action policies creates a complexity of legal requirements that affect personnel evaluations. Personnel evaluators should be knowledgeable about and adhere to all legal requirements of their evaluations. Stakeholders who are poorly informed about the legal rights of evaluatees and others affected by the evaluation may unwittingly ignore or abuse these rights, thereby harming the evaluatee. Evaluators who knowingly or unknowingly violate an evaluatee's legal and ethical rights may be subject to a grievance under a collective bargaining agreement, litigation through state or federal courts, or professional sanctions. Failure to respect the legal and ethical rights of evaluatees and to show courtesy may deny some evaluatees the opportunity to participate in and succeed at a position to which, by virtue of previous employment, they are entitled.

Compliance with the legal requirements pertinent to a particular evaluation will not necessarily prevent legal challenges. However, adherence to pertinent legal requirements should help minimize legal complications while simultaneously promoting ethical and sound professional evaluations.

GUIDELINES

A. Ensure that the institution's or agency's personnel evaluation policies and procedures are in compliance with the rights of evaluatees derived from the law and collective bargaining agreements and that they comply with both the substantial and procedural due process requirements.

B. Comply with equality of opportunity and diversity requirements that are subject to applicable laws by making decisions to recruit, hire, train, promote, transfer, or compensate evaluatees based solely on merit and qualifications and without regard to race, national origin, color, religion, gender, disability, sexual orientation, age, height, weight, or political affiliation (see A8, Bias Identification and Management).

C. Examine evaluation policies, procedures, and consequences on a regular schedule to ensure that evaluations are not de jure or de facto biased against members of any group (see A8, Bias Identification and Management).

D. Engage, as needed, an attorney who is very familiar with laws governing employment and personnel evaluation in the local context to help minimize legal complications.

E. Communicate personnel evaluation policies and the procedures to be followed in a timely manner, including criteria to be met, form of follow-up procedures, and severance packages. Use language that is understandable to all stakeholders.

F. Review evaluatee progress and provide constructive feedback regularly, letting each evaluatee know clearly, in written form and in a timely manner, if there are any deficiencies that must be corrected (see U5, Functional Reporting).

G. Implement procedures to appeal the results of an evaluation, and request and obtain a third party review of any evaluation activity or report deemed unfair or inaccurate (see P6, Conflict of Interest; U3, Evaluator Qualifications; A8, Bias Identification and Management; A11, Metaevaluation).

H. Take appropriate, feasible steps to help an evaluatee address concerns and return to an acceptable level of service based on a constructive discussion of problems and the criteria to be met for an acceptable level of performance (see P1, Service Orientation). Provide reasonable time and a clear deadline for an employee to correct deficient performance (see U1, Constructive Orientation).

I. Provide an evaluatee with sufficient advance notice of contemplated actions and the decision-making criteria to be applied before enacting a dismissal process (see P1, Service Orientation). Finalize the decision to dismiss an evaluatee only after the decision has been authorized institutionally (F2, Political Viability; A1, Valid Judgments).

J. Notify need-to-know officials about the facts of a termination, while limiting and guarding the information, to avoid unnecessary embarrassment to the involved parties (see P3, Access to Personnel Evaluation Reports; P4, Interactions With Evaluatees).

K. Document the assessment meetings, data, and process (see U3, Evaluator Qualifications; A4, Documented Purposes and Procedures; A7, Systematic Data Control).

COMMON ERRORS

A. Failing to define and invoke clear institutional personnel policies on such matters as equality of opportunity, affirmative action, and sexual harassment (see A1, Valid Judgments; A8, Bias Identification and Management).

B. Waiting to consult an attorney until a problem arises in a personnel evaluation instead of consulting one prospectively to review policies and help prevent such problems.

C. Advising evaluatees that their personnel evaluation files are not liable to disclosure without first consulting pertinent state law (see P3, Access to Evaluation Information).

D. Failing to initiate and document needed remedial or dismissal proceedings.

E. Assuming that a personnel evaluator will be liable for defamation if he or she presents a negative, but fair and sound, evaluation.

Illustrative Case 1: Failure to Consider All Applicable Laws
Description

A school board decided to send out a call for proposals for a comprehensive evaluation system directed toward all school-based personnel, including administrators, teachers, and support staff. The contract would encompass training of evaluators and initial implementation of the districtwide system. After a close assessment of the proposals submitted, the board awarded the contract to an out-of-state consulting firm whose track record appeared very strong. The firm proposed a system used in previous evaluations with similar-sized school districts. The system called first for formative evaluation procedures involving all staff followed by summative evaluations approximately six months later.

When the early stages of implementing the new system proceeded smoothly, the board was confident that it had selected an appropriate consulting firm and personnel evaluation system. Nevertheless, a sizable number of members of the education union were anxious and defensive about being evaluated, even though extensive discussions had occurred between the consultants and the union. This created lingering apprehension in the union about the personnel evaluation system. As a result of the summative evaluations, four teachers were dismissed. Two teachers, with the support of their union, appealed unsuccessfully to the board's appellate committee. They then appealed to the appropriate state jurisdiction. One appeal at this level arose from a perceived lack of sustained good-faith effort to help the teacher succeed as a consequence of the formative evaluation. The other was based on the teacher believing that she did not receive reasonable notice of the need to remedy deficiencies supported by a timeline and steps required to strengthen performance. Both appeals to state court were based on the school district's failing to fully comply with state laws pertaining to personnel evaluation. Both appeals were successful.

The outcomes of the court actions surprised the school board because the consulting firm had not advised them of the state requirements for follow-up. Inevitably, these results led to a diminution in confidence about the evaluation system, with the union vowing to undermine it even further without appropriate modification.

Illustrative Case 1: Failure to Consider All Applicable Laws
Analysis

While the school board acted properly in examining the credentials of the firm that received the contract, their inquiries did not go far enough. In particular, legal consequences of the failure to warn and prepare the board for compliance with state laws invalidated much of the consulting firm's good work. The consultants had never won a contract in the school board's state. They erroneously assumed that state laws in relation to personnel evaluation did not differ much from state to state and that different states did not give differing emphases to similar laws.

Litigation may occur when any legal aspects associated with a personnel evaluation are ignored. If the board had consulted an attorney who was an expert in laws governing the evaluation of education personnel in the district's specific setting, the chance of using legally inappropriate evaluation procedures could have been reduced. While the successful appeals to the state court may not have spelled the death knell to the new personnel evaluation system, the board was left with much lost ground and goodwill to recover (see U3, Evaluator Qualifications).

Illustrative Case 2: Overcoming Resistance to Change
Description

A school district in a unionized state had a strong teachers' association. The current president of the association, Mr. Kowalski, had served for many years as a teacher and administrator in the district. Although the district had not faced major controversies in the past few years, Mr. Kowalski was known for his ability to work through minor conflicts concerning such issues as contracts to find equitable solutions for both sides. This district had a reputation for strong student achievement scores and a stable teaching force. The community and the schools maintained a good relationship. The local press often ran positive articles highlighting student accomplishments in sports and academics. Letters to the editors by disgruntled parents were rare.

Following the retirement of the superintendent, the board hired as superintendent Dr. Lemas, a woman from another state that did not have teacher unions. Dr. Lemas had a reputation for being a strong leader. She had led her previous district through a controversial merger and had implemented several major restructurings of both the high school and middle school.

During her first six months, Dr. Lemas completed her own assessment of the district's needs through a process of focus groups, interviews, and reviews of documentation, including all district manuals and policies. She concluded that the district was not getting much mileage from the current system of teacher evaluation, which was a version of the 20-year-old state model of checklists and rating scales. She found a high correlation between years of experience and superior ratings. Veteran teachers, without exception, were ranked superior, while new teachers were rated much lower overall. Since the rating scales were strongly tied to evaluator observations, thus increasing their subjectivity, she began to explore other evaluation methods that might provide more data sources with stronger criteria.

During her assessment of the district, Dr. Lemas quickly discovered the power of the teachers' association. The Memorandum of Understanding (MoU) between the association and the district was carefully negotiated each year and served to hold both sides accountable. The section on teacher performance appraisal was very clearly spelled out. Teachers and administrators liked the current model. Dr. Lemas began focusing on this part of the MoU as she talked to teacher groups and principals. While no one thought the current model offered any hope for change, they also did not think change was necessary. After all, their test scores were good, the community was happy, and teachers liked working in the district. Dr. Lemas decided that changing the personnel evaluation system was one battle she could not undertake at this point because there did not seem to be a strong enough concern to effect change in this area.

Two years later, new state accountability measures were put into effect, and the district test scores began to drop. District office administrators involved principals in examining teaching practices. Among other things, they found a substantial lack of alignment between instruction and the new state standards. Teachers were continuing to teach units and lessons from the previous curriculum that had been moved to other grade levels or eliminated from the new curriculum; nevertheless, these teachers continued to receive the superior ratings on evaluations.

The association representatives and the district administrators recognized the need to change teacher practice by addressing several areas, one of which was the model of teacher evaluation. They concluded that a task force should be formed to study the best possible method to offer teachers constructive feedback and opportunities for professional development. Following a year of investigation into various evaluation models, they settled on one and began modifications to make it fit their district.

In developing this new model, the task force examined its current teacher evaluation manual to build on strengths and correct deficiencies. One major deficiency in the current manual was the lack of procedures and policies to prevent de jure or de facto bias against groups of individuals. There also were no procedures to ensure bias control among the evaluators, so that members of any group based on factors such as race, religion, gender, or sexual orientation would be protected. The task force reviewed several model policies and procedural manuals from other districts before developing its own. It was careful to include requirements for evaluator training in the area of bias identification as well as to ensure that all evaluation criteria allowed for ratings solely on the basis of merit and qualifications specifically related to the job requirements.

Following extensive reviews by teachers and administrators in the district, the school board and the teachers' association approved the new system of teacher evaluation. It was adopted as part of the MoU between the district and the association.

Illustrative Case 2: Overcoming Resistance to Change
Analysis

Although Dr. Lemas, the new superintendent, concluded from her initial assessment of the district that the current system of teacher evaluation lacked substance, she wisely recognized that at that time she did not have the political backing to institute a major change. Any effort to do so might have been met with great opposition and possibly could have derailed other, more pressing, efforts.

The new accountability standards forced the district to recognize the need to change and to begin the process of examining current practices on a much broader scale. Involvement by the teachers' association as well as district- and school-level administrators ensured greater overall buy-in to change. The establishment of the task force lent credibility to the process because it examined various evaluation models and carefully constructed one that would meet the demands of this district.

The broad involvement of teachers and administrators in the review process ensured that the new policies would be written in clear language understandable to all users. This review also offered the opportunity for employees of diverse backgrounds to provide input into the language and policies designed to safeguard against discrimination. The addition of specific policies and procedures to address such issues increased the legal viability of the new system of teacher evaluation by bringing it into compliance with federal, state, and local laws.

Supporting Documentation

Andrews, H. A. (1985). *Evaluating for excellence.* Stillwater, OK: New Forums Press.

Andrews, H. A. (1995). *Teachers can be fired.* Peru, IL: Catfeet Press.

Bridges, E. M. (1985). *The incompetent teacher: The challenge and the response.* Philadelphia: Falmer Press.

Malos, S. B. (1998). Current legal issues in performance appraisal. In J. W. Smither (Ed.), *Performance appraisal: State of the art in practice* (pp. 49–94). San Francisco: Jossey-Bass.

Millman, J., & Darling-Hammond, L. (Eds.). (1990). *The new handbook of teacher evaluation: Assessing elementary and secondary teachers.* Newbury Park, CA: Sage.

Rebell, M. A. (1990). Legal issues concerning teacher evaluation. In J. Millman & L. Darling-Hammond, (Eds.), *The new handbook of teacher evaluation: Assessing elementary and secondary school teachers* (pp. 337–355). Newbury Park, CA: Sage.

Rossow, L. F., & Parkinson, J. (1991). *The law of teacher evaluation.* Dayton, OH: Education Law Association (formerly National Organization for Legal Problems in Education, Topeka, KS).

Scriven, M. (1997). Due process in adverse personnel action. *Journal of Personnel Evaluation in Education, 11*(2), 127–137.

Shinkfield, A. J., & Stufflebeam, D. L. (1995). *Teacher evaluation: Guide to effective practice.* Boston: Kluwer.

Stufflebeam, D. L. (1999b). Using professional standards to legally and ethically release evaluation findings. *Studies in Educational Evaluation, 25,* 325–334.

Stufflebeam, D. L., & Pullin, D. (1998). Achieving legal viability in personnel evaluations. *Journal of Personnel Evaluation in Education, 11*(3), 215–230.

Stufflebeam, D. L., & Pullin, D. (2001). *Legal viability checklist for personnel evaluations and personnel evaluation systems.* Retrieved September 23, 2005, from http://www .wmich.edu/evalctr/checklists/legal_viability.htm

Sullivan, K. A., & Zirkel, P. A. (1998). The law of teacher evaluation: Case law update. *Journal of Personnel Evaluation in Education, 11*(4), 367–380.

Tucker, P. D., & Kindred, K. P. (1997). Legal considerations in designing teacher evaluation systems. In J. H. Stronge (Ed.), *Evaluating teaching: A guide to current thinking and best practice* (pp. 59–90). Thousand Oaks, CA: Corwin Press.

Valente, W. D. (1985). *Education law: Public and private.* St. Paul, MN: West.

Zirkel, P. A. (1996). *The law of teacher evaluation: A self-assessment handbook.* Bloomington, IN: Phi Delta Kappa Educational Foundation (in cooperation with the National Organization on Legal Problems in Education).

U

UTILITY STANDARDS

Summary of the Standards

Utility Standards   Intended to guide evaluations so that they will be informative, timely, and influential.

U1   **Constructive Orientation**   Personnel evaluations should help institutions develop human resources and encourage and assist evaluatees to perform in accordance with the institution's mission and goals.

U2   **Defined Uses**   The intended users and uses should be identified in policies and guidelines at the beginning of an evaluation process.

U3   **Evaluator Qualifications**   The evaluation system should be developed, implemented, and managed by people with the necessary skills, training, and authority.

U4   **Explicit Criteria**   Systems of evaluation should have clear, specific criteria directly related to the required job expectations for the evaluatees.

U5   **Functional Reporting**   Reports should be clear, timely, accurate, and germane to the purpose of the evaluation.

U6   **Follow-Up and Professional Development**   Personnel evaluations should lead to appropriate professional development.

U1   Constructive Orientation

> **STANDARD**   Personnel evaluations should help institutions develop human resources and encourage and assist evaluatees to perform in accordance with the institution's mission and goals.

Explanation.   Evaluations are constructive when they promote the success of students, educators, and the education organization of which they are a part. They are constructive when they guide selection and retention of proficient personnel, reinforce good practice, provide direction for improving performance, clarify needs for professional development, recognize outstanding performance, assist in terminating incompetent personnel, promote professionalism, and foster collegiality.

Evaluations are not constructive if they are used (a) merely to comply with perfunctory bureaucratic requirements for accountability, (b) essentially to control or intimidate, or (c) solely for the purpose of dismissal, ignoring other uses.

Rationale.   When personnel evaluation is constructive, it encourages and supports educators and their organization (i.e., university, college, training institute, district, or school) in fulfilling goals and responsibilities, including adherence to systems of accountability. Constructive evaluations provide educators with information and professional feedback that build their professional self-knowledge, increase their enthusiasm, and enhance their efficacy as practitioners. Such evaluations aid organizations in selecting and retaining proficient personnel, reinforcing strong professional practice, encouraging professional development, and fostering cooperation. Educators and institutions that achieve such beneficial characteristics are better able to provide high quality services to students and to maintain their effectiveness and positive self-image through periods of stability or change.

Evaluations that emphasize negative or punitive assessments discourage educators and promote resistance to evaluation and its goals. Evaluations that identify performance weaknesses but do not provide information or support to correct deficiencies contribute little to the organization.

GUIDELINES

A. Review the mission and goals of the organization to determine if the evaluation system provides the necessary support for all personnel in meeting organizational goals (see P1, Service Orientation).

B. Involve a representative group of evaluation participants in designing and developing the personnel evaluation system, including the definitions of the evaluation criteria and performance standards and the roles of stakeholders in light of current organizational mission statements and goals (see P2, Appropriate Policies and Procedures; F2, Political Viability).

C. Communicate to all interested parties the intended positive, constructive uses of evaluation results. Conceptualize personnel evaluation as an important part of professional development and the attainment of institutional goals (see U6, Follow-Up and Professional Development).

D. Ensure that structures are in place to develop evaluatees' areas in need of improvement as identified through the personnel evaluation system.

E. Define and clarify criteria and performance standards for all positions to ensure alignment with the roles and responsibilities of the various positions to the mission statement and goals of the organization (see A1, Valid Judgments; U4, Explicit Criteria).

F. Create a shared understanding among stakeholders of the purposes and procedures of the personnel evaluation system to facilitate adoption and high levels of implementation (see U2, Defined Uses; F2, Political Viability).

COMMON ERRORS

A. Assuming that personnel evaluation practices, procedures, and objectives are self-explanatory and acceptable to all parties.

B. Failing to align the criteria and standards of the evaluation system with the roles and responsibilities of the evaluatees or the goals and mission of the organization.

C. Failure to provide oversight of the personnel evaluation system to ensure that all evaluations are conducted in a professional manner with constructive comments and suggestions aligned with organizational goals (see P4, Interactions With Evaluatees).

D. Failure to provide structures for following up the results of the personnel evaluation (see U6, Follow-Up and Professional Development).

Illustrative Case 1: Transitioning to a New Evaluation System
Description

A school district developed and adopted standards of quality work for students. This initiative was designed to change classroom practice by permeating every aspect of instructional practice in all classrooms. The traditional system of teacher evaluation currently in place (a checklist of teacher behaviors during an announced observation by an administrator) did not appear to support these new practices. A complete review of the district's existing system determined that the traditional system lacked alignment with the newly adopted quality work standards. It did not address the quality of work students were asked to do or the assessment practices of the teachers.

Teachers thought the old system promoted a "dog and pony show" by creating inflated ratings and offering little incentive for growth and no encouragement for teacher professionalism. Teachers also reported that the old system had been used solely "to get rid" of teachers without providing them any opportunity for growth.

The superintendent, Mr. Klein, invited principals to help form a district committee to address the need for a new teacher evaluation system and to select interested teacher-leaders from the schools to participate. Mr. Klein wanted to ensure that all those affected by evaluation would be heard. The committee was charged with investigating alternative models of teacher evaluation from other states and districts.

Under the guidance of Mr. Klein and the assistant superintendent for instruction, the committee reviewed various systems of teacher evaluation before selecting one that appeared to fit the district's needs. The new evaluation system was aligned with current national and state teacher standards and promoted teacher collegiality and professional dialogue with administrators. The committee then modified the system's criteria to better support the district's goals and mission statement. The teachers wanted to make sure that the criteria were clear and could be used for self-assessment as well as evaluation. The principals wanted to make sure that the process supported credible feedback directly related to the district's goals.

Once the modifications were complete, the committee presented the new evaluation system for review by the faculties at each school. After this review, the committee presented the new system to the school board for approval before beginning training to implement it in the next school year.

Illustrative Case 1: Transitioning to a New Evaluation System
Analysis

In this case, the superintendent, Mr. Klein, recognized general dissatisfaction with an existing system of teacher evaluation that did not promote the district's new goals that now focused on quality student work. This district selected a teacher evaluation system that supported its expectations for teacher practice by aligning evaluation with its goals for student work, thus increasing its likelihood of meeting these goals. By creating a districtwide committee comprised of representatives of all intended user groups, Mr. Klein ensured alignment with the roles and responsibilities of each group, creating more buy-in. Inviting review by faculties of all the schools ensured that there would be a wide understanding of the new system's purpose. Finally, the school board was more likely to approve the new system because of the widespread input from both teachers and administrators. While this method of adoption was certainly more labor and time intensive, it was more likely to produce an evaluation system that would be constructive in terms of evaluatee acceptance and meeting district goals.

Illustrative Case 2: Failure of an Executive-Directed Evaluation
Description

Enthusiastic about the idea of publicly recognizing outstanding faculty, the board of trustees and Dr. Ferguson, the president of a state university, decided to conduct a special evaluation of the faculty. Accordingly, Dr. Ferguson asked department chairpersons to use this special evaluation to nominate between 1 percent and 5 percent of their faculty for an honorary award. Chairpersons were asked to submit their nominations within two weeks of the request and to maintain silence about their nominations to avoid any delay or disruption of the process.

When the nominations were submitted, Dr. Ferguson and the university deans selected faculty and made their choices public, first to the faculty in a special news release and then to the community through the local newspaper. The reaction of faculty was one of general outrage toward the evaluation process, its secrecy, and their exclusion from the process. Faculty members asked, "What does one do to deserve this award?" The standard reply was, "You know who the outstanding faculty members are and why they are the best. Read their publications. Sit in one of their classrooms and see what they do." Those who did not receive awards and yet believed they were worthy resented the lack of information. They felt their contributions to the university and to their academic fields were not recognized or appreciated.

Illustrative Case 2: Failure of an Executive-Directed Evaluation
Analysis

The board, the deans, and President Ferguson failed to involve the department chairpersons and faculty in planning an evaluation process that informed the award program. While excellence in teaching and research are undoubtedly part of the university's mission statement and institutional goals, this evaluation plan was not used constructively to encourage or assist those evaluated to meet these goals. The advice and support of department chairpersons and faculty were neither sought nor considered. Chairpersons were informed of the purpose of the evaluation, but given only vague guidance as to the criteria, standards, and procedures to be used. Faculty members were excluded except as the objects of evaluation and were not even informed that an evaluative process was occurring.

The deans and President Ferguson demonstrated little awareness of the faculty's sensitivities or professional roles. The evaluation permitted criteria and standards to vary from department to department. This promoted a sense of unfairness. Additionally, the secrecy surrounding the evaluation was bound to engender fear and distrust. The evaluation process, in short, stood as little more than an apparent pretext for permitting the deans and Dr. Ferguson to make awards. It transformed an opportunity into a costly and demoralizing experience.

Full employee involvement is as important as a strong executive desire for efficient and effective personnel evaluation programs. Cooperation among university executives, college and department administrators, and faculty in planning an evaluation program is essential to promote respect and acceptance for its outcomes. When evaluations are used solely to select an elite group for recognition, the opportunity to support institutional goals and assist all in meeting these goals is lost.

President Ferguson or his administrative representatives could have worked openly with faculty to explore the need and direction for change in the faculty evaluation system and the purposes it might serve. The president could have requested faculty participation in planning the program and sought faculty agreement on the evaluation's purpose, instruments, and procedures. If the value of the awards program to the university was suspect, the program could have been reconsidered and revised before implementation.

Involvement of evaluatees would have increased communication among the faculty and given them the opportunity to shape a program that would be amenable to both their professional values and their need for recognition.

Supporting Documentation

Grantham, T. C., & Ford, D. Y. (1998). Principal instructional leadership can reverse the under-representation of black students in gifted education. *NASSP Bulletin, 82,* 100–109.

Hoerr, T. R. (1998). A case for merit pay. *Phi Delta Kappan, 80*(4), 326–327.

Marshall, M. (1998). Using teacher evaluation to change school culture. *NASSP Bulletin, 82*(600), 117–119.

McGrath, M. J. (2000). The human dynamics of personnel evaluation. *School Administrator, 57*(9), 34–38.

Peterson, K. (2004). Research on teacher evaluation. *NASSP Bulletin, 88,* 60–79.

Rettig, P. R. (1999). Differentiated supervision: A new approach. *Principal, 78*(3), 36–39.

Sobel, D. M., Taylor, S. V., & Anderson, R. E. (2003). Teacher evaluation standards in practice: A standards-based assessment tool for diversity-responsive teaching. *The Teacher Educator, 38*(4), 285–302.

Van der Linde, C. H. (1998). Clinical supervision in teacher evaluation: A pivotal factor in the quality management of education. *Education, 119*(2), 328–334.

U2   Defined Uses

STANDARD   The intended users and uses should be identified in policies and guidelines at the beginning of an evaluation process.

Explanation.   Personnel evaluators should identify and consult with each user group to clarify the purpose(s) of the evaluation and how these groups will use evaluation results and findings. User groups of personnel evaluations typically include supervisors, institutions of employment (e.g., school districts, colleges, and universities), state agencies in charge of licensure or certification, and evaluatees. Evaluations are typically used to meet the demands of selection, certification, identification of staff development needs, accountability, promotion, awarding tenure, salary determination, special recognition, and terminating employment (see Uses of the Standards, Introduction; P1, Service Orientation; U1, Constructive Orientation).

Rationale.   Personnel evaluations should be guided by their intended use. This requires that the users be identified and consulted, their information needs specified, and the intended uses of information clarified. This identification helps ensure that an evaluation is targeted properly and produces useful information. By focusing the evaluation on the agreed-upon user groups and the uses of the information, it also safeguards against misuse of information. Information applied to any other than its intended use or provided to other than the intended users may produce damaging side effects. For example, if information is provided to unintended users, evaluatees may come to distrust the evaluation system and withhold information, believing that it may be misused.

GUIDELINES

A. Identify and consult potential audiences, especially primary users, to clarify their needs for personnel evaluation information.

B. Invite the evaluatees to help determine evaluation goals, uses, forms, methods, and audiences (see F2, Political Viability).

C. Identify issues and construct evaluation methods that are relevant to information needs and proposed uses (see A2, Defined Expectations).

D. Reach formal agreements with all parties involved to assure that they understand and are committed to the intended use of the evaluation information (see P2, Appropriate Policies and Procedures; F2, Political Viability).

E. Restrict use of evaluation information and findings to uses and users specified in formal evaluation agreements (see P3, Access to Evaluation Information).

F. Monitor the evaluation process to ensure tight connections between the collected information, intended uses, and actual uses (see A11, Metaevaluation).

COMMON ERRORS

A. Assuming that all users have identical or similar needs that will be met by the same type information.

B. Assuming too narrow or broad an audience and use for the evaluation.

C. Making unilateral decisions about which data will be most useful for which users.

D. Determining after the fact how information will be used rather than doing this as part of the evaluation system design.

E. Ignoring restrictions on the use of given information by sharing it with those not identified as legitimate users (see P3, Access to Evaluation Information; A7, Systematic Data Control).

F. Failing to document agreements on intended use (see P2, Appropriate Policies and Procedures).

G. Failing to provide a structure for continued monitoring of evaluations (see A11, Metaevaluation).

Illustrative Case 1: Violating Trust by Misusing Data
Description

Mr. McCarthy, an elementary school principal, was a firm believer in using evaluation to improve performance. He sought the assistance of the district staff developer in designing a system that could be used for teacher improvement in leading classroom discussions. The stated purpose of this formative evaluation was to help each teacher identify performance strengths and weaknesses in leading class discussions and to set goals for improvement in this area. Mr. McCarthy and the staff developer assured the teachers that the evaluation's only purpose was to help each teacher and that the teachers and the district staff developer would be the only users of the evaluation information. Mr. McCarthy, while participating in collecting data through classroom observation, would not use the information for personnel decisions. For that purpose, he would use the formal district evaluation system for summative evaluation of teachers. Teachers were also assured that they would not be compared with other teachers but would have private use of the information about themselves to improve their performance and set goals.

The staff developer, Mr. McCarthy, and several teachers developed an observation checklist that provided information only on the teacher's use of classroom discussion. Results of these formative observations were to be used only as a guide in selecting teacher goals and providing formative feedback on teacher progress. After discussion and modification, the teachers accepted this checklist. The faculty was divided into pairs of teachers. Mr. McCarthy arranged to cover classes while peers observed each other, met to review the observation data, and coached one another on improving classroom discussions.

The initial observations were made, goals were set, and coaching for improvement occurred from January through April. A second set of observations was conducted at the end of April, and the completed checklists were sent to the district staff developer. The district staff developer could see positive results as measured by the classroom observation checklists and feedback from teachers. Excited by such promising results, he shared these results with Mr. McCarthy.

In May, severe state and federal budget cuts required the principal to rank the teachers in the building for pink-slipping or a reduction in force. Most principals in the district rank ordered the teachers on the basis of seniority, but Mr. McCarthy selected teachers for dismissal based on the formative evaluation results. He incorrectly assumed that teachers would accept this unintended use of the evaluation information, since it seemed to be based on merit rather than seniority. Outraged that their trust in both the principal and the formative evaluation system had been violated, the teachers refused to participate further in this project and were reluctant to support Mr. McCarthy in other initiatives. The district staff developer also was outraged by the misuse of data shared with Mr. McCarthy and sided with the teachers.

Illustrative Case 1: Violating Trust by Misusing Data
Analysis

This case illustrates the problems of using data to serve unintended uses. The district staff developer and the principal, Mr. McCarthy, had assured teachers that information from this formative evaluation process would not be used in ways other than those promised and that only the district staff developer would have access to all the data. The staff developer, excited by the results, shared the outcomes with Mr. McCarthy, which was the first violation of trust. When an outside circumstance—the need for layoffs—required the rank ordering of teachers, Mr. McCarthy was faced with a difficult choice. He could have followed the practice of other principals and ranked teachers according to seniority rather than merit. However, he thought that some of the least senior teachers were more effective and that the data he needed to support his view were available through the formative evaluation process. In weighing the use of the data, Mr. McCarthy concluded that, while the data were collected with the intention that they be used only for improvement, the opportunity to create a more effective faculty was more important than violating the faculty's trust. Unfortunately, although he may have believed in his motives, he negated his effectiveness by seriously alienating the faculty.

Proper safeguards should have been established to ensure that the formative evaluation information would be used only for its intended purposes and would be available only to designated parties, in this case the district staff developer and the individual evaluatees. Since the principal was not an identified user of the evaluation information, the district staff developer should have reported composite data to Mr. McCarthy to support the effectiveness of the program instead of sharing the evaluation results of individual teachers. Once privy to this information, however, the principal should not have used it to rank order the teachers for the purpose of decisions about retention and dismissal. This was a clear violation of the intended use. If used for termination of faculty, it almost certainly would have resulted in litigation.

Since Mr. McCarthy felt so strongly about selection of retention by merit rather than seniority, he could have approached all parties involved and proposed a revised memorandum of understanding concerning this evaluation plan. Once fully informed of his intentions, the parties to the evaluation might have signed a memorandum of agreement (see P2, Appropriate Policies and Procedures) confirming the rules for access to the data and use of the evaluation data for this revised purpose. Such a formal agreement would have precluded violation of the rules, retained the faculty's confidence in the principal, and extended a successful collaborative effort to improve faculty effectiveness in the classroom.

Illustrative Case 2: Changing the Culture Surrounding Evaluations
Description

Members of a school board charged Dr. Vargas, a new superintendent, with devising a plan for awarding merit pay to teachers. While the current system of evaluation appeared to be fair and was accepted by the teachers, principals, and teachers' organization, it had not been used for merit pay in the past. In reviewing the process, Dr. Vargas and district administrators determined that the evaluation system primarily had been used to provide teachers with feedback. No teacher in the district had ever been dismissed solely as a result of poor performance. In fact, no teacher in the district had ever been rated on this evaluation system as being less than satisfactory in all areas. Most teachers were rated at the exemplary level.

In reviewing these documents, this puzzled Dr. Vargas, who knew that in the past year three of the district's 15 schools had been designated as low performing schools on state accountability measures. How, she wondered, could the students of "exemplary" teachers be falling so far behind? After reviewing the process and its criteria, she decided that the evaluation process itself did not need to change; however, its use and implementation did. A major concern for her was the scoring process. There seemed to be an inflation of scores not based on data collected.

Dr. Vargas and the district office administrative team began a thorough review of all the evaluation documentation of the past two years. They found that, in many cases, principals were dating all observations on one day—the day before the records were due in the central office. The comments from some principals appeared to be the same for most, if not all, of the teachers they supervised. In some cases, the principal rated all teachers as exemplary in all areas with little or no differentiation of scores. This indicated to Dr. Vargas that lack of oversight had resulted in the evaluations being treated merely as paperwork to be completed and turned in with no follow-up. The evaluations certainly were not being used for the purposes of differentiating between effective and ineffective teachers and identifying specific teacher strengths and weaknesses as stated in the current district policy. Based on these evaluations, there was no way to improve teacher quality, let alone identify teachers for merit pay.

Dr. Vargas modeled the evaluation process with each principal through the principal evaluation system. Each principal received feedback on individual strengths and weaknesses, as well as ratings that differentiated performance among the principals. Dr. Vargas also provided specific feedback to each principal on the implementation of the teacher evaluation system at his or her school. All principals received additional training in the process with the assurance that a system of periodic oversight at the district office would be in place.

Through a series of meetings and discussions with all involved in the evaluation process, Dr. Vargas garnered support for the plan that merit pay would apply to principals as well as teachers and be based on the summative evaluation process. Before this plan went into effect, the district policy was changed to reflect that the teacher and principal evaluation processes would include identification for merit pay in addition to the original purposes of identifying strengths and weaknesses and identifying incompetent teachers.

Illustrative Case 2: Changing the Culture Surrounding Evaluations
Analysis

The intended uses of an evaluation system can be well defined in district policy, but the actual implementation may not meet these expectations. In this case, a lack of oversight allowed principals to complete forms solely to meet deadlines and without completing the required data collection. This short-circuited the intended use of identifying and addressing weaknesses in teacher practice and resulted in inflated evaluation scores that masked poor instructional practices that were negatively impacting student achievement.

Dr. Vargas recalled the intended uses of the evaluation and added merit pay, but she did so by including all groups involved in the process (see F2, Political Viability). By clearly identifying and reinforcing the uses of the evaluation data, she increased the level of implementation within the schools and made personnel evaluation a top priority rather than perfunctory paperwork.

Supporting Documentation

Fenstermacher, G. D., & Richardson, V. (2005). On making determinations of quality in teaching. *Teachers College Record, 107*(1), 186–212.

Grantham, T. C., & Ford, D. Y. (1998). Principal instructional leadership can reverse the under-representation of black students in gifted education. *NASSP Bulletin, 82*, 100–109.

Hoerr, T. R. (1998). A case for merit pay. *Phi Delta Kappan, 80*(4), 326–327.

Marshall, M. (1998). Using teacher evaluation to change school culture. *NASSP Bulletin, 82*(600), 117–119.

Oldham, A. (2004). Lessons learned about standards-based teacher evaluation systems. *Peabody Journal of Education, 79*(4), 126–137.

Ponticell, J. A., & Zepeda, S. J. (2004). Confronting well-learned lessons in supervision and evaluation. *NASSP Bulletin, 88*, 43–59.

U3   Evaluator Qualifications

STANDARD   The evaluation system should be developed, implemented, and managed by people with the necessary skills, training, and authority.

Explanation.   Institutions should take great care in appointing, training, supporting, and monitoring the people who develop, implement, and manage personnel evaluation systems. Appropriately qualified people should be placed in charge, and their authority and responsibility to oversee and conduct valid and reliable personnel evaluations should be clearly established. Administrators, faculty, and others who implement evaluation plans should be trained in the institution's specific evaluation policies and procedures.

The institution must manage the evaluation system to ensure that evaluators have the appropriate authority and position to conduct evaluations. In addition, all evaluators must engage in regularly updated training and information on the evaluation process. A system of oversight must be in place to maintain the integrity of the process. This oversight should include ways to monitor records, reports, documentation, and evaluator training needs. If evaluators are poorly trained or do not carry their evaluations through effectively, the evaluation reports will be of little use to stakeholders.

Rationale.   The acceptance of an evaluation depends on the evaluatee's perceptions of the evaluators' qualifications as evidenced by their performance of the evaluation. To ensure credibility, an evaluator should be recognized as having the authority to evaluate, be sufficiently trained in the evaluation procedures, demonstrate knowledge about the evaluatee's position as well as the appropriate criteria for evaluation, and be as free as possible of conflict of interest and bias (see P6, Conflict of Interest; A8, Bias Identification and Management). The evaluator must also implement the system of evaluation with fidelity, so that the evaluatee is able to trust that the evaluator followed the intended procedures of the evaluation plan. If there are questions concerning fidelity of implementation, there more likely will be challenges by evaluatees. The evaluatees might resist the use of evaluation reports related to their employment status if the question of fairness is raised. Qualified evaluators bring credibility to the process and contribute to its constructive use.

GUIDELINES

A. Establish the authority and responsibilities of the evaluators.
B. Provide the appropriate professional development to ensure that all evaluators have the necessary knowledge and skills. Professional development of evaluators should include, but is not limited to, the following: principles and practices of sound personnel evaluation, performance appraisal techniques, methods for motivating others, training in sensitivity to diversity, conflict management skills, and an understanding of the law as it applies to education personnel evaluation.
C. Develop evaluators who can use the criteria of the evaluation system effectively to create useful reports.
D. Monitor the evaluation system to ensure that all evaluators are maintaining correct procedures (see A11, Metaevaluation).
E. Monitor the evaluation system to ensure that all evaluators respect diversity among their faculties and staff.

COMMON ERRORS

A. Allowing unqualified or untrained persons to conduct personnel evaluations.
B. Failing to plan and prepare carefully for observations, feedback sessions, and other evaluation activities.
C. Failing to provide appropriate professional development to newly hired personnel who will function in the role of evaluator before conducting evaluations.
D. Failing to provide appropriate safeguards, including training and oversight, against the influence of personal bias in the outcomes of the evaluation.
E. Failing to provide ongoing professional development to all evaluators to maintain the high level of skill needed to produce reliable, valid reports and documents.

Illustrative Case 1: Lack of Evaluator Training Triggers a Grievance
Description

Mr. Singh, a new high school principal, scheduled performance evaluation reviews beginning with a veteran English teacher, Mrs. Walsh. Mrs. Walsh had taught at the school long before Mr. Singh arrived. Although he had worked as a principal in other districts, Mr. Singh was new to this district. He had not used this district's particular form of teacher evaluation before but was confident of his prior experience with another evaluation system, so he opted out of attending the district training on this system.

Mr. Singh dreaded Mrs. Walsh's performance review because he knew that he would have to give her some negative comments and lower scores than she had received in the past. It seemed to him that her class had been chaotic all year, with students constantly moving around, talking, and roaming the hallways. He knew he would have to address this in the review conference. Throughout the year, he had tried to be encouraging and hoped that she would improve, but her classes seemed to go along as usual with no change.

Mr. Singh had planned to complete the required three formal classroom observations, but thought that he had seen enough from two observations and his occasional walks down this teacher's hallway. A busy schedule prevented him from getting into Mrs. Walsh's classroom for the third required observation. Realizing that he had not had time to complete her performance review and that Mrs. Walsh was scheduled to meet with him during her planning period that day, Mr. Singh hurriedly pulled out the district form and completed it. In his rush to complete the form, he stressed all the documented deficiencies of performance, such as lack of structure and control of students, without noting her obvious strengths in certain areas. He noted that the form asked him to record her comments to present evidence concerning her performance. He had not thought about that. The other evaluation systems he had used had relied solely on his observations. He entered a "not applicable" in those spaces. He also made several errors in completing the form.

When meeting with Mrs. Walsh, Mr. Singh handed her the form and asked for her signature as he had with other evaluation systems. She refused to sign without going over the comments and ratings. She was surprised and hurt that her compassion for and nurturing of her at-risk students did not seem valued by this principal, who appeared not to understand or support her philosophy of interactive teaching. Mrs. Walsh stated that she got the impression that all Mr. Singh valued was that students be kept quiet and at their seats all day. She also questioned the insufficient observation data, given that a third observation was never completed and that only deficiencies were noted. In addition, she complained about not being given the opportunity to address his concerns or explain that her classes were interactive and project-based; thus, students were involved in authentic writing that required some out-of-class interviews and research. She noted that no comments were provided as rationale for low rating scores in some areas. From past experience, Mrs. Walsh knew these were required in this teacher evaluation system.

During this conference, Mrs. Walsh pointed out that her past performance evaluations had always been exemplary and well done by the previous principal who had followed evaluation procedures carefully with fair comments that addressed both strengths and weaknesses. Mr. Singh then became flustered and admonished her against comparing principals in terms of evaluations. Mrs. Walsh became defensive and demanded that Mr. Singh have a content area expert evaluate her performance. The interview ended with Mrs. Walsh in tears and Mr. Singh red in the face. When Mrs. Walsh left the office, she immediately contacted her professional organization to begin a grievance process against Mr. Singh.

Illustrative Case 1: Lack of Evaluator Training Triggers a Grievance
Analysis

This case illustrates the dangers of common errors caused by lack of training and district oversight in conducting performance evaluations. In this case, the evaluator, Mr. Singh, relied on training and experience with another type of teacher evaluation. The fact that he "opted out" of district training indicates a lack of oversight on the part of the district to ensure that all evaluators are certified and have completed adequate training. The district should require training of all evaluators before their beginning the evaluation process. Violations of procedure to this magnitude damage the value of feedback and the resulting reports.

Errors arising from lack of familiarity with the evaluation system diminish the credibility of the evaluator. Although Mr. Singh may have had good grounds for concern over Mrs. Walsh's performance, he failed to use the process to help address his concerns. By failing to follow the procedures of the evaluation correctly (i.e., failure to complete all required observations and errors in completing the forms), Mr. Singh left himself open to a grievance. What should have been a constructive exchange became a mutually harmful confrontation (see P4, Interactions With Evaluatees; U1, Constructive Orientation). Mr. Singh lost his credibility as an evaluator with Mrs. Walsh and any colleagues that she could influence. Mr. Singh also became involved in a time-consuming grievance process that could have been avoided.

To benefit from performance evaluation, the evaluatee must see the evaluator as a fair and credible source of information. It is essential that all procedures of an evaluation process (e.g., number and deadlines of observations, correct use of forms, scheduling of conferences) be followed (see A4, Documented Purposes and Procedures).

The evaluator must prepare for the interview and offer specific examples of the evaluatee's strengths and weaknesses that are directly keyed to the position description. It is helpful for the evaluator to spend some time at the beginning of the interview reviewing the areas of agreement on performance to establish a shared perception of at least some aspects of the performance. For those evaluatees who fall significantly below expectations, the evaluator must provide a formal, written performance improvement plan, complete with goals for improvement, institutional support to be provided, dates by which the goals must be met, and evidence to be used in assessing progress (see U6, Follow-Up and Professional Development).

Illustrative Case 2: Supervising the Evaluation Process
Description

A district hired five new building-level administrators at the start of the school year. Each new principal and assistant principal would be responsible for conducting personnel evaluations. As part of their induction into the district, the assistant superintendent, Miss Liwang, designed and conducted training on the procedures and forms of the personnel evaluation system. With the use of the district's electronic data management system, she was able to closely monitor all the data entries from her office, such as classroom observations and lesson plan reviews. She also could provide each new administrator with immediate electronic feedback on the quality of his or her comments and observation notes. In this manner, Miss Liwang was able to provide ongoing oversight and support of the evaluation process throughout the year. In addition, all new administrators were assigned accomplished colleagues as mentors. Mentors and new administrators met monthly throughout the first year in collaborative meetings that focused on evaluation along with other leadership responsibilities.

Illustrative Case 2: Supervising the Evaluation Process
Analysis

When this district hired new administrators, training in the evaluation system became one of the top priorities. While other duties were addressed, this district recognized the value in placing expectations of effective evaluation into the new administrator's role. Recognizing that instruction and student learning are linked to teacher quality, this district approached teacher evaluation as an integral part of the expectations for instructional leadership. Building qualified evaluators required not only initial training in the forms and process, but also additional support through the mentoring program and oversight by the assistant superintendent, Miss Liwang.

This district used an electronic data management system that allowed immediate, ongoing oversight, so that errors or poor quality reports were either avoided entirely or corrected before the summative report. This increased the utility of the reports to the district, evaluators, and evaluatees. New administrators were confident and competent in their roles and responsibilities in the evaluation process in this district. Schedules and consistent high quality evaluations were maintained without interruption. Relationships built among the administrators in their evaluation-focused activities not only strengthened evaluation procedures but also provided support and useful induction into the district. The design of the evaluation development process maximized growth for the participants with ongoing review and dialogue, immediate feedback, and personal support.

Supporting Documentation

Darling-Hammond, L. (2003). Keeping good teachers. *Educational Leadership, 60*(8), 76–77.

Rettig, P. R. (1999). Differentiated supervision: A new approach. *Principal, 78*(3), 36–39.

Sobel, D. M., Taylor, S. V., & Anderson, R. E. (2003). Teacher evaluation standards in practice: A standards-based assessment tool for diversity-responsive teaching. *The Teacher Educator, 38*(4), 285–302.

Van der Linde, C. H. (1998). Clinical supervision in teacher evaluation: A pivotal factor in the quality management of education. *Education, 119*(2), 328–334.

U4   Explicit Criteria

STANDARD   Systems of evaluation should have clear, specific criteria directly related to the required job expectations of the evaluatees.

Explanation.   The evaluation system must outline clear expectations for performance in language that is easily understood and interpreted by both evaluators and evaluatees (see A2, Defined Expectations). An evaluation system should have a clear alignment between the explicit criteria defined by job expectations and the rating scale, rubric, or other method used to judge the performance. Criteria also are important in designing an evaluation process. Explicit criteria must be considered when developing procedures for conducting the evaluation process, so that the procedures used to gather evaluative information result in the intended interpretation of performance expectations (see P2, Appropriate Policies and Procedures). Not defining the criteria explicitly opens the opportunity for individual interpretation and jeopardizes the usefulness of results.

Rationale.   Evaluation reports become the basis for important personnel decisions such as promotion, dismissal, and granting tenure, as well as judgments about the practice and professional development needs of evaluatees. The criteria used to interpret expectations not only must be relevant, but also must be legally defensible by conforming to the intended purposes and uses of the evaluation.

Without explicit criteria, bias is more readily introduced to the evaluation. Through evaluators' individual interpretations, an evaluation may deviate significantly from the intended expectations. Vague wording and recommendations that stray too far from the criteria diminish the worth of the evaluation, while strict adherence to well-formed criteria results in usable feedback and valid reports.

GUIDELINES

A. Ensure that all criteria for job performance expectations are stated explicitly in the evaluation procedures.
B. Align evaluation criteria with current job descriptions.
C. Conduct periodic reviews of evaluation criteria to ensure continued alignment with organizational goals.

D. Provide regular reviews of evaluation criteria involving input from evaluators, evaluatees, and other key stakeholder groups to ensure continued shared understanding of criteria and alignment with job descriptions.

E. Align documentation and reports with the criteria to address only identified professional roles and responsibilities in the evaluation report and ensure that extraneous comments beyond these roles and responsibilities are neither included nor accepted.

F. Provide continuous oversight of the evaluation process to ensure that evaluators interpret and use criteria appropriately in all evaluation reports.

G. Provide copies of written evaluation reports to evaluatees in advance of an evaluation conference, if possible, and ensure that all parties share an understanding of the criteria used.

H. Use the agreed-on criteria to provide a rationale for and justification of evaluation findings.

I. Allow evaluatees to append clarifications, remarks, and rebuttals to the evaluation report by providing a written policy with guidelines on how to do so (see P2, Appropriate Policies and Procedures).

COMMON ERRORS

A. Basing the evaluation report on vague recollections or data that are irrelevant to job duties and responsibilities as outlined by criteria.

B. Failing to explain criteria to evaluatees at the beginning of the process.

C. Failing to relate the criteria to the defined expectations (see A2, Defined Expectations) in a manner that is easily understood by both evaluators and evaluatees.

D. Trying to please users of the evaluation by reflecting an individual's preconceived strengths or weaknesses without current data.

E. Introducing bias on the part of the evaluator by allowing subjective interpretation of data unrelated to the criteria.

F. Failing to update criteria when job descriptions or job responsibilities change.

G. Restricting the criteria to a subset of job expectations; for example, relying on an external measure such as standardized test scores as the only criterion for teacher performance.

H. Using one set of criteria (e.g., for classroom teachers) to evaluate another role (e.g., guidance counselors) for convenience or in the absence of a clearly defined system for the latter role.

Illustrative Case 1: Vague Evaluation Criteria Produce Counterproductive Results
Description

A university student service office was having morale problems, and the agency head, Mr. Fetterman, decided first to identify the issues and then address them through employee evaluations. Since he preferred the judgment of someone external to the situation, he asked a faculty colleague who was also a friend to serve as the evaluator. This colleague, Dr. Bhatia, was a respected senior member of the faculty but had no experience as an evaluator beyond the usual service on tenure and promotion committees. Nevertheless, she agreed to conduct the evaluation as a favor.

Dr. Bhatia did not want to appear as a representative of management, so she tried to be friendly and form casual relationships with the persons being evaluated. She failed to take immediate notes, but thought that her impressions of the employees' performance levels would be adequate. Since Dr. Bhatia was not as familiar as Mr. Fetterman with the duties of all the employees, and she did not fully understand the criteria of the evaluation system, she based her impressions on a general sense of what employees told her about their job duties and responsibilities.

In addition, Dr. Bhatia was uneasy about officially recording employee problems and deficiencies. Consequently, her official report to Mr. Fetterman was largely positive, and she communicated her negative impressions of the situation and certain employees in an informal session with him. Mr. Fetterman weighed these informal comments as heavily as the formal written reports shared with employees. Thus, certain remediation plans were put into place to address reported weaknesses of employees. The employees were confused by the difference between the largely positive individual written reports that they had received and the negative treatment some were experiencing from Mr. Fetterman. Morale declined further because the situation was exacerbated by the lack of explicit criteria, which resulted in poorly used evaluation reports.

Illustrative Case 1: Vague Evaluation Criteria Produce Counterproductive Results
Analysis

No clear criteria were used in these evaluations to guide collection and analyses of data before writing the evaluation reports. Since the reports given to employees were based on evaluator impressions rather than agreed-on criteria, confusion and poor morale resulted. The tendency of the evaluator, Dr. Bhatia, to be positive in the written evaluations but to make negative informal reports further destroyed the credibility of the evaluations, harmed the situation they were intended to relieve, and probably undermined the usefulness of future evaluations in that office. The negative aspects could not be justified or addressed satisfactorily since they were not included in the written evaluation reports. This caused confusion because the agency head was essentially reacting to a different set of evaluation results from those provided to the evaluatees.

Dr. Bhatia should have insisted on receiving clear criteria on which to judge employees against the expectations of their jobs. She entered her task with little more than a general impression of what "good" employees should look like. This resulted in confusion and poor reporting practices. Dr. Bhatia also was uncomfortable reporting on unsatisfactory performance without solid criteria to form the basis for her judgment. Once criteria were clarified and established, she should have written her final reports accordingly. The reports given to the employees should have been completed with strengths and weaknesses as well as a justification for the judgments. No additional information outside the report should have been shared with Mr. Fetterman to influence his actions. Even if shared, Mr. Fetterman should not have used the informal negative evaluation results because they were not included in the written report given to the evaluatees.

Mr. Fetterman erred in using an inexperienced and untrained evaluator, especially in a sensitive, negative situation (see U3, Evaluator Qualifications). He should have determined whether the evaluator was capable of carrying out a frank, objective evaluation and producing a straightforward, accurate report. If Dr. Bhatia did not meet those standards, Mr. Fetterman should have employed a qualified alternate.

Illustrative Case 2: Updating Evaluation Criteria to Reflect the Job
Description

Mrs. Davison, the supervisor of school nurses in a large district, decided that the evaluation process for nurses was outdated because it did not include some recent changes in procedures. She worried that some of the nurses were not implementing these changes as thoroughly as they should due to lack of accountability and feedback. In an effort to reinforce the new practices, Mrs. Davison decided to include them in the evaluation criteria for school nurses.

Mrs. Davison called the nurses together to review the changes and offer comments on the wording and meaning of the new criteria. Most nurses agreed that the new instrument reflected their current job requirements much more closely. After a year of evaluation using the updated criteria, Mrs. Davison found far more instances of correct implementation of the new policies. Many nurses reported greater satisfaction with the fairness and effectiveness of their evaluations.

Illustrative Case 2: Updating Evaluation Criteria to Reflect the Job
Analysis

When job requirements change substantially, evaluation criteria must be updated to reflect those changes. Both the evaluator and the evaluatee can feel frustrated if misunderstandings result from poorly written or obsolete criteria that fail to reflect the current job adequately. In addition, implementation of new, critical job requirements may not occur if the vehicle for feedback and support from supervisors is missing. In this case, the nurses were given the opportunity to review and comment on the new criteria before they were put into place. This step helped assure that the evaluation criteria were aligned with job expectations.

By allowing the nurses the opportunity to review the changes in their evaluation process, the supervisor gained valuable buy-in from the evaluatees. It would have been even more effective if the nurses had initial input into the creation of the new criteria. Involving at least representatives of the evaluatees in revision processes leads to both greater buy-in and a stronger evaluation process because the language will tend to reflect that used by the group being evaluated.

Supporting Documentation

Kimball, S. M., White, B., Milanowski, A. T., & Borman, G. (2004). Examining the relationship between teacher evaluation and student assessment results in Washoe County. *Peabody Journal of Education, 79*(4), 54–78.

Peterson, K. (2004). Research on teacher evaluation. *NASSP Bulletin, 88,* 60–79.

Reeves, D. R. (2004). Evaluating administrators. *Educational Leadership, 61*(7), 52–58.

Sawyer, L. (2001). Revamping a teacher evaluation system. *Educational Leadership, 58*(5), 44–47.

Sobel, D. M., Taylor, S. V., & Anderson, R. E. (2003). Teacher evaluation standards in practice: A standards-based assessment tool for diversity-responsive teaching. *The Teacher Educator, 38*(4), 285–302.

Taylor, L. K., & Shawn, J. (2003). The long and winding road to accountability. *Leadership, 32*(3), 32–33.

Thomas, G. (1999). The core work of school leaders. *Thrust for Educational Leadership, 28*(5), 24–26.

Vanscriver, J. H. (1999). Developing rubrics to improve teacher evaluation. *High School Magazine, 7*(2), 32–34.

U5   Functional Reporting

STANDARD   Reports should be clear, timely, accurate, and germane to the purpose of the evaluation.

Explanation.   Those in charge of coordinating or conducting evaluations not only should use sound assessment practices, but also should take care in producing the resulting reports. All personnel evaluations should result in clearly written reports based on data collected during the process that reflect the criteria of the job performance. These reports should accurately reflect performance; inflation of ratings or reports that omit deficiencies are to be avoided. Evaluators should help users understand the reported results of the evaluation to pursue appropriate actions. Little is gained if the evaluatee is handed a vaguely written report or provided with informal verbal feedback that fails to address major job performance issues. In addition to clarity and accuracy, reports also must be issued in a timely way. Lapses in time may seriously diminish the impact of an evaluation as well as violate procedural requirements.

Rationale.   When results are clear, timely, accurate, and germane to the purpose of the evaluation, follow-up actions such as faculty development and personnel actions follow naturally and effectively. When reports lack these required characteristics, appropriate follow-up actions are unlikely to occur or may be flawed in important ways. For example, a well-written and documented report that is completed on schedule can be used as a basis for a personnel action. That same report submitted after the required completion date likely will result in a grievance or other litigation if a personnel action is based on that report. Similarly, even the most accurate, timely report will lose its ability to influence performance if not clearly understood by all users.

GUIDELINES

A. Ensure that all reports can be justified and supported by documented evidence of performance.
B. Review the language in reports in terms of clarity and relevance to criteria.
C. Ensure that all scores or ratings included in reports reflect the performance level of the evaluatee accurately.
D. Provide all written reports to users within specified time frames of the process.
E. Conduct a conference with the evaluatee to ensure clear understanding of the evaluation outcomes and allow necessary questions.

F. Allow the evaluatee to submit any written comments or disagreements with the results of the evaluation within a specified time.

G. Ensure that each evaluatee signs and dates his or her evaluation report following a review conference, with the understanding that while a signature may not indicate agreement with the results, it does confirm that the report was formally reviewed.

H. Include a description of the disposition of the evaluation in the report including follow-up activities based on experience and performance level (e.g., master teacher, marginal teacher, new teacher).

I. Include follow-up activities as part of the written record, and maintain records of instances in which the evaluatee did or did not act on recommendations from evaluations.

J. Follow up as warranted, especially with evaluatees who have been unsatisfactory or are in danger of job termination.

K. Provide any necessary written notices of termination or nonrenewal of a contract by the appropriate date as specified in the written evaluation policies and procedures.

L. Maintain the report as well as other evaluation records in a secure location to ensure access only by defined users.

M. Provide oversight of all records and documentation maintained by evaluators.

COMMON ERRORS

A. Failing to keep superiors and officials informed of serious performance problems when they are identified.

B. Inflating scores on evaluation reports.

C. Not including deficiencies discussed with the evaluatee and the response by the evaluatee in the report.

D. Failing to use the evaluation information appropriately in personnel decisions.

E. Assuming that all appropriate users, including the evaluatee, will understand and will use the information.

F. Failing to record the accurate date on a written report.

G. Failing to conference with the evaluatee to ensure clear understanding of the results of a written report.

H. Failing to obtain an evaluatee's signature and date following a conference concerning a written report.

I. Failing to provide written reports on a timely basis.

J. Writing reports that do not address key elements of job performance.

Illustrative Case 1: A Principal's Deficiency in Evaluating Teachers
Description

A middle school principal, Mr. Morelli, suddenly realized that all of his written evaluation reports were due to the district office by that afternoon. He had managed to keep up with the required observations and other data collection procedures such as checks on lesson plans, attendance records, and so forth, but other pressing responsibilities had caused him to put off completing all the formal evaluation records. To his dismay, he found that he had six teacher evaluations and six evaluation conferences to complete. Of these six teachers, two had serious deficiencies in performance. The more he thought about it, however, the more Mr. Morelli convinced himself that it was pointless so late in the school year to write up their deficiencies and try to resolve them. If he wrote up the deficiencies, he would have to include an action plan for improvement and a report on what had been accomplished. He knew that he would not have time to write up the action plan, much less get it started before the end of the year, so he rationalized that his evaluation reports would only be stuck in a file, and he could still address these teachers' deficiencies without writing a formal action plan.

Having decided this, he began immediately to complete the evaluation forms. His intention was to address the deficiencies he had noted in his informal observations of the two teachers, but not to include those deficiencies in his written reports. On each final report, he indicated that the teacher was performing at a satisfactory level although this was not the case for at least two teachers.

Illustrative Case 1: A Principal's Deficiency in Evaluating Teachers
Analysis

This principal, Mr. Morelli, became trapped by the time crunch felt by all school-level administrators, but failed his own responsibility to the school and students. He reduced feedback from his observation to a task that he could check off and send to the district office. In addition, several errors in his procedure prevented his school and teachers from benefiting from the evaluations. First, Mr. Morelli did not write reports that would be useful in identifying teacher strengths and weaknesses and thus lead to suggested follow-up and improved performance. Second, by not reporting known deficiencies, he not only denied these teachers the opportunity to improve, but also condoned their poor practice, which allowed them to continue. While he met his deadline, he compromised his effectiveness as an evaluator and principal.

Mr. Morelli should have placed a higher priority on accurately completing his teacher evaluations instead of compromising the process. His written reports lacked a full reporting on known deficiencies and did not include suggestions for follow-up and professional improvement. Written evaluation forms record a teacher's performance on specific criteria over time. These reports must accurately reflect performance to be useful to the teacher and any other user of evaluations, or, as in this case, credibility of both the evaluator and the evaluation system is lost.

Illustrative Case 2: A Collective Effort to Improve Reporting
Description

Dr. Karp, a superintendent of a small school district, reviewed the paperwork associated with the principal evaluation system in place and determined that the format of the formal written reports did not reflect the process. It also did not allow adequate documentation of suggested follow-up plans for improvement. The current system was primarily a checklist of completed duties rather than a true report of performance. During the summer break, Dr. Karp began conducting meetings with the principals and school board members to redesign the form. Each group brought to the table its own reporting needs. School board members were more interested in overall school performance and principal management of facilities. Principals tended to want more formal feedback on their performance as instructional leaders. While the process of evaluation in place had evolved into one that would provide such feedback, the forms themselves could not be used to convey feedback in these areas. Working with the central office staff, the superintendent considered the needs of stakeholders to develop a more appropriate form. This form was reviewed and adopted by the school board as part of the personnel evaluation policy.

Illustrative Case 2: A Collective Effort to Improve Reporting
Analysis

In this case, the superintendent, Dr. Karp, recognized the importance of having written reports in a format that supported the evaluation criteria and the needs of all user groups. The written reports needed to provide not only documentation of the performance of an evaluatee, but also the means to improve the general performance of an organization. This superintendent also was aware of the value of inviting input from other users of the report—the evaluatees (principals) and superiors (school board).

Written reports provide documentation of the evaluation process and its suggested follow-up. Therefore, to be useful to an evaluation process, written reports must be in a format conducive to recording strengths, weaknesses, and follow-up according to the data collected and analyzed during the course of an evaluation. Any comments about the report should be pertinent to the evaluation itself and reflect the criteria. This increases understanding and usefulness for all users.

Supporting Documentation

Pigford, A. B. (1987). Teacher evaluation: More than a game that principals play. *Phi Delta Kappan, 69*, 141–142.

Rettig, P. R. (1999). Differentiated supervision: A new approach. *Principal, 78*(3), 36–39.

Sobel, D. M., Taylor, S. V., & Anderson, R. E. (2003). Teacher evaluation standards in practice: A standards-based assessment tool for diversity-responsive teaching. *The Teacher Educator, 38*(4), 285–302.

Van der Linde, C. H. (1998). Clinical supervision in teacher evaluation: A pivotal factor in the quality management of education. *Education, 119*(2), 328–334.

Zimmerman, S., & Deckert-Pelton, M. (2003). Evaluating the evaluators: Teachers' perceptions of the principal's role in professional evaluation. *NASSP Bulletin, 87*, 28–37.

Zirkel, P. A. (2004, March/April). Evaluating teachers. *Principal, 83*(4), 10–12.

U6 Follow-Up and Professional Development

STANDARD   Personnel evaluations should lead to appropriate professional development.

Explanation.   The development of a high quality staff should be a key focus of any personnel evaluation system. Credible feedback from trained evaluators who base their judgment on the criteria of the evaluation system is crucial. Feedback stemming from the evaluation should address both areas of strength and areas needing improvement. The system should be designed to obtain information that can lead to the preparation of an individual professional growth plan for each evaluatee and plans for an in-service staff development program.

Rationale.   Unless evaluation results are used to improve staff performance, the quality and adequacy of educational services likely will remain unchanged or even decline. Educators are deeply aware of and committed to the value of lifelong learning and professional development. Evaluation systems that promote professional growth through such vehicles as self-assessment, peer review, coaching, mentoring, and individual growth plans should lead to higher job performance levels among staff. Empowering evaluatees to play a key role in their own growth helps build trust and respect between evaluators and evaluatees and promote staff morale.

GUIDELINES

A. Provide timely, credible evaluation feedback (see P4, Interactions With Evaluatees).
B. Identify performance areas that need reinforcement or improvement or are areas of strength (see P5, Comprehensive Evaluation).
C. Provide specific, constructive ways to build on strengths and address weaknesses.
D. Begin evaluation conferences on a positive note, avoiding an adversarial posture and emphasizing support for the evaluatee as a professional and the promotion of professional growth and improvement.

E. Use evaluations to allocate resources for improving performance, and provide resources and support for that purpose (see F3, Fiscal Viability).

F. Encourage, train, and assist educators to assess and improve their own performance (see U3, Evaluator Qualifications).

G. Promptly reinforce improvement by an educator involved in remediation and professional development activities.

H. Give recognition and encouragement to outstanding performance (see P4, Interactions With Evaluatees; P5, Comprehensive Evaluation).

I. Provide evaluators with support personnel or services to assist in collecting and analyzing needed information when those tasks exceed their professional training and expertise or their availability.

J. Ensure that all professional development meets the standards for high quality as outlined in federal legislation and professional standards (see P7, Legal Viability).

COMMON ERRORS

A. Failing to recognize and respond to both the strengths and weaknesses of an evaluatee's professional qualifications or performance (see P5, Comprehensive Evaluation).

B. Failing to determine whether the educator is provided with sufficient resources and support to do the job or to look at the work context (see A3, Analysis of Context).

C. Making unreasonable recommendations for improvement that cannot be supported by the organization (see F3, Fiscal Viability).

D. Not linking growth plans to the institution's mission statement and goals and the individual's current job assignment or possible future job assignment (see U1, Constructive Orientation).

E. Writing up short-term "quick fixes" for professional development not aligned with the goals of the institution or the criteria of the evaluation.

F. Failing to prioritize in the growth plan what is to be accomplished by what date.

G. Allowing too much or too little time for completing all or any part of the plan.

H. Failing to foster a climate of support and growth for evaluatees.

I. Failing to follow up on plans to ensure that the evaluatee is meeting all requirements and showing improvement.

J. Failing to provide timely and germane feedback to the evaluatee on the progress of the plan for professional development.

Illustrative Case 1: A Failure to Communicate
Description

A new fifth-grade teacher, Mr. Laroque, was enthusiastic about his job and knew his subject matter quite well, but found classroom management to be a challenge with students at this age level. The principal, Ms. Walsh, observed his classroom during a formal observation visit and two informal walk-throughs during the first two months of the school year. Although Ms. Walsh realized that Mr. Laroque was having trouble managing his students, she thought there was little that she could do at that time given the demands of a large school. She was reluctant to offer any specific suggestions that might require resources she did not have to offer. She hoped Mr. Laroque would seek help from more experienced teachers or would learn to deal with difficult students on his own by the end of the year. Although Ms. Walsh documented the incidences of poor management in her written report, she did not offer any suggestions for improvement.

At the end of the evaluation period, Ms. Walsh informed Mr. Laroque that his performance in the area of student management was substandard based on documentation she had collected throughout the year. He was stunned that his classroom management was scored so poorly on his summative evaluation given that he had not received any negative feedback throughout the year. Ms. Walsh informed him at this point that he would be kept on probationary status for the next school year in the hope that he would improve his classroom management.

Illustrative Case 1: A Failure to Communicate
Analysis

When someone does not want to take action or does not know what action to take, it is easy to avoid action by saying that there are no resources available to improve the situation. However, in most situations, there are options that could be identified and explored. Ms. Walsh thought that she did not have the time to look into what these options might be, given the current level of resources in the school. Mr. Laroque, working in a self-contained classroom and new to the school and the profession, did not know where to turn for assistance. He could have been reluctant to admit to his more experienced colleagues that he was having problems. Since the principal did not specifically address his classroom management after her classroom observations, Mr. Laroque believed that his difficulties in classroom control must not be as serious a problem as he originally thought.

Ms. Walsh and Mr. Laroque should sit down together and identify specific areas of his classroom management approach that are most problematic, so that they can develop possible strategies for improving his skills in specific problem areas. If Mr. Laroque had a mentor, the mentor then could be included in the discussions for improvement in classroom management. Low-cost options might include asking Mr. Laroque to observe another teacher during his planning periods, providing videotapes on classroom management techniques, or asking him to attend a workshop on this topic in an adjacent district. Many online resources are also available that could offer support and suggestions at little, if any, cost. Mr. Laroque should be encouraged to conduct a self-assessment of his teaching to determine the cause for the poor behavior of his students. It is quite possible that poor planning or poor instructional strategies are the fundamental cause of his student management problems.

Illustrative Case 2: Using Data Management to Serve Follow-Up Efforts
Description

The superintendent and assistant superintendent of instruction in a district decide that the information collected by the teacher evaluation system is not used to its full potential. Teachers are rated by evaluators on their individual strengths and weaknesses, but nothing is actually done as a result of this rating. An enormous percentage of the staff development funds is being spent on outside consultants to conduct districtwide workshops. Many teachers who attend the workshops are already proficient in the strategy taught, yet may need help in other areas.

The district administrators investigated an electronic data management system to help them manage the large volume of data generated by teacher evaluation reports. Managing paper files had become too cumbersome and costly in terms of manpower. The electronic system allowed them to maintain databases and generate reports based on evaluation ratings to determine the needs of individual teachers. This permitted teachers to engage in the type of professional development needed, thus avoiding wasted resources. As part of this effort to link teacher evaluation to professional growth, all teachers created their own professional growth goals and plans linked directly to the criteria in the evaluation system. This encouraged teachers to examine and incorporate the evaluation criteria directly into teaching practice.

Illustrative Case 2: Using Data Management to Serve Follow-Up Efforts
Analysis

This district found a way to incorporate teacher evaluation into the professional development plans, thus eliminating wasted resources and efforts. By using evaluation ratings and feedback to generate their own growth goals, teachers improved the connection between the evaluation criteria and their individual practice.

In this case, the district found an electronic data management system that enabled them to generate queries and reports in such a way that this process was more feasible than if they had relied on paper files. It was essential that the evaluators conducted the evaluations in such a way that the ratings and reports provided accurate data about the performance levels of the teachers.

Supporting Documentation

Bunting, C. E. (1998). Self-directed teacher growth: Helping it happen in schools. *Schools in the Middle, 8*(1), 21–23.

Deojay, T. R., & Novak, D. S. (2004). Blended data. *Journal of Staff Development, 25*(1), 32–36.

Dufour, R. (2000). School leaders as staff developers: The key to sustained school improvement. *Catalyst for Change, 29*(3), 13–15.

Honaker, C. J. (2004). How leaders can enrich the school environment. *Kappa Delta Pi Record, 40*(3), 116–118.

Howard, B. B., & McColsky, W. H. (2001). Evaluating experienced teachers. *Educational Leadership, 58*(5), 48–51.

Marshall, M. (1998). Using teacher evaluation to change school culture. *NASSP Bulletin, 82*(600), 117–119.

National Staff Development Council. (2001). *Standards for staff development* (Rev. ed.). Oxford, OH: Author.

Steele, B. (1997). Coaching teachers in assessment. *Scholastic Early Childhood Today, 11*, 11.

FEASIBILITY STANDARDS

Summary of the Standards

Feasibility Standards   Intended to guide personnel evaluation systems to ensure ease of implementation, efficiency in use of time and resources, adequacy of funding, and viability from a political standpoint.

F1   **Practical Procedures**   Personnel evaluation procedures should be practical and efficient.

F2   **Political Viability**   Personnel evaluation policies and procedures should identify, engage, and be responsive to stakeholders.

F3   **Fiscal Viability**   Adequate time and resources should be provided for personnel evaluation activities.

F1   Practical Procedures

> **STANDARD**   Personnel evaluation procedures should be practical and efficient.

Explanation.   Personnel evaluation procedures should provide data and information that can be interpreted validly without disrupting the instructional or training activities being conducted by the evaluatee or impeding the learning of students. They should be practical enough to provide useful feedback and efficient enough to do so without hampering the work of the institution and its staff. This is accomplished best through the implementation of procedures that are integrated into the regular operations of the school or institution. In general, procedures should obtain the information needed within the budgetary and resource constraints of the organization. Such procedures also should align with system goals and policies, and they should conform to recommended practices in the evaluation field.

Rationale.   Evaluatees must be provided with full opportunities to demonstrate their knowledge, skills, and attitudes, so that sound and justifiable judgments can be made about their performance. Steps must be taken to ensure that adequate resources and time are available for the evaluation. Impractical procedures can be inefficient and needlessly disruptive, detracting from individual performance and organizational efficiency. They also can impair the credibility of the institution's administration and lower staff morale. Consequently, evaluators should avoid evaluation procedures that are cumbersome to implement, overly expensive, overly complex, needlessly obtrusive, or superficial. Systems of personnel evaluation often may appear comprehensive yet require procedures that cannot possibly be followed given the resources of the institution.

GUIDELINES

A. Develop evaluation priorities and align personnel evaluation procedures with those priorities to ensure that the most important evaluation matters are addressed effectively.

B. Identify available resources and policy requirements before designing data-collection procedures.

C. Select procedures that provide necessary information with minimal disruption (see A4, Documented Purposes and Procedures).

D. Avoid unnecessary duplication of information that already exists.

E. Define in familiar language all concepts or key terms of the evaluation system (see U4, Explicit Criteria).

F. Define the roles of evaluators (see U2, Defined Uses).

G. Help evaluatees and others involved in the evaluation understand the evaluation procedures through periodic orientation sessions (see P1, Service Orientation).

H. Delineate the procedures by which evaluatees can exercise their rights to review data about their performance (see P2, Appropriate Policies and Procedures; P3, Access to Evaluation Information).

I. Review procedures periodically to assess whether they are still appropriate or need to be altered (see P2, Appropriate Policies and Procedures; A11, Metaevaluation).

J. Encourage evaluatees and others involved in their evaluations to suggest ways by which evaluation procedures can be made more efficient and useful.

K. Ensure that all documentation developed for personnel evaluation is necessary and useful for the purposes and intent of the evaluation.

COMMON ERRORS

A. Using unnecessarily complex procedures for information collection.

B. Arbitrarily adding or omitting procedures while the evaluation is in progress.

C. Failing to consider situational factors that might influence evaluatee performance (see A3, Analysis of Context).

D. Disrupting ongoing instruction.

E. Disregarding complaints about evaluation procedures (see P7, Legal Viability).

F. Unduly stressing practicality over accuracy.

G. Disregarding stated timelines, resulting in a cost overrun (see F3, Fiscal Viability).

Illustrative Case 1: An Efficient Evaluation of Principals
Description

The central office administrators of a large school district designed a plan for evaluating the instructional leadership of building principals. The plan included 20 performance categories selected by central office administrators as important dimensions of the principal's role as an instructional leader. The district's personnel director, with the help of a consultant and two principals who had recently retired from the district, initially developed these categories. The evaluation plan required documentation of performance derived from interviews with the principals, members of their teaching staffs, and representatives of the parents' associations for their schools.

Once the plan was developed, four central office administrators were assigned to supervise and evaluate the principals. They were given four days of training, after which they expressed many concerns. They wondered if they understood the plan well enough to use it, had enough time to conduct all required activities, or had sufficiently clear directions regarding the use of evaluative information for personnel decision making. In response to their concerns, the central office staff and the consultant met. They noted that there was overlap among some of the 20 criteria and therefore reduced the number to 12. The consultant then carefully described what each criterion meant and the types of behavior or knowledge that could be used to tell if the criterion had been met. Together they developed a four-point rating guide to promote consistent evaluations of the principals. In a letter to each principal, they clarified how the evaluation information was to be used and what follow-up procedures were to be made available to principals identified as needing improvement.

After the evaluations were completed and the principals had received their reports, they were surveyed to determine what they thought of the evaluation process and their evaluations. Collectively, they noted that the performance dimensions were consistently assessed among the principals; the evaluators kept in mind the knowledge and behaviors corresponding with each criterion; the time required to collect information from teachers, parents, and principals was not excessive; and the written reports were clear and informative and contained suggestions for follow-up activities. Consequently, while there was variation among the ratings of the principals, as a group they reacted positively to the evaluation.

Illustrative Case 1: An Efficient Evaluation of Principals
Analysis

The district's goal to enhance the performance of principals as instructional leaders was worthwhile. The initial plan included more dimensions than could reasonably be assessed and appeared to some evaluators to lack clarity. Had these concerns not been addressed, the practical feasibility of the plan might have been jeopardized. Appropriate changes were made, and the problematic elements of the evaluation were clarified. The data collection procedures were practical for this district. The reports provided to the principals reflected what was set out in the evaluation plan and contained justified conclusions (see A10, Justified Conclusions) and opportunities for follow-up (see U6, Follow-Up and Professional Development) that were based on defensible information (see A5, Defensible Information).

Illustrative Case 2: An Overly Ambitious Evaluation Plan
Description

Dr. Silva, dean of a graduate school, allocated a large percentage of his annual budget for evaluating the leadership of the school's four department heads. This decision followed falling enrollments in all four departments over the course of several years. Dean Silva and the four department heads collaboratively agreed on seven major performance criteria including ratings by employers on the level of job readiness and preparation of the departments' graduates. The dean then contracted with an outside consultant who prepared an evaluation plan based on input from the four department heads and representatives of faculty, students, and graduates. In an effort to address the many concerns of all stakeholders, the procedures were extremely comprehensive.

The evaluation plan initially proceeded well. Included in the procedures were (1) staff and student interviews about departmental leadership, (2) the dean's review of policy decision-making methods and approaches to curriculum development, (3) surveys of faculty and staff to determine departmental morale, (4) review of written communication within and between the four departments, and (5) interviews with employers of graduates from each program. Each step required detailed narratives and summaries of the data collected in relation to the evaluation plan's criteria, often resulting in pages and pages of narrative.

Concerns arose, however, about the collection of information from the employers, mainly because the department heads noted that too much evaluation funding and time were being directed to this aspect of the evaluation. This part of the study proved more demanding than anticipated, and the costs of conducting these off-site interviews in terms of travel, time, and effort for evaluators far exceeded that required for the other procedures. As a result, it became clear that many other planned procedures for internal department evaluations would be omitted or glossed over since the consultant had allocated a majority of the funding and resources to the collection of data from the employers of graduates. The four department heads expressed to Dean Silva their anxiety about the altered balance of the evaluation and the movement away from the accepted plan.

The final evaluation reports of the four department heads consisted of long narrative reports that lacked any summary or scoring. The reports also tended to be skewed heavily toward the employers' assessment of graduates, a situation the department heads found unacceptable. They argued that the evaluation of the leadership of their departments was inadequate and too strongly biased toward only one of the seven performance criteria. The dean found that the procedures in the plan were overwhelming to implement regardless of the resources. In reality, it took an unreasonable amount of time and effort to fully implement such a comprehensive plan.

Illustrative Case 2: An Overly Ambitious Evaluation Plan
Analysis

Dean Silva's goal to evaluate the leadership of the department heads was commendable, particularly in light of declining enrollments in the four departments. While the evaluation plan appeared sound, its execution was flawed by a lack of practicality. What appeared to be comprehensive became overwhelming. Because of the imbalance between the internal and external evaluations, the procedures employed resulted in information that was of doubtful use in drawing conclusions about the department heads' leadership. The high cost of focusing the evaluation on graduates' success as employees with a resulting reduction in attention to the other six designated criteria of leadership abilities inevitably undermined the credibility of the evaluation and hopes for strengthened department leadership.

The plan should have focused on a more even-handed exploration of the seven criteria with reasonable procedures for reporting and scoring the data. In this case, the plan's procedures fell out of alignment with its intentions, mainly because too little consideration was given to the allocation of evaluator time and the cost for examining each of the seven criteria. The process became unbalanced and unwieldy, whereas more careful planning of time lines and cost could have led to an evaluation that would have produced the required information.

Supporting Documentation

Anderson, L., & Wilson, S. (1997). Critical incident technique. In D. L. Whetzel & G. R. Wheaton (Eds.), *Applied measurement methods in industrial psychology* (pp. 89–112). Palo Alto, CA: Davies-Black Publishing.

Pearlman, M., & Tannenbaum, R. (2003). Teacher evaluation practices in the accountability era. In T. E. Kellaghan & D. L. Stufflebeam (Eds.), *International handbook of educational evaluation* (pp. 609–642). Dordrecht, The Netherlands: Kluwer.

Peters, L. H., & DeNisi, A. S. (1990). An information processing role for appraisal purpose and job type in the development of appraisal systems. *Journal of Managerial Issues, 2*(2), 160–175.

F2   Political Viability

> **STANDARD**   **Personnel evaluation policies and procedures should identify, engage, and be responsive to stakeholders.**

Explanation.   Political viability refers to the conditions of trust, willingness to engage, and general support needed to conduct evaluations effectively to serve students, the institution, and the persons being evaluated. To achieve this viability, personnel policies and procedures should provide all stakeholders and users of evaluations with a common, acceptable understanding of the purposes and procedures of the evaluation (see U2, Defined Uses; P2, Appropriate Policies and Procedures). While an institution's board or senior administrator is officially responsible for the evaluation policies, purposes, and procedures, the board or senior administrator should work cooperatively with stakeholders to ensure that appropriate and acceptable policies and procedures are established (see P1, Service Orientation).

Political viability requires that a system of personnel evaluation be transparent, in that all procedures and policies are defined and communicated to all users with the idea of engaging them in their development and implementation. While the results of a personnel evaluation must be safeguarded carefully and maintained in confidence, this level of confidentiality does not apply to the procedures of the system itself. This requirement often competes directly with efficiency. It can be time consuming and costly to answer questions and clarify issues raised by stakeholders and to involve them in planning and reviewing evaluation procedures. Nevertheless, the extent of effort likely will be commensurate with the consequences of the decisions and the utility of the findings.

Rationale.   If personnel evaluation policies and procedures are understandable, cooperatively developed, acceptable to all interested parties, and officially adopted, they are likely to ensure continued cooperation among stakeholders and users. Such cooperation fosters support for the program, commitment to its purposes, acceptance of its methods, effective implementation, confidence in the reports, and trust in evaluation outcomes. In general, evaluatee support will result only if the evaluation system is officially mandated, proves to be fair, is amenable to criticism and correction, provides a due process period for correcting deficiencies, and duly recognizes quality performance.

If evaluation plans and procedures are not politically viable, misunderstandings or disruptions are likely to occur, and the efforts of those charged with carrying out evaluations likely will be ineffectual.

GUIDELINES

A. Identify all stakeholder groups (see U2, Defined Uses).
B. Involve all stakeholder groups including staff, instructors, managers, department chairpersons, supervisors, administrators, equity officers, evaluation specialists, policy board members, union representatives, and pertinent external groups in developing and reviewing personnel evaluation policies and procedures (see U2, Defined Uses).
C. Develop and implement a policy for collecting and evaluating any deficiencies in the evaluation system suggested by stakeholder groups.
D. Provide sufficient time and opportunity for concerned individuals and groups to help develop, review, and revise personnel evaluation policies.
E. Review personnel evaluation policies periodically to assess if they are still appropriate or need to be altered (see P2, Appropriate Policies and Procedures; A11, Metaevaluation).

COMMON ERRORS

A. Assuming that cooperation happens automatically by failing to understand the sources of organizational power and politics of the organization.
B. Failing to allow sufficient time to field-test and install a new personnel evaluation plan.
C. Collecting, but failing to address pertinent criticisms and recommendations during the policy development process.
D. Disregarding feedback provided by individuals and groups invited to review the system's overall effectiveness.
E. Failing to adequately orient new members of the organization or its external constituencies to the personnel evaluation system.
F. Attempting to evaluate the performance of an individual in the absence of official organizational procedures on personnel evaluation.
G. Changing the purpose of an evaluation system (e.g., adding a merit pay plan) as a public relations exercise without carefully determining and validating the rationale and procedures to be employed.

Illustrative Case 1:
Haste Jeopardizes a Program's Viability
Description

Dr. Liebowitz, the superintendent of a large metropolitan school district, wanted to select staff and train them for promotion to more senior administrative positions within the school district. His long-range goal was to establish an administrative academy in the district that would serve this purpose. Each year, staff members that were nominated as having high administrative potential would have an opportunity to attend the academy to have their administrative skills assessed and to receive training. Dr. Liebowitz learned of a leadership workshop to be offered in a nearby city in six weeks. He saw this as an opportunity to gain firsthand information about how to establish such an academy and to start the screening process quickly.

When he returned from the workshop, Dr. Liebowitz asked three associate superintendents to identify personnel in the district who had some administrative experience and had demonstrated potential to be effective administrators. The associate superintendents nominated 20 principals, supervisors, and unit directors. Dr. Liebowitz formed a screening committee, including the three associate superintendents and two assistant superintendents, to interview the nominees who were interested in the program and to recommend the five most highly qualified individuals.

Several weeks later and during an administrative cabinet meeting, a letter signed by all the principals in the district was read. The letter criticized the superintendent for failing to identify the criteria for selecting administrative leaders or providing all administrators with the opportunity to participate in the training. The letter further criticized the superintendent for using favoritism and the "buddy system" as the basis for the selections made. Since so many misunderstandings had occurred, Dr. Liebowitz concluded that acceptance of the program was unlikely. The plan for the academy was suspended.

Illustrative Case 1:
Haste Jeopardizes a Program's Viability
Analysis

While the idea of a leadership academy for new and prospective school administrators in the district had merit, the superintendent, Dr. Liebowitz, jeopardized its initial acceptance, and perhaps its eventual success, with hasty implementation. He was forced into a defensive position and at that point thought his only choice was to drop the idea.

Dr. Liebowitz should have taken steps to first ensure the appropriate involvement of his administrative staff in an evaluation plan to select the candidates (see A4, Documented Purposes and Procedures). Working collaboratively with these people, he could have identified the criteria for selection, who should be selected as evaluators, how the evaluation results would be used, who would be eligible to be considered for selection, the number of applicants to be selected, and the nature of the training program. He could have asked stakeholders for their ideas, listened to their suggestions, and been as responsive as possible to their views. If Dr. Liebowitz expected the system to have any permanency, he could have assured them of involvement in periodic reviews of the system. He might have constituted this group as a standing committee charged with helping to plan and periodically review the administrative academy.

Illustrative Case 2: Good Intentions Gone Awry
Description

The board of a small school district decided that all building personnel would be evaluated annually. A small committee was formed consisting of two board members, two district level administrators, and one parent who had urged the board to have staff evaluated for personnel and institutional improvement. The board assumed that the committee was representative of the district and thus thought that no further consultation was needed. The selected system of personnel evaluation was a published model that had succeeded elsewhere. The district hired a consultant to train the committee and two district office senior administrators in how to perform the evaluation tasks. The consultant conducted a small pilot study, which also assured the board that the proposed budget was adequate and that the process was not too cumbersome for principals.

Concerns were raised at all staff levels when schools received the document outlining the evaluation procedures. For many, the proposed personnel evaluations came as a complete surprise. Others had some inkling of what was to transpire but doubted whether the data-gathering methods and criteria for judgment were appropriate for their situations. These and other apprehensions were relayed to the board and evaluation committee, but were generally ignored in the belief that concerns would be allayed once evaluations commenced and their benefits were realized. Worried staff members were told that the document outlining the evaluation procedures represented the board's personnel evaluation policy and that there was no recourse.

When the personnel evaluation system was implemented at the beginning of the new school year, the staff found the methodology inappropriate because it varied little among the different roles, for example, guidance counselors, media specialists, classroom teachers, teaching assistants, and so forth. Their concerns gave way to frustration, resentment, and even anger. While the staff were willing to focus on professional improvement, particularly if improvement in student learning would be an outcome, they could not see how the evaluation process would be effective in identifying appropriate follow-up activities, including possible in-service education and training. They also were worried about the fairness of the process if it was not viewed as valid for some of the areas.

The evaluation committee could not satisfactorily answer these and other concerns that arose as the evaluation progressed. One teacher wrote to the super-intendent, expressing the feelings representative of many others: "This evaluation process is supposed to be about me and my professional improvement, but I feel left out in the cold about the whole business."

By the end of the year, a considerable proportion of staff had not been evaluated because of the lack of time. Some staff members had refused to be assessed. The board, alarmed by the failure of what they considered was the right course of action, debated whether to abandon the scheme entirely or modify it after full consultation with all involved personnel.

Illustrative Case 2: Good Intentions Gone Awry
Analysis

The first mistake the board made was to assume that there was no need for collaboration among all concerned groups. The committee lacked membership from key stakeholder groups including principals, teachers, and support staff. Without input from these key groups, there would be little chance of buy-in or support. Other major deficiencies in the scheme flowed from this prime omission. The personnel evaluation policy should have evolved from a collaborative effort, together with the procedures and processes necessary to make evaluations acceptable for professional development and the kind of personnel improvements that the board quite rightly was seeking. Whether or not an "off-the-shelf" system should have been adopted should have depended on its harmony with the evaluation policies and procedures and the evaluation criteria (see P1, Service Orientation; U4, Explicit Criteria). When concerns were raised about the evaluation system, the board should have addressed them.

The board had little recourse except to begin again if members sincerely wished to introduce a worthwhile, and generally acceptable, personnel evaluation system. Such a process must not be adopted or implemented until sound policies based on broad school-community consultation are in place (see U1, Constructive Orientation; P7, Legal Viability). Users of the evaluation system and other pertinent groups such as parents need to be fully informed of the purpose, implementation, and review of personnel evaluation in their district (see P1, Service Orientation).

In this case, the teachers and staff did not object to evaluation per se, but rather to the way in which this system was selected and implemented. The same process, with input from all concerned stakeholder groups that resulted in necessary modifications, may well have been successful in achieving desired goals. From the start, however, the evaluation failed to attend to matters of political feasibility. That failure resulted in large financial and political costs to the superintendent, school board, and district.

Supporting Documentation

Duke, D. L. (1990). Developing teacher evaluation systems that promote professional growth. *Journal of Personnel Evaluation in Education, 4,* 131–144.

Glasman, N. S., & Heck, R. H. (2003). Principal evaluation in the United States. In T. E. Kellaghan & D. L. Stufflebeam (Eds.), *International handbook of educational evaluation* (pp. 643–670). Dordrecht, The Netherlands: Kluwer.

Helm, V. M. (1997). Conducting a successful evaluation conference. In J. H. Stronge (Ed.), *Evaluating teaching: A guide to current thinking and best practice* (pp. 251–269). Thousand Oaks, CA: Corwin Press.

Iwanicki, E. F. (1990). Teacher evaluation for school improvement. In J. Millman & L. Darling-Hammond (Eds.), *The new handbook of teacher evaluation: Assessing elementary and secondary school teachers* (pp. 158–171). Newbury Park, CA: Sage.

Keig, L. (2000). Formative peer review of teaching: Attitude of faculty of liberal arts colleges toward colleague assessment. *Journal of Personnel Evaluation in Education, 14*(1), 67–87.

Manatt, R. P. (1988). Teacher performance evaluation: A total systems approach. In S. J. Stanley & W. J. Popham (Eds.), *Teacher evaluation: Six prescriptions for success* (pp. 79–108). Alexandria, VA: Association for Supervision and Curriculum Development.

McConney, A., Wheeler, P. H., Wiersma, W., Millman, J., Stufflebeam, D., Gullickson, A., et al. (1996). *Teacher evaluation kit and data base of CREATE products* [CD-ROM]. Kalamazoo: Western Michigan University, Center for Research on Educational Accountability and Teacher Evaluation.

Millman, J., & Darling-Hammond, L. (Eds.). (1990). *The new handbook of teacher evaluation: Assessing elementary and secondary teachers.* Newbury Park, CA: Sage.

Shinkfield, A. J., & Stufflebeam, D. L. (1995). *Teacher evaluation: Guide to effective practice.* Boston: Kluwer.

Stronge, J. H. (1995). Balancing individual and institutional goals in educational personnel evaluation: A conceptual framework. *Studies in Educational Evaluation, 21,* 131–151.

Stronge, J. H. (Ed.). (1997a). *Evaluating teaching: A guide to current thinking and best practice.* Thousand Oaks, CA: Corwin Press.

Stronge, J. H. (1997b). Improving schools through teacher evaluation. In J. H. Stronge (Ed.), *Evaluating teaching: A guide to current thinking and best practice* (pp. 1–23). Thousand Oaks, CA: Corwin Press.

Stronge, J. H., Helm, V. M., & Tucker, P. D. (1995). *Evaluation handbook for professional support personnel.* Kalamazoo: Western Michigan University, Center for Research on Educational Accountability and Teacher Evaluation.

Stronge, J. H., & Tucker, P. D. (1999). The politics of teacher evaluation: A case study of new design and implementation. *Journal of Personnel Evaluation in Education, 13*(4), 339–360.

Valentine, J. W. (1992). *Principles and practices for effective teacher evaluation.* Boston: Allyn & Bacon.

F3   Fiscal Viability

> **STANDARD**   Adequate time and resources should be provided for personnel evaluation activities.

Explanation.   Sound systems of personnel evaluation require adequate human and fiscal resources to function effectively. These costs typically are viewed as system and personnel costs. The system must have trained personnel evaluators, support staff, administrative staff, the involvement of all stakeholders, and, when needed, the help of outside experts. An organization also must consider the necessary facilities and equipment to store and control the documentation generated through personnel evaluation (see P3, Access to Evaluation Information). Personnel costs include evaluators who require time and financial support to receive adequate training in the instruments and procedures, collect the data and information, analyze and interpret the data and information, write up reports, report findings to evaluatees and other legitimate users, and plan follow-up activities. Similarly, there are personnel costs for the associated activities of the support staff and district administrators that oversee and manage the personnel evaluation reports (see A11, Metaevaluation).

Expectations for personnel evaluations must be balanced against the resources available to provide evaluations that yield consistent, valid, and useful information. In organizations where such resources are limited, the system may need to be tailored to accommodate such limits. The test of fiscal viability is whether the allocation of human and other fiscal resources is sufficient to conduct meaningful and useful evaluations.

Rationale.   Resource allocation is a visible demonstration of an organization's commitment to personnel evaluation. Without adequate resources, an evaluation effort is prone to inappropriate compromises, shortcuts, and omissions. When limited resources impede professional, efficient evaluation practice, evaluation data likely will be of limited use or have negative consequences for evaluatees, their employers, or both (see A1, Valid Judgments; U1, Constructive Orientation). Appropriate allocation of resources certainly provides the necessary tools for success; however, resource support alone will not guarantee a successful personnel evaluation program. Evaluators, evaluatees, and others must use these resources and the resulting information effectively (see U1, Constructive Orientation; U6, Follow-Up and Professional Development).

The justification for expenditures for personnel evaluation may include, but is not limited to, the following:

- Improved retention of quality personnel
- Improved personnel performance
- Improved services to students and clients
- Improved operation and general welfare of the organization

GUIDELINES

A. Identify the purpose(s) of the evaluation and how the resulting information will be used and by whom (see U2, Defined Uses).
B. Estimate the time and financial costs of needed evaluation resources, such as data collection instruments, materials, secretarial support, computer support, and analyses.
C. Compare the estimated costs with the amount of money available to ensure that the resources and support are sufficient to achieve the stated evaluation purposes.
D. Estimate the personnel time required to conduct each personnel evaluation to decide on the frequency of evaluations and to allocate staff time accordingly.
E. If sufficient resources cannot be committed, modify the objectives and procedures, keeping in mind the need for consistent, valid, and useful information.
F. Ensure that resources for evaluation are used effectively and efficiently (see A11, Metaevaluation).
G. Search for new ideas that will help evaluators complete personnel evaluations that serve the needs of the evaluatees and their students most efficiently.

COMMON ERRORS

A. Failing to allocate adequate resources to allow for evaluation of all evaluatees in a timely, accurate, and acceptable manner.
B. Failing to allocate human and fiscal resources to develop and maintain the personnel evaluation system.
C. Failing to allocate adequate resources to provide appropriate training of evaluators and users of the evaluations (see U3, Evaluator Qualifications; U6, Follow-Up and Professional Development).
D. Failing to allocate adequate resources to review and streamline processes used for personnel evaluation (see A11, Metaevaluation).
E. Adopting data collection procedures that may appear to yield important and useful information but are so time consuming, difficult to use, or costly that the likelihood of effective implementation is nonexistent (see F1, Practical Procedures).
F. Wasting resources by collecting irrelevant data or conducting poorly developed, nonuseful evaluations (see F1, Practical Procedures; P2, Appropriate Policies and Procedures).

G. Failing to follow up personnel evaluations with appropriate and effective actions or decisions, resulting in wasted resources or rework (see U6, Follow-Up and Professional Development).

Illustrative Case 1: Inadequate Resources Undercut a Promotion Evaluation
Description

Two elementary school principals and one high school principal applied for the position of executive director of human resources in their district. The superintendent, Dr. Barker, and his two assistant superintendents, were selected by the school board to evaluate the suitability of the three applicants. Dr. Barker chaired the evaluation committee and was in charge of organizing and implementing the evaluation procedures, which would occur over a three-month period. All involved parties agreed that the evaluation system that had been used successfully in past years for the evaluation of professional personnel in the district would be used with modifications to be made by an external consultant to match the specific qualifications of the associate superintendent position.

The evaluation was to start in February. However, the start date for the evaluation of the three applicants was postponed twice. The first postponement occurred because the consultant did not complete the modifications on time, while the second postponement was due to the fact that the modifications, when received, were unsatisfactory. These delays put pressure on the evaluation procedures, because the timely appointment of an executive director of human resources was essential. The current executive director was retiring at the end of the school year, and the new person was needed to take part in recruiting and hiring teachers and planning for the new school year.

Funding for the evaluations was to come from the district's personnel evaluation budget. However, just as the evaluations of the three principals were due to begin, a review of the evaluation budget revealed that most of the available funds had already been spent. With the end of the school year near at hand, the district could not allocate more money to the evaluation; the district's total budget for the current fiscal year was effectively exhausted. Due to both time and funding pressures, the evaluation committee reduced the length of the evaluation period from six weeks to two weeks. Committee members communicated this information to the three principals, who were dismayed at the major change to the evaluation plans and their lack of opportunity to have input to the change. The evaluation problems were further exacerbated because Dr. Barker often was absent because of previous commitments, thereby limiting his involvement in the evaluation sessions.

Despite these major concerns, the two-week evaluations went forward, with all three principals becoming increasingly disgruntled with what they considered a poor, unprofessional process. Collectively, they decided to withdraw their applications, resulting in a fourth principal being appointed as an acting executive director, a situation that suited no one.

Illustrative Case 1: Inadequate Resources Undercut a Promotion Evaluation
Analysis

This district began the process of selecting a new executive director of human resources, intending to be fair and thorough in finding the best fit for this important district position. Despite these intentions, poor planning and insufficient financial resources led to inadequate time allocations available for evaluating the three principals. Insufficient funding resulted in rushed evaluations that were not carried out satisfactorily in the limited two-week period. Dr. Barker should have been aware of his other commitments that would prevent him from participating in the evaluations as planned. His lack of involvement indicated his lack of total commitment to the project, thus limiting its overall credibility.

The financial resources available for personnel evaluation should have been examined more closely before any planning began, with an application to the board for additional funding if necessary. Sufficient funding is essential to the success of any evaluation. Bearing in mind his other commitments, the superintendent either should have played a minor role or not have participated as a member of the evaluation committee. Further, the unprofessional conduct of the evaluations that resulted from the reduction of time and inadequate funding allocation may have damaged the image of the personnel evaluation system being used for internal promotions.

Supporting Documentation

Horn, J. (2001). *A checklist for developing and evaluating evaluation budgets.* Retrieved April 22, 2005, from http://www.wmich.edu/evalctr/checklists/ evaluationbudgets.pdf

McConney, A., Wheeler, P. H., Wiersma, W., Millman, J., Stufflebeam, D., Gullickson, A., et al. (1996). *Teacher evaluation kit and data base of CREATE products* [CD-ROM]. Kalamazoo: Western Michigan University, Center for Research on Educational Accountability and Teacher Evaluation.

Monteau, P. (1987). Establishing corporate evaluation policy: Cost versus benefit. In L. S. May, C. A. Moore, & S. J. Zammit (Eds.), *Evaluating business and industry training.* Boston: Kluwer.

Shinkfield, A. J., & Stufflebeam, D. L. (1995). *Teacher evaluation: Guide to effective practice.* Boston: Kluwer.

Stronge, J. H. (1995). Balancing individual and institutional goals in educational personnel evaluation: A conceptual framework. *Studies in Educational Evaluation, 21,* 131–151.

Stronge, J. H. (2003). Evaluating educational specialists. In T. E. Kellaghan & D. L. Stufflebeam (Eds.), *International handbook of educational evaluation* (pp. 671–694). Dordrecht, The Netherlands: Kluwer.

A ACCURACY STANDARDS

Summary of the Standards

Accuracy Standards Intended to guide personnel evaluation systems to ensure that an evaluation is technically adequate and complete to produce sound information appropriate for the purpose of making sound judgments.

- **A1 Valid Judgments** Personnel evaluations should promote valid judgments about the performance of the evaluatee that minimize risk of misinterpretation.

- **A2 Defined Expectations** The evaluatee's qualifications, role, and performance expectations should be defined clearly.

- **A3 Analysis of Context** Contextual variables that influence performance should be identified, described, and recorded.

- **A4 Documented Purposes and Procedures** The evaluation purposes and procedures, planned and actual, should be documented.

- **A5 Defensible Information** The information collected for personnel evaluations should be defensible and aligned with the evaluation criteria.

- **A6 Reliable Information** Personnel evaluation procedures should produce reliable information.

- **A7 Systematic Data Control** The information collected, processed, and reported about evaluatees should be reviewed systematically, corrected as appropriate, and kept secure.

A8   Bias Identification and Management   The evaluation process should provide safeguards against bias.

A9   Analysis of Information   The information collected for personnel evaluations should be analyzed systematically and accurately.

A10 Justified Conclusions   Conclusions about an evaluatee's performance should be justified explicitly to ensure that evaluatees and others with a legitimate right to know can have confidence in them.

A11 Metaevaluation   Personnel evaluation systems should be examined systematically at timely intervals using these and other appropriate standards to make necessary revisions.

A1   Valid Judgments

STANDARD   Personnel evaluations should promote valid judgments about the performance of the evaluatee that minimize risk of misinterpretation.

Explanation.   Validity refers to the degree to which judgments concerning an evaluatee's job performance are trustworthy. Based on the procedures of the evaluation system being used by the evaluator, judgments in personnel evaluations can result from multiple sources including classroom observations, interviews, student surveys, peer assessments, portfolio assessments, project assessments, and student achievement data. To enhance the validity of the inferences drawn from personnel evaluations, the procedures and data sources should be linked to the purposes and intended uses of the evaluation. Evaluators should always provide sufficient opportunity for the evaluatee to demonstrate the knowledge, skills, attitudes, or behaviors being evaluated or risk making judgments without a defensible basis.

It is incorrect to say that a specific assessment method is valid. Rather, it is the judgment drawn from the information obtained from a particular method that must be valid or trustworthy. The evaluator must follow procedures, analyze all appropriate data, and report judgments based on the explicit criteria of the evaluation system to protect the validity of the evaluation results.

Rationale.   Validity is the single most important issue in personnel evaluation. If the evaluation is to serve its intended purpose, then the resulting judgments must be accurate, defensible, and based on a sound system of evaluation. In the absence of such evidence, the inferences drawn and the decisions made about an evaluatee may be unsupportable, capricious, and without merit. Invalid judgments can do great harm to both the individual and the organization. If an evaluator rates performance levels too high, the evaluatee may not seek necessary professional development opportunities, become complacent with substandard work, and weaken the ability of the organization to achieve its goals. On the other hand, if judgments are made about an individual based on bias, lack of evidence, or misuse of the instrument, the organization may stand to lose someone who could have been a positive asset.

GUIDELINES

A. Ensure that data sources and procedures accurately assess the knowledge, skills, attitudes, and behaviors identified in the purposes and explicit criteria of the evaluation system (see U4, Explicit Criteria).

B. Use multiple assessment methods best suited for the intended purposes of evaluation to substantiate findings and ensure that comprehensive and consistent indications of an evaluatee's performance are collected (see A5, Defensible Information).

C. Use more than one observer or rater and check interrater consistency (see A6, Reliable Information).

D. Ensure that inferences from assessment instruments adapted from another context are valid for the intended purpose and use.

E. Consider the backgrounds and cultural experiences of evaluatees when interpreting their performance (see A8, Bias Identification and Management).

F. Ensure that evaluators are well trained in conducting evaluations to ensure sound evaluation practices and avoid systematic biases such as the "halo effect," in which a general impression or previous rating influences the present rating (see U3, Evaluator Qualifications; A8, Bias Identification and Management).

G. Document unanticipated circumstances that interfere with the collection of data (see A3, Analysis of Context).

H. Prepare a scoring procedure to guide the process of judging a performance or product before the assessment is performed.

COMMON ERRORS

A. Using an assessment procedure for a purpose for which it was not intended (e.g., using an evaluation instrument designed for classroom teachers to evaluate guidance counselors or media center coordinators).

B. Concentrating solely on the parts of the performance to be evaluated that are the easiest to assess, such as teacher behaviors rather than student learning.

C. Using information simply because it is available without assessing its authenticity or appropriateness for the current evaluation.

D. Allowing newly hired or novice administrators to conduct evaluations before they receive training in the system and instruments.

E. Assuming that a procedure yields information that can be interpreted validly solely because it seems reasonable or is common practice.

F. Failing to confirm or refute alleged strengths or weaknesses of an individual through observing and documenting performance and discussing it with that person.

G. Failing to include information that has been identified as relevant to the evaluation purpose.

H. Failing to take account of factors over which the evaluatee has no control, such as an interrupted classroom observation.

Illustrative Case 1: A Narrow Assessment
Description

The board of education for a large school district required that the principal of each school evaluate all teachers based on four announced observations throughout the school year. The intent of these observations was to provide teachers with an evaluation of their performance and, where needed, to identify areas for individual improvement. Mrs. Nguyen, the principal of a large, urban, elementary school, made one scheduled observation for each teacher at the end of September, November, February, and April. After each visit, she completed a one-page evaluation form that provided ratings on the following criteria: management of student behavior, skill in presentation, monitoring of instruction, and organization of the classroom. A copy of the completed form was shared with the teacher within one week of each observation to encourage follow-up actions. During the last month of school, Mrs. Nguyen met with each teacher to examine and discuss trends, consistencies, and inconsistencies in the results of the four observations, the changes the teacher had made, the extent to which the teacher had met the individual objectives set at the end of the previous year, and what teaching objectives and changes the teacher planned to make during the next year.

Illustrative Case 1: A Narrow Assessment
Analysis

The board policy required multiple assessments throughout the year, and the discussions that occurred after each observation provided a timely way for teachers to know how they were performing and what changes, if any, needed to be made. Likewise, the end-of-year summative evaluation of the four formative observations, coupled with the degree to which the teachers met the goals and objectives they set for themselves at the end of the previous year and their plans for the next year, reflect an attempt to relate the evaluation findings to appropriate follow-up actions (see U6, Follow-Up and Professional Development).

Nevertheless, the judgments based on such a narrow scope of data may not be valid. Since the teachers knew when they were to be observed, there was the opportunity for them to teach to the instrument during the observed class, thus not fully representing their overall performance on days they were not observed. This would result in an inaccurate judgment of performance. To remedy this, unscheduled observations should be made to validate findings obtained from scheduled observations.

Although there seems to be an alignment between the instrument's criteria and the method for collecting data, this type of evaluation is focused too narrowly to provide enough data to judge a classroom teacher's total scope of job responsibility accurately. Other factors crucial to sound evaluation should have been included in the evaluation process: for example, student engagement, assessment of learning, alignment of instruction with curriculum, and so forth.

The principal, Mrs. Nguyen, followed the procedures prescribed in the evaluation instrument according to board policy, but her judgments based on such a narrow scope would endanger the validity of any judgment of performance. The school board should examine its procedures for teacher evaluation to include analyses of such evidences as samples of the teachers' instructional materials and student assessments and, as needed, obtain independent peer assessments from other teachers in the school or from a supervisor in the district office who is responsible for instruction, curriculum, or professional development. Additionally, as part of the evaluation process, evaluators should consider the extent to which student needs are being met.

Illustrative Case 2:
A Thorough Administrative Evaluation
Description

The school board of a medium-sized district was aware that several of the school principals in the district had been in their positions for more than 20 years. The board was concerned that many of these principals were not familiar with more recent developments in education and the increasing use of technology for teaching and learning. They acknowledged that the principals were familiar with the use of computers for administrative purposes, but thought this was a rather limited use, given recent improvements in software for teaching and learning. Consequently, board members asked the superintendent, Dr. Laird, to evaluate all principals to determine their needs for professional development and to plan and fund training sessions and study leaves.

Dr. Laird had previously attended a workshop in which the Personnel Evaluation Standards were presented and illustrated. Therefore, he referred to the standards to design an evaluation that would yield data that could be interpreted validly in terms of the strengths and weaknesses of each principal. To maximize the usefulness of the evaluation, he thought it necessary to assess all facets of administration so as to place the need for follow-up in context and to avoid stressing technology at the expense of other knowledge and aspects of administration. Dr. Laird established a working group of two administrators nominated by the principals, two teachers or administrators selected for knowledge of technology, two teachers nominated by the local teachers' association, and two parents nominated by the district parent council. This working group helped design the evaluation and oversee its implementation. Dr. Laird believed teacher and parent input would be valuable in ensuring that all facets of administration were assessed.

The advisory committee recommended hiring a consultant with experience in personnel evaluation, and a written agreement, including a budget, was established to develop a comprehensive evaluation system. The evaluation would include developing a survey of teachers' and parents' views of their school principal, observation and interview instruments for each principal, and an analysis and reporting procedure to allow a valid interpretation of each principal's strengths and weaknesses. The consultant agreed to do the work for a fee that was accepted by Dr. Laird and the advisory board.

The consultant was told that the purpose of the evaluation was formative and that the information obtained in the evaluation would be used to establish appropriate follow-up and professional development. She prepared two survey forms and instruments for observations and interviews that contained comparable items. The advisory committee reviewed the questionnaires and instruments and found that they contained relevant and representative items that would yield information that could be interpreted regarding a principal's strengths and weaknesses in the areas of administration, school leadership, knowledge of teaching and learning, and knowledge and use of technology for the same purposes. In keeping with the purpose of the evaluation, the advisory committee asked that one question—Would you reappoint your principal next year?—be removed because it went beyond the formative purpose of the evaluation. With the removal of this question and some minor revisions, the advisory committee recommended approval of the questionnaires and schedules.

The questionnaires were administered, and the observations and interviews were completed during January and February. The consultant recommended that profiles (one for parents, one for teachers, one of what was observed, and one for what was found in the interviews) be developed for the principals as a group. The profiles indicated the average view of the principals and the extent of disagreement among those providing the observations. The consultant also developed individual profiles that compared each principal with the group profile. She recommended that each profile be interpreted with the advice of the advisory committee.

The group profile and interpretation were reported at the April board meeting. The board found the profiles and interpretation to be useful and instructed Dr. Laird to distribute the individual profiles, which they had not seen, to the principals, with a request to prepare a follow-up action plan addressing weaknesses. All the principals agreed that their individual profile accurately reflected their knowledge and expertise in technological issues. They complied with the request to submit in-service plans and asked that such evaluations be conducted on a regular five-year schedule. Appropriate follow-up activities at the district level were developed using the group-level results and the follow-up requests made by the principals, again using an advisory committee of principals, teachers, and parents.

Illustrative Case 2:
A Thorough Administrative Evaluation
Analysis

Dr. Laird's knowledge of *The Personnel Evaluation Standards* and his desire to follow the standards, combined with the decision to employ an experienced personnel evaluator as a consultant, resulted in an evaluation that yielded a comprehensive and relevant set of information that could be interpreted validly in terms of the strengths and weaknesses of the principals as a group and of each principal as an individual. Along with direct observations and interviews, Dr. Laird included teacher and parent input that was valuable in ensuring that all facets of administration were assessed. The method of reporting at the group level (i.e., mean level of performance accompanied by a measure of variability) and at the individual level added to the validity of the inferences drawn and decisions made. Last, the existence of a written agreement and accompanying budget clearly set forth the expectations for both the district and the consultant, thereby avoiding difficulties or surprises. The process could have been improved by adding training for the principals to ensure their understanding of the instrument.

Clearly, there was a constructive orientation (see U1, Constructive Orientation). Formative purposes were maintained and meaningfully addressed (see U2, Defined Uses) and confidentiality respected (see P3, Access to Evaluation Information). Last, the purposes for the evaluation were met and the promised feedback provided (U6, Follow-Up and Professional Development).

Supporting Documentation

Abadiano, H. R., & Turner, J. (2004). Professional development: What works? *The New England Reading Association Journal, 40*(2), 87–91.

Airasian, P. W., & Gullickson, A. (1994). Teacher self-assessment: Potential and barriers. *Kappa Delta Pi Record, 31*(1), 6–9.

Airasian, P. W., & Gullickson, A. (1997). Teacher self-evaluation. In J. H. Stronge (Ed.), *Evaluating teaching: A guide to current thinking and best practice* (pp. 215–247). Thousand Oaks, CA: Corwin Press.

American Association of School Administrators. (1978). *Standards for school personnel administration* (3rd ed.). Seven Hills, OH: Author.

American Educational Research Association, American Psychological Association, & National Council on Measurement in Education. (1999). *Standards for educational and psychological testing.* Washington, DC: American Educational Research Association.

Athanases, S. (1994). Teachers' reports of the effects of preparing portfolios of literacy instruction. *The Elementary School Journal, 94,* 421–439.

Bernardin, H. J., & Beatty, R. W. (1984). *Performance appraisal: Assessing human behavior at work.* Boston: Kent.

Coker, H., Medley, D., & Soar, R. (1980). How valid are expert opinions about effective teaching. *Phi Delta Kappan, 62,* 131–134.

Darling-Hammond, L., & Youngs, P. (2002). Defining "high qualified teachers": What does "scientifically-based research" actually tell us? *Educational Researcher, 31*(9), 13–25.

Haertel, E. (1991). New forms of teacher assessment. *Review of Research in Education, 17,* 3–29.

Hoy, W. K., & Tarter, C. J. (1995). *Administrators solving the problems of practice.* Boston: Allyn & Bacon.

Linn, R. L., Baker, E. L., & Dunbar, S. B. (1991). Complex, performance-based assessment: Expectations and validation criteria. *Educational Researcher, 20*(8), 5–21.

Messick, S. (1989). Validity. In R. L. Linn (Ed.), *Educational measurement* (3rd ed., pp. 13–103). Washington, DC: American Council on Education.

Messick, S. (1994). The interplay of evidence and consequences in the validation of performance assessments. *Educational Researcher, 23*(20), 13–23.

Millman, J., & Darling-Hammond, L. (Eds.). (1990). *The new handbook of teacher evaluation: Assessing elementary and secondary teachers.* Newbury Park, CA: Sage.

Rowan, B., Chiang, F., & Miller, R. J. (1997). Using research on employee's performance to study the effects of teachers on students' achievement. *Sociology of Education, 70,* 256–284.

Sanders, W. L., & Rivers, S. P. (1994). The Tennessee value-added assessment system (TVAAS): Mixed-model methodology in educational assessment. *Journal of Personnel Evaluation in Education, 8,* 299–311.

Shulman, L. (1988). A union of insufficiencies. Strategies for teacher assessment in a period of reform. *Educational Leadership, 46,* 36–41.

Society for Industrial and Organizational Psychology. (2003). *Principles for the validation and use of personnel selection procedures* (4th ed.). Bowling Green, OH: Author.

Wright, S. P., Horn, S. P., & Sanders, W. L. (1997). Teacher and classroom context effects on student achievement: Implications for teacher evaluation. *Journal of Personnel Evaluation, 11,* 57–67.

A2   Defined Expectations

> **STANDARD**   The evaluatee's qualifications, role, and performance expectations should be defined clearly.

Explanation.   Personnel evaluations should be based on the position of the evaluatee and the requirements and responsibilities that a person in that position is expected to meet. All parties to the evaluation must have the same understanding of these expectations (see U4, Explicit Criteria) before the evaluation process is designed and implemented. Deliberations and agreements concerning these expectations should (a) be in accordance with local agreements, rules, and regulations; (b) align with institutional or company goals and programs; and (c) reflect the best available evidence concerning the duties most crucial to staff and organizational success.

Personnel expectations have three parts:

1. Position qualifications—the experience, knowledge, skills, and licenses, degrees, or certificates judged to be necessary to carry out the position's responsibilities and fulfill the performance expectations.
2. Position responsibilities—the tasks and responsibilities performed by the person holding the position.
3. Performance outcomes—the results expected from the evaluatee's job performance.

These parts should be defined before hiring or assigning the person to the position based on the needs of the organization. The performance objectives should be derived from one or more of the following: the tasks specified in the job description, required professional activities associated with the position, and consideration of the context in which the job is to be performed.

Personnel should be evaluated on each of these three components to ensure that the knowledge, skills, and performances corresponding to each component are present. For example, has a teacher completed a teacher education program relevant to the grade level and subject matter the teacher is assigned to teach and met all state requirements for licensure? Did the teacher cover the prescribed content in the allotted time, and did students demonstrate learning? Did a university professor publish a sufficient number of articles in refereed journals, direct dissertations, and obtain competitive research grants and contracts? The evaluatee must be informed of these expectations before the start of an evaluation period, particularly one involving high stakes decisions such as tenure or renewal of a contract.

Rationale.   A carefully developed and sufficiently detailed description of the role, responsibilities, qualifications, and performance objectives is a prerequisite to creating a sound personnel evaluation. Failure to delineate the qualifications and expectations and how the outcomes will be measured can lead to incorrect inferences. Incorrect inferences can inhibit appropriate follow-up activity or result in unjustified dismissal.

GUIDELINES

A. Develop position qualification specifications from state licensure regulations, school board or other institutional policy documents, department requirements, and professional standards.

B. Develop job descriptions based on systematic job analyses conducted specifically for this purpose or from information available in public sources such as electronic or paper job postings.

C. Obtain position description information from as many knowledgeable sources as possible, including but not limited to the following:
   - Persons currently holding the position.
   - Supervisors and other decision makers.
   - State requirements (e.g., "highly qualified" teaching requirements).
   - Applicable contracts and labor agreements.
   - Position descriptions.
   - Letters of appointment.
   - Review of literature.

D. Specify significant role tasks, duties, responsibilities, and performance objectives in detail. A clear specification of an individual's role might include the following:
   - Knowledge of content area.
   - Instructional organization and design.
   - Noninstructional duties.
   - Interactions with the community.
   - Interactions with students and peers.
   - Assessment and evaluation procedures.
   - Participation in professional development activities.
   - Research record (publications, presentations, grants).
   - Service to the profession.

E. Make clear the relative importance and performance level of each standard used to define success in the position (see U4, Explicit Criteria).

F. Investigate and resolve any discrepancies in the position description between the role of the evaluatee and the expectations associated with that role when they are not in agreement.

COMMON ERRORS

A. Developing a position description that addresses part but not all of the performance objectives.

B. Failing to keep a position description up to date and accurate due to external factors, such as the introduction of technology.

C. Specifying a position in terms of desirable traits, attitudes, and personality characteristics, rather than as needed qualifications, tasks, duties, and expected performance outcomes.

D. Significantly changing a job requirement (such as level of degree) without cause or discussion with the evaluatee.

E. Failing to adequately align job requirements and expected tasks with performance outcomes.

Illustrative Case 1: Defining Expectations
Description

A new superintendent of schools, Ms. Kass, asked for the job description used to evaluate teachers in the district. She was provided with a memo that contained a list of four criteria:

1. Knowledge of the content area.
2. Effective communications.
3. Effective interaction with students, parents, and peers.
4. Participation in professional development activities.

Ms. Kass thought that while these criteria were relevant, the list could be expanded to more fully prescribe what a sound teacher evaluation should include. She asked the personnel director for the district to chair and form a committee of teachers and administrators in consultation with the local teachers' association. Six teachers—two at the elementary level, two at the middle school level, and two at the senior high level— were approached and agreed to serve. Three principals, one from each grade level configuration, also agreed to serve on the committee. Ms. Kass then met with the committee, shared her concerns about the existing criteria, and asked that the committee first draw up a list of duties that teachers should be expected to perform. Once developed and agreed on, they were to share the list with teachers and parent councils at each school in the district to ensure that the list was comprehensive, fair, and understandable.

Following a review of the literature, the committee members agreed that the teacher performance variable was one of the most powerful predictors of student performance. With this in mind, they proceeded to develop a list of essential behaviors, using what they had gleaned from the literature and their own collective experiences. The list, and its description, follows.

One of the most powerful predictors of student performance is teacher performance. Therefore, a teacher should be able to do the following:

- Examine and respond to the individual and collective needs of students.
- Demonstrate up-to-date knowledge of principles of learning.

- Demonstrate up-to-date knowledge of the curriculum and course content.
- Employ a variety of teaching techniques that address the approved curriculum.
- Maintain class control and good rapport with the students and their parents or guardians.
- Be accessible to help individual students solve learning problems.
- Maintain clear and complete records on student participation and progress.
- Regularly evaluate student progress and provide specific feedback to students, including reinforcement of successes and concrete steps for improvement.
- Conduct meaningful parent-teacher or child-led parent conferences, with the identification of appropriate follow-up.
- Maintain a clear, up-to-date day planner for use by a substitute teacher when needed.
- Participate in relevant in-service professional development activities.
- Periodically evaluate and update course content, procedures, and materials.
- Demonstrate and model understanding of research relevant to effective teaching.
- Maintain positive working relationships with school staff.

The teachers and parents who took part in the review believed that the list was comprehensive, so no additions were suggested. Both groups thought the list was fair and indicated that they had a clear understanding of the activities to be used when evaluating a teacher. Further, the executive of the local teachers' association likewise judged the list to be complete and fair and suggested that it be adopted.

Illustrative Case 1: Defining Expectations
Analysis

The superintendent, Ms. Kass, was correct in thinking that the initial list of factors to be considered for evaluating teachers in her district could be improved. It was too broad and vague to suggest either specific job tasks or performance outcomes. She included all stakeholders in reviewing the list to ensure that it was comprehensive and acceptable. This also created greater buy-in by the teachers and administrators, the primary users of the evaluation.

The committee further clarified the role of the teacher and identified what had been done in other teacher evaluations before developing the list of what they considered to be essential teacher behaviors. Further, all parties possessed the same understanding of what the expectations were prior to the evaluation of a teacher.

Illustrative Case 2: Misaligned Outcomes
Description

A beginning assistant professor in psychology, Dr. McGinnis, was given a faculty handbook by the chair of the psychology department. The chair advised her to read the contents to better understand the roles, responsibilities, and expectations of faculty members. The handbook, which had not been updated in many years, described the expectations for tenure and promotion in terms of excellence in campus teaching, scholarly activity related to the faculty member's area of expertise, and professional service related to academic areas of expertise. Further, it stated that the three areas would be considered equally at the time the decision was made regarding granting tenure and concurrent promotion to associate professor. Anxious about receiving tenure and promotion, Dr. McGinnis worked diligently on the three areas and refused assignments outside her academic area.

The department chair was critical of Dr. McGinnis's seeming unwillingness to accept assignments that were crucial to the greater good of the department, the faculty, and the university. Specifically, he mentioned that she had refused to teach an additional outreach course off campus for which she would have been paid extra and that she also had declined to serve as the department's representative on the university faculty association. Dr. McGinnis pointed out that teaching off campus was not an expectation that was included in the faculty handbook and that serving on the faculty association was not her area of expertise and would take away time for research at a time when she was attempting to establish her career. She also noted that during the last two years she had served on the department's selection committee for graduate students. Despite acceptable teaching evaluations and a credible program of research, the department chair did not support the granting of tenure and promotion.

Illustrative Case 2: Misaligned Outcomes
Analysis

This case exemplifies problems that arise when there is a lack of attention and specificity regarding statements related to faculty role and responsibilities. When a faculty handbook is assumed to contain the operating procedures to be followed by faculty, it is critical that the handbook be specific and current. In this case, it was vague and out of date. Dr. McGinnis, anxious about tenure and promotion, adhered to the procedures and was ultimately denied tenure and promotion. Seemingly the department chair was working with a different set of criteria.[2]

The faculty handbook should have been clear regarding current expectations of faculty. To ensure that the faculty handbook reflected the current expectations, it should have been reviewed regularly, especially after a change in leadership (see A11, Metaevaluation). Dr. McGinnis should not have been penalized by the department chair for adherence to a document that was presented as the guidebook to be followed. To prevent future problems, the responsibility for keeping the faculty handbook current, accurate, and clear should be assigned and assessed annually. In addition, policies should be adopted that will ensure that all faculty are aware of any changes in policy or expectations as reflected in the faculty handbook.

While the faculty handbook is the primary point of contention here, it is noteworthy that the department chair did not follow up with the faculty member to ensure a common understanding of expectations. Had the chair or faculty member taken that simple step to confirm understandings, changes to the handbook and professorial expectations likely would have proceeded directly without misunderstandings and acrimony.

Supporting Documentation

Bernardin, H. J., & Beatty, R. W. (1984). *Performance appraisal: Assessing human behavior at work.* Boston: Kent.

Bernstein, E. (2004). What teacher evaluation should know and be able to do. *NASSP Bulletin, 88,* 80–88.

Educational Testing Service. (1998). *The Praxis series.* Princeton, NJ: Author.

Haertel, E. (1991). New forms of teacher assessment. *Review of Research in Education, 17,* 3–29.

Hoy, W. K., & Tarter, C. J. (1995). *Administrators solving the problems of practice.* Boston: Allyn & Bacon.

Interstate New Teacher Assessment and Support Consortium. (1995). *Next steps: Moving toward performance-based licensing in teaching.* Washington, DC: Council of Chief State School Officers.

Millman, J., & Darling-Hammond, L. (Eds.). (1990). *The new handbook of teacher evaluation: Assessing elementary and secondary teachers.* Newbury Park, CA: Sage.

National Board for Professional Teaching Standards. (1997). *What teachers should know and be able to do.* San Antonio: The Psychological Corporation.

National Commission on Teaching and America's Future. (1996). *What matters most: Teaching for America's future.* New York: Author.

National Staff Development Council, in cooperation with the National Association of Elementary School Principals. (1995a). *Standards for staff development (elementary school ed.).* Oxford, OH: Author.

National Staff Development Council, in cooperation with the National Association of Secondary School Principals. (1995b). *Standards for staff development (high school ed.).* Oxford, OH: Author.

National Staff Development Council. (1995c). *Standards for staff development (middle school ed.).* Oxford, OH: Author.

Rebore, R. W. (1997). *Personnel administration in education.* Englewood Cliffs, NJ: Prentice Hall.

Shulman, L. (1988). A union of insufficiencies. Strategies for teacher assessment in a period of reform. *Educational Leadership, 46,* 36–41.

A3   Analysis of Context

STANDARD   Contextual variables that influence performance should be identified, described, and recorded.

Explanation.   Certain contextual variables may have a temporary impact on an evaluatee's job performance within a specific time span. Any contextual variable that may influence a person's job performance should be noted on the appropriate data collection forms or report. To ignore such variables could lead to an invalid interpretation of the evaluation findings, giving a false impression of the evaluatee's performance (see A9, Analysis of Information). Contextual variables do not include those associated with race, gender, creed, or sexual orientation, because those are not considered to be contextual in nature (see A8, Bias Identification and Management).

Contextual variables may result from personal experiences that include death in the family, long-term illness, change in family structure, or any other traumatic or unusual life experience that might potentially lower an evaluatee's job performance for a period of time. These life situations and experiences affect persons in various degrees and for various lengths of time. When an evaluator is aware of such a circumstance that has the potential of affecting typical job performance, the situation should be noted in the evaluation document to ensure an accurate analysis of performance (see A9, Analysis of Information).

In addition to the contextual variables caused by personal experience, a person's job performance also may be impacted by organizational contexts. Among the many contextual factors that can adversely influence performance are those associated with organizational structure and process, leadership and supervisory practices, financial resources, and decision-making policies. Contextual variables also include community characteristics such as educational priorities and support and characteristics of major stakeholders such as parents. Time, space, and availability of materials and equipment are resources that can influence performance, as can various human resources, including support services and the availability of professional expertise. Many of these factors are beyond the control of the evaluatee, yet may have detrimental effects on job performance.

Contextual factors also encompass working relations, the kind and amount of discretion allowed an employee, and the support and contributions of colleagues. Other contextual factors influencing performance may be short term such as a fire drill or sick child during a classroom observation. In this case, the evaluator may decide to discontinue the observation. If continued, the evaluator must make note of the disturbance in the evaluation report whether or not there appeared to be significant impact on the performance observed.

Contextual factors can either constrain or facilitate performance. Therefore, conditions that are likely to affect performance should be considered to identify their possible impact on performance for both the evaluator and the evaluatee. In the evaluation report, contextual factors should be referenced both to provide a fair and valid interpretation of the assessment of a performance (see A8, Bias Identification and Management; A9, Analysis of Information) and to determine how the job description, the employee's approach, or the institution's support of the employee could be revised to better address recurrent environmental influences. Contextual influences should not be used to rationalize poor performance that would occur otherwise (see A10, Justified Conclusions).

Rationale. Failure to take account of extenuating circumstances beyond the control of the evaluatee threatens the validity of the evaluation process (see A1, Valid Judgments). Moreover, it is in everyone's best interest for the institution to look at environmental influences to help employees become more effective (see U6, Follow-Up and Professional Development; P4, Interactions With Evaluatees).

On the other hand, evaluatees must work in dynamic, complex settings, and it is part of their everyday responsibility to assess and address environmental influences. Personnel evaluations should examine contextual factors, both to provide a fair and valid assessment of performance and accomplishments and to consider how the employee and institution might address future environmental influences more effectively. The evaluator and the evaluatee must not simply cite personal factors and contextual influences as mitigating circumstances that justify substandard performance.

GUIDELINES

A. Identify and record specific contextual variables that might affect the work environment.
B. Record short-term, unexpected incidences that occur during data collection, regardless of the immediate appearance of influence on performance.
C. Develop a written policy to guide decisions about how contextual information will be accounted for in making interpretations and evaluation decisions, and make the policy available to evaluatees.
D. Provide evaluatees with the opportunity to discuss their performance, especially if it was deemed deficient or unacceptable (see P4, Interactions With Evaluatees).

COMMON ERRORS

A. Allowing contextual factors to become an excuse for poor performance that may have been unrelated to these factors.

B. Allowing contextual variables to influence the collection of data but not the interpretation of performance.

C. Failing to identify and consider important contextual factors that affect the performance of evaluatees with different cultures and values.

D. Failing to make explicit which personal and contextual variables are being considered or disregarded.

E. Overestimating or underestimating the influence of contextual variables when assessing performance.

Illustrative Case 1: Masking Poor Performance
Description

Mrs. Reynolds, a second-grade teacher with tenure and 15 years of teaching experience in a large urban school district, was known among her peers for being ineffective in teaching reading. Third-grade teachers easily identified which students had been in her class the year before based on their low reading skills. These teachers knew that Mrs. Reynolds' students had to receive additional tutoring and help prior to the end-of-grade test in reading. Every year, a small number of concerned parents requested that their children not be assigned to her class.

Following a succession of negative evaluations, the principal recommended certain changes in Mrs. Reynolds' preparation and teaching activities. He developed a plan of action to improve her practice in teaching reading. Consequently, Mrs. Reynolds asked to be transferred to a new school in the district and accepted a position in an inner city school. In approving the transfer, the superintendent stipulated that, within two years, she must obtain a satisfactory evaluation from her new building principal.

Mrs. Reynolds continued to teach as before, and early in the second year of her probationary period, the school's third-grade teachers complained to the principal that students coming from her class were far behind in reading. The principal's evaluation showed that Mrs. Reynolds had not implemented any of the previous principal's recommendations, was typically unprepared and disorganized, made no attempt to address the widely varying educational levels and needs of her students, and actually spent little time in teaching reading.

In his evaluation report to the area superintendent, the principal noted that under normal circumstances he would recommend that a teacher with this record be dismissed. However, he further observed that circumstances in the neighborhood and school were so bad that whether or not a teacher taught well was inconsequential. Turnover among students averaged 90 percent annually. Absenteeism was high. Many students showed a lack of interest in education and disrespect for school property. Students in a given class often could not speak one another's first language, and many were not fluent in English. In his report, the principal noted that someone had to "baby-sit" these kids and that Mrs. Reynolds was at least meeting this need. Thus, he recommended to the area superintendent that she be taken off probation due to what he considered to be contextual factors possibly influencing her poor performance.

Illustrative Case 1: Masking Poor Performance
Analysis

The first principal in this case called for changes in the teacher's practice based on evaluations and poor student outcomes. He believed that Mrs. Reynolds had managed to obtain tenure earlier and lapsed into poor practices due to a lack of effort on her part, not context within her school. The first principal recognized that the poor performance could possibly be improved through corrective action. He also based his recommendations on the actual performance and job expectations for teachers in his school (see A2, Defined Expectations; U6, Follow-Up and Professional Development).

Unfortunately, it is all too common for marginal teachers to be allowed to transfer rather than to improve their teaching. It is even more unfortunate when a district allows this to happen to a school with more challenged populations requiring more skilled teachers. Once a marginal teacher has been identified and placed on a plan of action, it is unfair to the teacher and the students to disrupt that plan, even when the teacher attempts to circumvent it. In this case, the area superintendent displayed an obvious lack of concern for the overall well-being of the district in allowing a marginal teacher to avoid a plan of action by transferring to what may have been perceived as a less demanding school.

The second principal in this case excused Mrs. Reynolds' poor performance by attributing it to what he considered to be contextual variables within the school's community. His obvious low expectations for student performance and lack of understanding of the cultural diversity of his school community prevented him from making sound judgments on personnel performance in this case. Such poor judgment resulted in a perpetuation of marginal teaching.

If Mrs. Reynolds' poor performance could be directly related to such conditions as lack of classroom space, inadequate student materials, poor curriculum, or lack of community and school outreach programs, and so forth, then contextual variables would rightfully play a part in her evaluation. In this case, however, the second principal made the all too common mistake of accepting poor performance based on his own lack of understanding of the nature of the organizational and environmental structures that could be put into place to meet the needs of diverse populations of students.

Illustrative Case 2: An Overburdened Professor
Description

The director of an executive MBA program at a large university sat down to prepare evaluations of two key untenured faculty members. Both professors had the same job responsibilities and expectations although with different content areas. Given the same responsibilities and expectations, the director felt comfortable comparing the two in terms of their output. He noted that Professor Albertson seemed to exhibit good performance in most areas over the last semester, with excellent evaluations from students in his classes, good reviews from the graduate and undergraduate students he supervised, and positive input from other faculty for various administrative projects that were his duties. While the director noted some areas regarding improvement (e.g., timeliness of feedback to his advisees and students in courses), he was prepared to give a positive evaluation overall.

The director was somewhat less positive about Professor Bolton, who had been on the faculty longer and whom he generally thought of as the more capable of the two based on prior evaluations. The evaluations from courses led by Professor Bolton over the last semester were uncharacteristically varied. While most were glowing, one class on legal issues had garnered very negative evaluations. Further, Professor Bolton's advisees were very positive about her performance in many areas but noted that she had been later than usual in getting things to them, somewhat curt in meetings, and generally less available to assist them.

Before writing his evaluation report, the director examined the self-evaluations of the two professors. He had asked both professors to note any constraints on their performance that should be considered in evaluation. While both professors had noted some typical constraints (e.g., tight budgets, insufficient clerical support), he was somewhat surprised by the lengthy reply from Professor Bolton. She noted that she thought her performance had been adversely affected in the past few months by a number of factors. The first was that she had been asked at the last minute to take over the course on legal issues and the other work of a colleague who needed to go on maternity leave earlier than expected. She was concerned that the course went poorly due to the lack of adequate preparation time. Another concern was that a major lawsuit on sexual harassment was filed in the business school during the time of the course. She quickly discovered that the students in the class had strong feelings about the suit—one way or another—and had brought their animosity into the classroom, which may have caused them to skew their opinions of her teaching. Professor Bolton also noted that her colleague's maternity leave was handled in such a way that the absent professor's regular duties were not distributed over several people but were all assigned to Professor Bolton. Therefore, she had to assume additional roles on two committees and become an active player in a college public relations project requiring extensive travel. These factors contributed to her lack of preparation, follow-up with students, and stressed attitude.

Based on this information, the director tempered his evaluations appropriately. He made note of these contextual variables in the final evaluation report.

Illustrative Case 2: An Overburdened Professor
Analysis

By asking for information on performance constraints, the director became aware of unusual circumstances that affected the performance of Professor Bolton. Consequently, he was able to take the circumstances into account in his evaluation of her performance.

The executive MBA program as a whole might want to revisit how the work of coworkers on leave is distributed to others. The director might work with Professor Bolton on how to handle student expectations about availability when one has a heavy travel schedule and how to effectively use electronic communications to mitigate availability problems during those travel periods. Professor Bolton might set some goals regarding how she might seek help if asked to cover content areas where she is less knowledgeable and also how to handle a hostile audience in a class. Such discussions will help prevent the constraints from operating in the future and will also better equip Professor Bolton to handle such constraints if faced with them again.

Supporting Documentation

Bernardin, H. J., Hagan, C. M., Kane, J. S., & Villanova, P. (1998). Effective performance management: A focus on precision, customers, and situational constraints. In J. W. Smither (Ed.), *Performance appraisal: State of the art in practice* (pp. 3–48). San Francisco: Jossey-Bass.

Clift, R. T., Veal, M. L., Holland, P., Johnson, M., & McCarthy, J. (1995). *Collaborative leadership and shared decision making.* New York: Teachers College Press.

Harrison, M. I. (1994). *Diagnosing organizations: Methods, models, and processes* (2nd ed.). Thousand Oaks, CA: Sage.

Millman, J., & Darling-Hammond, L. (Eds.). (1990). *The new handbook of teacher evaluation: Assessing elementary and secondary teachers.* Newbury Park, CA: Sage.

Rebore, R. W. (1997). *Personnel administration in education.* Englewood Cliffs, NJ: Prentice Hall.

A4 Documented Purposes and Procedures

> **STANDARD** **The evaluation purposes and procedures, planned and actual, should be documented.**

Explanation. A system of evaluation must provide documented procedures for conducting evaluations so that there is consistency and clear understanding by all stakeholders concerning the purposes and procedures to be followed (see P2, Appropriate Policies and Procedures; U2, Defined Uses; and F2, Political Viability). An evaluator should always document fully all procedures and data collected throughout an evaluation period in accordance with stated procedures. Documentation of both planned and actual evaluation purposes and procedures provides stakeholders with a clear idea of the intended purposes and procedures to be followed and the actual purposes addressed and procedures employed in an evaluation. This information allows assessment of the alignment of purposes with procedures and the impact any changes may have had on the evaluation findings and decisions. Differences can be identified and reconciled or at least taken into account when interpreting findings.

Documentation of an evaluation's purposes and procedures also has other uses. It provides vital information to anyone who wishes to evaluate the evaluation (see A11, Metaevaluation) and provides clarification in cases of litigation (see P7, Legal Viability). The documentation can be used to inform the conduct of similar evaluations in other settings, and the descriptions provide good case material for use in training personnel evaluators. This documentation also should be used to help prevent misuse of evaluation information. Where there is a perceived risk of misuse, those responsible for evaluations should work to prevent such misuse.

Rationale. The effectiveness of an evaluation is linked to how well the evaluator, evaluatee, and other stakeholders understand and accept the evaluation purposes and procedures. Systematic documentation of the entire evaluation process helps ensure that the evaluation will be equitable, fair, and legal. Deviations from intended purposes and procedures can produce unintentional erroneous results. The nature of any deviation must be documented and accounted for, so that the evaluatee and other users of the evaluation can interpret results properly and avoid follow-up actions detrimental to the evaluatee, the employer, or both. All appropriate personnel should be helped to understand and invited to evaluate the design and implementation of the actual process.

GUIDELINES

A. Develop and make available to employees a written document regarding evaluations, including purposes, areas covered, sources of information, guidelines for analyzing data, making interpretations, and drawing conclusions.

B. Inform employees in a handbook or written document about the organization's personnel evaluation system. Elements to consider include these:
- Why evaluations are conducted and how the information collected will be used (see P1, Service Orientation; U2, Defined Uses).
- How evaluation forms for various job categories have been developed and are maintained to reflect up-to-date information regarding job requirements and performance levels (see A2, Defined Expectations).
- Specific criteria for promotion, salary increases, merit awards, bonuses, and termination.
- Timeline for evaluations .
- Who conducts the evaluations.
- How evaluators are trained to conduct observations and rate performance (see U3, Evaluator Qualifications).
- The right of the evaluatee to discuss professional development purposes with the evaluator and to receive a written copy of the evaluation (see U6, Follow-Up and Professional Development; P4, Interactions With Evaluatees).
- Policies and procedures for appealing a decision (see P7, Legal Viability).
- Process for monitoring the personnel evaluation system (see A11, Metaevaluation).
- Whom stakeholders can contact if they have any questions (see U1, Constructive Orientation).

C. Ensure that personnel evaluators are trained to and do properly document their evaluation purposes and procedures, planned and actual. Accomplish this by engaging evaluators in periodic training and review of pertinent policies, and review documentation submitted by evaluators (see P2, Appropriate Policies and Procedures; A11, Metaevaluation; U3, Evaluator Qualifications).

D. Maintain appropriate records of evaluations, including their timing, the results for each evaluation, and any important deviations from the institution's approved evaluation system (see P2, Appropriate Policies and Procedures; A11, Metaevaluation).

E. Address in writing any issues raised by an evaluatee or other user of the evaluation, and reference the record of planned and actual evaluation procedures (see P7, Legal Viability).

F. Provide all employees and other users with feedback forms for suggesting improvements in the evaluation system (see F2, Political Viability; A11, Metaevaluation).

G. Periodically provide all employees with orientation and training in the evaluation process (see P2, Appropriate Policies and Procedures; A1, Valid Judgments; A6, Reliable Information).

COMMON ERRORS

A. Using an informal procedure that relies on undocumented materials and observations to make evaluation decisions.

B. Making an evaluation plan so inflexible that unanticipated events cannot be accommodated.

C. Failing to document deviations from the intended evaluation purposes or procedures.

D. Changing the evaluation plan without informing evaluatees.

E. Failing to review documentation submitted by evaluators.

F. Failing to review procedures followed by evaluators (e.g., maintaining deadlines, using correct forms, etc.)

Illustrative Case 1: Failing to Document Poor Performance
Description

The dean of a community college expressed concern to the head of a department about continuing complaints regarding Mr. Dobee, an instructor. The department head made a preliminary, informal investigation by observing one of Mr. Dobee's classes and talking privately with a few students. He received consistent and convincing information and concluded that Mr. Dobee was indeed doing a poor job. This conclusion seemed so obvious that the department head decided to forgo formal evaluation and documentation. He made no written record of the evaluation and did not inform the dean of his procedures, findings, or intended next steps.

Instead, he immediately met privately with Mr. Dobee and communicated his findings orally. He pointed out the wasted minutes during the class period, the instructor's apparent ignorance of his students' abilities, his habit of communicating to students that he held low expectations of their performance, his penchant for intimidating and embarrassing them, and his failure to return graded assignments or provide students with feedback on their work.

Mr. Dobee agreed that he needed to improve in these areas. He thanked the head for being honest with him and for identifying these shortcomings. He did not contest any of the department head's conclusions and did not request a written report. The department head concluded the meeting by telling Mr. Dobee to do better.

Six months later, the department head made an unscheduled visit to Mr. Dobee's classroom. After a half hour, he concluded that there had been no improvement. When he met with Mr. Dobee later that same day to discuss the observation, the instructor conceded that his teaching was poor and was not getting better. Consequently, the department head informed Mr. Dobee that his contract would not be renewed the following year. The verbal notice was followed by written confirmation and copied to the dean. The dean did not question the department head, and he did not meet with the instructor.

Mr. Dobee immediately began seeking other employment, but he could not find a job. He decided that he should not have accepted the dismissal notice and consulted with the faculty member in charge of faculty grievances. On reviewing the case, the faculty representative told Mr. Dobee, the department head, and the dean that Mr. Dobee did not have to accept the dismissal. The department head had failed to use the forms and procedures specified in the college's official evaluation plan. It did not matter that Mr. Dobee had agreed with the evaluations; an appropriate written record of the evaluation was not available for use in defense of the decision. The only written record contained confirmation of dismissal and did not describe the procedures followed or present the evidence obtained from any evaluations. There was little doubt that Mr. Dobee could successfully appeal the ruling. The dean agreed with the analysis, and the department head reluctantly withdrew the letter of dismissal.

Illustrative Case 1:
Failing to Document Poor Performance
Analysis

The termination decision was justified in the minds of the department head, the dean, and even the instructor, Mr. Dobee. The evaluations were viewed as fair and appropriate. Nevertheless, because specified procedures had not been followed and no record of the data collected or the time of collections existed, the evaluation could not be used to support a dismissal decision. The department head failed to specify the consequences of poor performance as required in the college's evaluation plan, and he did not record the steps followed in gathering data and providing feedback.

The dean regularly should have reminded all department heads of the requirements of the approved plan for personnel evaluations. The department head should have followed the plan and maintained records of the prescribed steps used to obtain evaluative information. The officials of the institution should have evaluated and improved the evaluation system to ensure that it would result in fair, justifiable conclusions to evaluations.

Illustrative Case 2:
Applying Revised Evaluation Procedures
Description

A sudden increase in population in the community and a new early retirement package caused the superintendent of a suburban district to predict that the local schools would need to hire several new teachers for the following school year. The school district had a formal evaluation procedure in place; however, due to previous stability in student enrollment and staffing, the written evaluation procedures were no longer being followed closely and in some cases were not appropriate. The district's head of personnel had evaluation experience and convened a task force consisting of two principals, six teachers, two community members, and herself. Their mandate was to review and revise the current evaluation procedures and update the teacher handbook.

Working with *The Personnel Evaluation Standards* as a guiding document resulted in a formal evaluation procedure that

- Detailed the purposes and procedures of the evaluation process for new teachers.
- Outlined the roles and expectations of administrators and senior teachers (evaluators) along with the new teachers (evaluatees) in the evaluation process.
- Included suggestions to support the evaluations of those teachers in nontraditional classroom procedures.
- Described the criteria for judgment and the resulting outcomes for those being evaluated.

The task force agreed that the demands on the administrators and teachers were reasonable and would lead to fair evaluations of new teachers. The team agreed to meet in cases of grievance and to reconvene the following spring to review the procedure. Three new teachers who experienced the evaluation would be included in this review. Further, to support the evaluation procedure, a teacher and an administrator agreed to act as ombudsmen for those conducting the evaluation or those being evaluated.

Administrators and senior teachers at each school completed a one-day workshop highlighting the purposes of the evaluation and the expectations of those completing the evaluation. Similarly, newly hired teachers were given the updated handbook and also completed two separate workshops. One was facilitated by the senior district administrator who led the task force, and one was led by their school administrator. These workshops focused on the format and structure of the evaluation.

The revised procedure, as outlined in the handbook and workshops, included a clear statement of the purposes of the evaluations (e.g., identification of acceptable level of performance, follow-up where indicated, and conditions for termination should follow-up not be taken or not lead to improved and acceptable performance), a form to use in obtaining peer and administrative evaluations, checklists for observations, a self-evaluation form, a list of objective performance indicators, tips for conducting evaluation feedback sessions and planning follow-ups, a list of developmental resources for strengthening teacher performance, contact information for the two ombudsmen, and due process procedures to be followed in the event of a grievance. At the completion of each workshop, participants signed a letter acknowledging that they had completed the workshop, received all relevant information, and understood the purposes, procedures, and possible results of the evaluation procedure.

All workshop participants were informed that the materials within the handbook would serve as formal documentation of the evaluation system. Those involved in evaluations were asked to document each evaluation clearly by obtaining signatures from all parties before forwarding copies of the materials to the head of personnel.

As a result of the new procedure, three of the newly hired teachers were required to complete supplementary workshops and training, and one teacher was released. Two of these teachers began grievance procedures, claiming that they were neither informed of the expectations nor of the resulting consequences. In responding to these teachers, task force members met to review their files. They noted that each of the teachers had attended the workshops and had received a copy of the handbook. Further, the specific evaluation files noted that the teachers had received consistent feedback regarding their teaching and expectations for improvement and further professional development. The teachers in question had signed these reviews. The task force agreed with the decisions, and the grievance proceeded no further.

Illustrative Case 2:
Applying Revised Evaluation Procedures
Analysis

The district recognized the need to update and ensure that the methods used in evaluation were relevant for the purposes of the evaluation, based on teaching expectations, and would lead to valid inferences regarding teacher performance (see A1, Valid Judgments). The revised procedures provided support to evaluators and evaluatees and a list of developmental resources for improving teacher performance. Further, specific procedures were in place to inform those involved in the evaluation and to document all evaluation-related events and materials. Each part of the evaluation system was documented in the teacher handbook that was given to all relevant employees. This information was supplemented by workshops and access to ombudsmen. These procedures ensured that all relevant employees were aware of the evaluation purposes, methods, and consequences and that they would have access to personnel who could address concerns about the evaluation procedure (see P1, Service Orientation). The detailed and signed documentation enabled the task force to support the original evaluation decisions and avoid further grievance.

Supporting Documentation

Clift, R. T., Veal, M. L., Holland, P., Johnson, M., & McCarthy, J. (1995). *Collaborative leadership and shared decision making.* New York: Teachers College Press.

Gilliland, S. W., & Langdon, J. C. (1998). Creating performance management systems that promote perceptions of fairness. In J. W. Smither (Ed.), *Performance appraisal: State of the art in practice* (pp. 209–243). San Francisco: Jossey-Bass.

Guthrie, J. W., & Reed, R. J. (1991). *Educational administration and policy: Effective leadership for American schools.* Boston: Allyn & Bacon.

Society for Industrial and Organizational Psychology. (2003). *Principles for the validation and use of personnel selection procedures* (4th ed.). Bowling Green, OH: Author.

Wolf, K. (1996). Developing an effective teaching portfolio. *Educational Leadership, 53,* 34–37.

A5   Defensible Information

> **STANDARD**   **The information collected for personnel evaluations should be defensible and aligned with the evaluation criteria.**

Explanation.   Information gathered in personnel evaluations provides the evidence used to form interpretations and make decisions and recommendations regarding an evaluatee's performance. It also is used for developing follow-up activities designed to improve evaluatee performance. As is true with any evidence, the defensibility of the information should be of prime concern. To be defensible, the information gathered must be of such a nature and extent that it can be reliably and validly interpreted (see A1, Valid Judgments). The evaluator must be able to support judgments based on the data collected and documented, so judgments never should be contradictory to documented evidence (see A4, Documented Purposes and Procedures).

Information collected for personnel evaluation may be obtained using a variety of assessment instruments and from a variety of sources, including the evaluatee's work samples, coworkers, supervisors, clients, and special reviewers. The data from these sources and instruments can be problematic if they are of such poor quality as to be of limited use. Although appropriate assessment methods and procedures increase the likelihood of gathering good information, their use does not necessarily guarantee it. Even when procedures are well described and followed precisely, unexpected circumstances may result in information that is not of the quality necessary to make valid interpretations (see A1, Valid Judgments; A3, Analysis of Context). Moreover, good procedures may result in information that is adequate for one evaluation purpose but not for another (see U2, Defined Uses).

An example of indefensible information would be ignoring any known sources of bias or error in the information obtained. For example, students' ratings of an instructor in a difficult course could be influenced by the difficulty of the course rather than reflecting only on the instructor's performance (see A8, Bias Identification and Management).

Another example might be the use of information or data from a source that is unrelated to the evaluation criteria set forth in the evaluation system, such as when a supervisor dislikes an employee's style of dress, but dress code is not included in the evaluation criteria. The evaluator cannot, in this case, use dress style as a way to lower judgment of an evaluatee's performance (see A8, Bias Identification and Management).

Use of a variety of sources and assessment methods helps ensure comprehensive and consistent indications of performance. At the same time, it helps identify any problems in the information. Independent data sources and methods should serve as cross-checks for one another. When they agree, the information and evidence have been corroborated. When they yield disparate results, additional investigation should be conducted to identify (a) the reason for the differences, (b) whether the differences render some or all of the information indefensible, and (c) what cautions should be put in place when interpreting the data. Differences may not mean the information is flawed. For example, students may be able to evaluate only certain aspects of a teacher's performance, whereas peers and supervisors will be able to evaluate other behaviors. Thus, some differences in evaluations conducted from diverse perspectives will be based on differences in the evaluatee's performance across settings.

For all types of records, steps should be taken to ensure that the data are correct and their integrity is maintained (see A7, Systematic Data Control). Failure to detect biases, inaccuracies, unauthorized changes, and other problems reduces the defensibility of the data and can result in inappropriate evaluation findings and decisions.

Rationale.   When personnel evaluators conscientiously use defensible information, their evaluations are more likely to promote the effective performance of job responsibilities and fulfillment of institutional missions. By monitoring and defending the quality of information on which an evaluation is based, the likelihood of valid interpretations of the evaluatee's performance increases, as does the appropriateness of follow-up recommendations.

GUIDELINES

A. Identify the information needed to address the purpose(s) and use(s) of the evaluation (see U2, Defined Uses).
B. Choose assessment methods and procedures that meet practical and defensible data collection constraints (see F1, Practical Procedures) while providing relevant information that can be interpreted reliably and validly (A1, Valid Judgments; A6, Reliable Information).
C. Describe the sources of information (evaluatee, administrators, students, parents, assessment instruments, student work samples, artifacts, etc.) that were used in the evaluation.
D. Use a variety of data-gathering methods (observation checklists, interviews, products) to help ensure comprehensive and consistent indications of performance.
E. Collect information that conforms to legal, ethical, and organization-based policies to promote confidentiality and privacy (see P7, Legal Viability).
F. Align collected evaluation information with the evaluation criteria to eliminate irrelevant data and assess the adequacy of collected data.

COMMON ERRORS

A. Failing to gather needed information from defensible information sources (e.g., student ratings, peer evaluations) because evaluation planning occurred too late to allow the information to be collected and used.

B. Selecting sources of information based on their availability rather than the need to have data from a specific source (e.g., administrators rather than colleagues and fellow staff).

C. Choosing assessment methods and procedures based on their ease of use rather than on their appropriateness for the questions and uses of the evaluation.

D. Assuming without supporting evidence that different information sources (e.g., students or parents) are comparable and equally valid (see A1, Valid Judgments).

E. Failing to ensure that work products submitted by an evaluatee (artifacts such as lesson plans, student work samples, publications, etc.) are indeed the products of the individual submitting them for evaluation.

F. Failing to document the source of data adequately, or basing an evaluation report on questionable data such as hearsay or supposition.

G. Assuming that defensible information appropriate for one evaluation situation will also be appropriate for another evaluation situation.

Illustrative Case 1: Coauthors as Data Sources
Description

The tenure review committee of a college was reviewing candidate materials submitted by individuals under consideration for tenure and promotion to associate professor. Each portfolio contained the following: (a) a copy of the annual yearly reports, which included a list of courses taught each year and the publications that either appeared in that year or, if not yet published, were accepted for publication; (b) a summary of the mandatory student evaluations of the faculty member's teaching; (c) a peer evaluation of the faculty member's teaching and teaching material; (d) samples of two published scholarly articles; and (e) six letters of reference where the sources of the reference were selected by the department chair from a list provided by the faculty member and the department.

In the case of a Dr. Bouvron, who had been endorsed by her department chair for the granting of tenure and promotion to associate professor, one of the tenure committee members noted that two of the external reviewers for Dr. Bouvron were also coauthors on several of the publications listed in her annual reports. The tenure review committee questioned whether the information provided by these individuals should be considered in making a tenure decision and decided, given the number of such coauthored articles, that the reviews of these two individuals should be disregarded.

Illustrative Case 1: Coauthors as Data Sources
Analysis

The department chair should have made certain that the individuals he requested as external reviewers were not closely related to the faculty member and that they disclosed any personal or professional relationships they had with the evaluatee. Failure to do so led the tenure committee to discount their evaluations, thereby reducing the contribution of the external reviews in the decision to be made (see A1, Valid Judgments).

The information provided by the coauthors would be considered indefensible in this case because of the potential for conflict of interest. A suggestion of bias on the part of the coauthors would further taint the information provided for the evaluation.

Guidelines regarding sources of information that are appropriate or inappropriate should be made explicit in a faculty handbook and applied consistently across the college. In addition, when presenting the evaluation information, the department chair should have noted any factors that might affect the interpretation of the information (see A8, Bias Identification and Management).

Illustrative Case 2:
Self-Promotion Is Not Self-Evaluation
Description

The superintendent of a medium-sized school district gave a very positive evaluation and recommendation for promotion to associate superintendent for Ms. Schultz, an elementary school principal with only two years of administrative experience. During her time as principal, Ms. Schultz met with the superintendent regularly to update him on the learning projects she had introduced at the school and how they were progressing. She consistently reported that the students were achieving the expected learning outcomes and that the sixth-grade students had performed above the state average on the state assessments in reading and mathematics. Additionally, she regularly sent e-mails to the superintendent in which she suggested new and innovative ways of dealing with problems. When other principals learned of the positive recommendation, they approached the superintendent to complain, stating that the principal was very dependent on her teachers, had claimed ideas as her own that were the product of group efforts, and was under budget because of cutting corners in maintenance.

Illustrative Case 2:
Self-Promotion Is Not Self-Evaluation
Analysis

The superintendent's reliance on self-reports of performance by the principal resulted in his making an evaluation based on indefensible information. When confronted about the evaluation, the superintendent was unable to justify his recommendation because he had not been thorough in conducting the evaluation.

While self-reports of progress and performance can be a useful source of information in making evaluations, particularly in cases where frequent observation is not possible or will not yield meaningful information, relying solely on self-evaluations can be problematic. The superintendent should have developed a means of gathering information from other sources (e.g., visits to the school, teacher and parent satisfaction surveys) so that he would be able to cross-check the findings and increase the reliability of the information obtained (see A6, Reliable Information).

Supporting Documentation

Atwater, L. E. (1998). The advantages and pitfalls of self-assessment in organizations. In J. W. Smither (Ed.), *Performance appraisal: State of the art in practice* (pp. 331–369). San Francisco: Jossey-Bass.

Dalessio, A. T. (1998). Using multisource feedback for employee development and personnel decisions. In J. W. Smither (Ed.), *Performance appraisal: State of the art in practice* (pp. 278–330). San Francisco: Jossey-Bass.

Kozlowski, S. W. J., Chao, G. T., & Morrison, R. F. (1998). Games raters play: Politics, strategies, and impression management in performance appraisal. In J. W. Smither (Ed.), *Performance appraisal: State of the art in practice* (pp. 163–208). San Francisco: Jossey-Bass.

Millman, J., & Darling-Hammond, L. (Eds.). (1990). *The new handbook of teacher evaluation: Assessing elementary and secondary teachers.* Newbury Park, CA: Sage.

A6   Reliable Information

> **STANDARD**   Personnel evaluation procedures should produce reliable information.

Explanation.   Reliability refers to the degree of consistency in the judgments formed based on data collected throughout an evaluation process. In a sound system of evaluation, every effort should be made to ensure that the results of an evaluation are based on data that are systematically collected and consistent in their findings. It is quite common, and perhaps even unavoidable, that errors in data collection occur when relying on such methods as classroom observation. If one observer collects data during an observation, there is always the likelihood that incidences may be missed or misinterpreted. Consistency should be sought across different indicators of the same criterion (internal consistency), across different contexts and occasions on which a behavior is observed (stability), and across different observers of the same behavior (observer agreement). In other words, if two or more evaluators are engaged in the evaluation process, it is important that each evaluator comes to a closely similar conclusion regarding the evaluatee's performance level. This can be enhanced through rigorous training of evaluators (see U3, Evaluator Qualifications). It can be enhanced further through the development of instruments that reduce subjectivity.

Reliability of evaluation information should be assessed directly. Different strategies are used to assess reliability depending on the type of data and nature of the decision to be made. In personnel evaluations, the clearest way to determine reliability of information is to compare the ratings of two or more evaluators using the same set of data. Because personnel evaluations are used to make high-stakes decisions, there should be very little disagreement, if any, concerning the level of performance or the nature of the data. For this reason, it is common practice for school administrators to share responsibility in collecting observation data, so that the same teacher will be observed by two or more administrators over the course of the evaluation period.

The choice of information-gathering methods should be guided by the need to avoid methods with poor consistency or reliability. Knowledge of the evaluation criteria and instruments that reflect these criteria greatly increase reliability across raters.

There is one strong caveat on reliability: it is necessary for validity but not sufficient to guarantee validity. In particular, bias on the part of the evaluator or a "halo effect" from evaluations in other settings may result in highly reliable though inaccurate judgments. For example, if the evaluator is biased in any way in respect to the evaluatee's race, gender, creed, culture, or any other aspect unrelated to job performance, this may influence the information collected for an evaluation, resulting in a wrong judgment (see A8, Bias Identification and Management). Likewise, conflict of interest should be monitored carefully in the event that relationships or circumstances outside the realm of the evaluation may exist that would produce inappropriate consistencies in data and either negatively or positively affect the results of the evaluation.

Rationale.   All evaluation decisions are affected by the reliability of the information used. Procedures that lack reliability also will lack validity. Personnel evaluation decisions can have substantial effects on evaluatees in terms of employment and future opportunities. Individual personnel evaluation instruments and the procedures used should have levels of reliability that are acceptable for the intended uses, with higher reliability required for those evaluations having higher stakes. The affected persons have a right to know what efforts were made to enhance reliability and the reliability levels achieved. In such instances, the steps to secure and confirm acceptable reliability ensure that the rights of evaluatees are protected.

GUIDELINES

A. Determine whether the nature of the information collected allows for consistency across situations and evaluators.

B. Wherever possible, choose information-gathering procedures that in the past have yielded data and information with consistent results for the intended use.

C. Ensure that the method used to determine reliability (e.g., internal consistency, stability, observer agreement, or decision consistency) for each data-gathering procedure is appropriate for that procedure and for the interpretation(s) to be made.

D. Clearly define the expected performance standards, including relevant performance criteria, and ensure that these standards are understood by all defined users (see A2, Defined Expectations; U4, Explicit Criteria; U2, Defined Uses).

E. Use procedures to enhance reliability and discern consistent patterns and trends (e.g., increased assessment form length, multiple observers and raters, variety of data sources, multiple occasions).

F. Develop and use standard assessment procedures for all evaluatees, and consider individual differences in responsibilities and needs.

G. Ensure that the procedures used for judging or scoring evaluatees' performances are applied consistently and monitored by developing protocols for judging performance and related products to reduce inconsistencies in scoring (see A11, Metaevaluation).

H. Provide adequate training to scorers and observers to ensure that they are alert to the kinds of mistakes likely to occur and how to avoid them (see U3, Evaluator Qualifications).

I. Check the consistency and agreement of scoring, categorization, themes, and coding by using two or more qualified raters who analyze the same set of data, information, or observations independently to ensure consistency in the results of the analyses.

J. Cross-check all data collection and interpretation procedures to guard against biases that produce high but spurious levels of reliability.

COMMON ERRORS

A. Assuming the information is adequately consistent when the reliability has not been determined.

B. Scoring performance tasks, including observations, when tired, distracted, or inattentive.

C. Failing to adhere to described measurement procedures or to document changes in procedures.

D. Assuming that the published reliability of a procedure is the same for different groups and situations inconsistent with the intended use of the procedure.

E. Confusing reliability with validity. Reliability is a necessary but insufficient condition for validity (see A1, Valid Judgments).

F. Failing to consider that unusual circumstances may have influenced the evaluatee's behavior and produced inconsistencies in findings (see A3, Analysis of Context).

G. Not controlling or managing bias or conflict of interest on the part of an evaluator, either of which may result in reliable but inaccurate information.

Illustrative Case 1: Inadequate Data Yields Unreliable Information
Description

Mr. Groach, the vice principal, conducted all the faculty evaluations in a middle school. These evaluations were used to determine who should receive merit pay and who should participate in corrective professional development. The school's principal required the vice principal to have sole responsibility for these evaluations and specified that each teacher was to be observed once during the latter part of the year. All observations were announced ahead of time to allow teachers to prepare.

During each observation, Mr. Groach made notes on what he was observing and how the students were behaving. After the visit, he used his notes to complete a two-page form using a five-point Likert-type scale that provided ratings on the following criteria: classroom management, time devoted to learning tasks, skill in presentation, engagement of students in the learning process, feedback to students, clarity of assignments, and overall effectiveness. A copy of the completed form was discussed with the teacher, after which both the teacher and the vice principal signed the form indicating agreement and acceptance of the evaluation.

Each year, Mr. Groach did not recommend any teacher for corrective professional development because all teachers received above satisfactory evaluations. While all the teachers in the school appeared to be effective based on the personnel evaluations, the school's overall student achievement scores began to drop significantly until the school was among the lowest performing in the district.

Illustrative Case 1: Inadequate Data Yields Unreliable Information
Analysis

The classroom observation procedure used in this school obviously was not adequate. The method of data collection in this case has several flaws. A single observation provides insufficient data because the information is not likely to be representative of a teacher's overall performance over time. A single observer is not adequate in this case. Data collected on one occasion by one evaluator is questionable because there simply is not enough information available to provide reliable judgment. Also, it is not possible to assess reliability of data and confirm its adequacy from a single observation per teacher.

These observations not only were narrow in focus, but also announced ahead of time, allowing teachers to prepare for the evaluation. Announced observations likely would lead to high consistency in rating but compromised validity. This occurs because teachers, knowing the high stakes of this observation, have the opportunity to adjust their teaching during that one class period to meet the criteria of the evaluation. Announced observations are questionable in many cases due to this likelihood of influencing the teacher's behavior to match expectations. Observations should capture a sample of the teacher's daily practice as closely as possible to assess overall performance level.

The student achievement data provide an indication of the lack of reliability in the information collected through this system of evaluation. In cases such as this, inflated teacher evaluation results often may mask poor practice that results in lower student achievement.

Illustrative Case 2: Discrepancies Among Evaluators
Description

A community college recently introduced a policy of obtaining performance evaluations for each instructor from an administrator, a supervisor, a peer, and a random sample of students. The instructor's union was satisfied with this aspect of the evaluation process because members thought that involving colleagues in the evaluation process would lead to better accountability and less bias in the ratings. The college's mandate was to meet the needs of the community, so an instructor may teach classes in the morning, afternoon, or evening. Typically, the evening classes serve community members interested in upgrading their skills or taking courses for personal fulfillment.

Evaluations were based on three separate observations and a review of class materials. While peer evaluations occurred during the morning and afternoon classes, the administrator and supervisor observations occurred during the evening classes, so as not to interfere with their daily administrative responsibilities.

One instructor, Ms. DeLeon, received a consistent evaluation in her last review, except for two areas. She was rated highly by the administrator, supervisor, peer, and a majority of the students in all areas of performance except in student expectations and the quality of assessment techniques. In terms of student expectations, the administrator and supervisor rated her performance as "satisfactory," and in terms of assessment techniques they both indicated "needs improvement." The peer and student evaluations did not suggest a problem in these areas of performance. When Ms. DeLeon inquired about the discrepancy, she was told that the rating process was valid since it was based on clearly outlined performance expectations and that there was no reason to appeal an overall positive evaluation. She left unsatisfied, wondering whether she needed to address her methods to engage and assess students since she was provided with such conflicting information.

Illustrative Case 2: Discrepancies Among Evaluators
Analysis

The instructor, Ms. DeLeon, was concerned about an apparent lack of reliability in evaluations of student engagement and assessment techniques. There are a number of plausible reasons for the discrepancy, including inconsistency in the instructor's performance over time, differences in the types of students in the classes, the format of daytime and evening classes, and the ways the observers view specific aspects of performance. In particular, it may be important to examine whether the causes for the differences in ratings were associated with evaluations based on daytime or evening classes. The poorer ratings came from evaluations based on evening classes, when it is more likely the administrator and supervisor would be tired after the day's work. Further, it may be that evening classes require a different set of expectations. In this regard, it would be important to determine if the evaluations of other evening classes exhibited similar discrepancies. If so, the evaluation procedure may need to be modified for such classes.

The administrator should have investigated the discrepant ratings so as to be able to provide an explanation for the differences or to revise ratings, if needed. Further, the reply the instructor received was based on confusion between reliability and validity. The college should routinely evaluate the interrater reliability of ratings. If there are particular dimensions of performance where interrater reliability is low, the reasons for the differences should be investigated, and the quality of rater training in that area should be reviewed.

Supporting Documentation

American Educational Research Association, American Psychological Association, & National Council on Measurement in Education. (1999). *Standards for educational and psychological testing*. Washington, DC: American Educational Research Association.

Brennan, R. L. (2001). *Generalizability theory.* New York: Springer-Verlag.

Brennan, R. L., & Johnson, E. G. (1995). Generalizability of performance assessments. *Educational Measurement: Issues and Practice, 14*(4), 9–12.

Cizek, G. J. (Ed.). (2001). *Setting performance standards: Concepts, methods, and perspectives.* Mahwah, NJ: Lawrence Erlbaum.

Feldt, L. S., & Brennan, R. L. (1989). Reliability. In R. L. Linn (Ed.), *Educational measurement* (3rd ed., pp. 105–146). New York: American Council on Education.

Guthrie, J. W., & Reed, R. J. (1991). *Educational administration and policy: Effective leadership for American schools.* Boston: Allyn & Bacon.

Howe, K., & Eisenhart, M. (1990). Standards for qualitative (and quantitative) research: A prolegomenon. *Educational Researcher, 19*(4), 2–9.

Kirk, J., & Miller, M. L. (1986). *Reliability and validity in qualitative research* (Qualitative Research Methods Series, No. 1). Newbury Park, CA: Sage.

Millman, J., & Darling-Hammond, L. (Eds.). (1990). *The new handbook of teacher evaluation: Assessing elementary and secondary teachers.* Newbury Park, CA: Sage.

Rebore, R. W. (1997). *Personnel administration in education.* Englewood Cliffs, NJ: Prentice Hall.

Shavelson, R. J., & Webb, N. M. (1991). *Generalizability theory: A primer.* Newbury Park, CA: Sage.

Society for Industrial and Organizational Psychology. (2003). *Principles for the validation and use of personnel selection procedures* (4th ed.). Bowling Green, OH: Author.

A7 Systematic Data Control

> **STANDARD** **The information collected, processed, and reported about evaluatees should be reviewed systematically, corrected as appropriate, and kept secure.**

Explanation. A review of personnel evaluation information should be conducted methodically, thoroughly, and regularly. Information should be checked for accuracy and completeness at every stage of collection, entry, storage, and retrieval. Needed corrections should be made and documented. The assessment information and the evaluation results must be recorded and protected by appropriate maintenance and security, particularly for evaluations that serve future personnel decisions such as career promotion or job retention. Access and retrieval of information should be restricted to those with legitimate rights to the information and analysis (see P3, Access to Evaluation Information). Systematic data control begins with sound policies that outline what information is confidential and who has access to such information (see U2, Defined Uses).

Handling information and maintaining quality control involves the following questions:

- What type of information will be retained?
- How will those who control the information be trained to maintain security and confidentiality of files?
- How and where will the information be stored?
- What procedures will be used and who is responsible for determining that the stored data and information are current, complete, correct, and secure?
- How long will the information be stored?
- What security arrangements are needed to limit access to only those users with a legitimate right (see P3, Access to Evaluation Information)?

The data and supporting documentation should be stored in an organized way to support ease of interpretation by those using the information to guide personnel evaluation decisions. Procedures for entering data into computer files or other data storage methods (e.g., portfolios) should be documented and verified to ensure integrity and compliance.

If data are maintained in an electronic data management system, safeguards must be taken to ensure that sufficient firewalls and security systems are in place to prevent unauthorized access to records or documents. All electronic or online data management systems should have access levels that limit the scope of access for each role (e.g., teacher, principal, assistant principal, district office supervisor), so that only those records that are appropriate for each role are accessible (see P3, Access to Evaluation Information).

Rationale.   Personnel decisions are important and should be made with confidence that their information basis is complete, accurately documented, organized, and secure. Failures in data control can render evaluations useless and have substantial legal ramifications for evaluators. Systematic data control minimizes the introduction of extraneous errors and safeguards against inappropriate access to or use of the evaluation data. While evaluators have limited control over such matters as sampling and measurement errors, they have considerably more control over scoring, coding, data entry, and analysis and can play an important part in minimizing errors in these areas. Periodically, evaluators should systematically review personnel records and information to ensure that errors are corrected. Undetected or uncorrected errors can distort the results of the data analysis and render the evaluation inaccurate and misleading. Similarly, evaluators must work to prevent the indiscriminate sharing of evaluation findings that can discredit the integrity of the evaluation system.

GUIDELINES

A. Use a systematic quality control process in which evaluators and designated knowledgeable personnel review policies, audit procedures for data inclusion, check the veracity of information, verify information procedures, and monitor the correct use of information.

B. Ensure that those responsible for collection, entry, and storage of information are familiar with the procedures and policies used to maintain security and limit access to information used for personnel evaluation. Maintain systematic documentation of procedures for future reference.

C. Ensure that people included in processing the information have the necessary training and background to perform their tasks accurately.

D. Systematically check for errors in entering, processing, and reporting recorded information.

E. Incorporate procedures that increase accuracy of data entry (e.g., double entry procedures).

F. Routinely check with people who contribute information to personnel files to ensure that the collected information is represented accurately.

G. Write a date and reason for data collection on each entry, so that files may be updated easily or used for longitudinal data analysis and not used for unintended or inappropriate purposes.

H. Require employees to sign each evaluation report placed in their file, indicating that they have seen the report and had an opportunity to discuss it.

I. Prepare duplicate data sets and keep a backup set in a secure location. This is especially important when there is a chance that fire, theft, computer malfunctions, data processing errors, or staff neglect can cause vital information to be lost. Label evaluation documents as ORIGINAL or COPY.

J. Systematic data control includes the elimination of out-of-date data. Set policy on how long and under what conditions data should be maintained. At appropriate times securely dispose of out-of-date data (original and backup copies) and document the disposal process. Periodically check data disposal processes to ensure proper disposition of old information and reports and that current evaluation data are not compromised in the disposition process.

K. Enact procedures to repair or remove data that is flawed or compromised, and document the actions taken.

L. Ensure that all electronic files are properly backed up within the system or with hard copies.

COMMON ERRORS

A. Assuming that the results from data entry procedures are accurate.

B. Readily accepting the accuracy of written, published, or stored information.

C. Failing to include or follow procedures for checking the accuracy of data entry, coding, storage, and retrieval due to time or other constraints.

D. Failing to maintain an audit trail for the data.

E. Allowing unauthorized persons access to privileged personnel information.

F. Failing to keep backup information up to date.

G. Failing to properly train technology personnel to maintain electronic databases.

Illustrative Case 1: Securing Electronic Personnel Files
Description

Dr. Patel, the superintendent of a school district employing more than 3,000 certified staff, received several complaints from members of the human resources department concerning the need for additional storage for personnel files. File cabinets were overflowing, and space for additional cabinets had been taken for use by the technology department with its increasing amount of equipment. The lack of adequate space had resulted in file cabinets being housed in hallways and other insecure areas.

Dr. Patel charged a committee of district-level administrators to investigate solutions to the problem. On their recommendation, the district invested in an electronic data management system that could store all personnel records on the district server. On approval, all new evaluations were immediately entered into the electronic system. Copies of all previous evaluations that were to be maintained were scanned for maintenance in electronic form. All out-of-date evaluation materials and reports were destroyed through a carefully monitored administrative process. The saving in physical storage space was enormous.

This system maintained personnel records, including licensure, area of certification, years of experience, current teaching level, and building assignment. It also allowed the district to maintain all personnel evaluation records with accurate time stamped and dated documentation of observations, evaluator entries, and other data concerning teacher performance. This increased the district administration's oversight of the evaluation process by providing a more accurate record of the evaluation process in a much more easily accessible manner. Within minutes, the district administrator could create a report documenting all data entries by evaluators for any given time period. This increased the fidelity of implementation of the district's teacher evaluation system.

Records could be maintained electronically and hard copies, such as the pages for signatures, produced only when needed, as in the case of a grievance. While paper files always ran the risk of being lost or damaged, the electronic files were backed up systematically on a regular basis. The system also allowed those administrators with a preset level of security clearance to access the records more easily from their own computers rather than through the cumbersome process currently in place to safeguard the paper files.

Illustrative Case 1: Securing Electronic Personnel Files
Analysis

Many districts rely on paper files and records for personnel data including evaluations. These files generally are housed in a central location requiring anyone needing access to physically go to that location and follow the necessary procedures to maintain security (see P3, Access to Evaluation Information). Electronic data management systems are becoming more and more popular. As districts and universities increase their technology capacities, this type of data management system provides easier access, greater security, and more reliable control of the data.

In this case, Dr. Patel and the administrative team implemented a data management system that not only solved their storage and security problems, but also offered an opportunity to provide greater oversight of the teacher evaluation procedures. For example, the electronic data management system accurately stamped the date and time for such entries as observations. That date stamp in turn helps ensure timely collection of evaluation information and increases the accountability of evaluators.

Illustrative Case 2: Proper Organization of Personnel Information
Description

With the annual review process about to occur among a large faculty at a midsized university, the dean responsible for reviewing the personnel files and making salary increment decisions suddenly became incapacitated due to a severe illness. The newly appointed associate dean, Dean Bakovic, having some experience in personnel evaluation, was asked by the academic vice president of the university to complete the task.

Due to the nature of the university expectations for faculty, the evaluation method was complex and required the use of extensive personnel information. Nevertheless, when beginning the task, Dean Bakovic was able to locate current written documentation regarding the evaluation procedures in the ill dean's filing cabinet. Similarly, relevant personnel information was stored in alphabetized files within a locked office cabinet. A second copy of the documentation and personnel files was stored electronically on the ill dean's computer. Dean Bakovic was able to access this information using a key and computer password provided by the ill dean's personal assistant.

The documentation clearly identified the procedures used to interpret the personnel information. The personnel files noted the dates of data entry into the computer along with the date of an accuracy check. All information in the files noted the date the faculty had reviewed their files, and the faculty member signed each file. The manner in which the files were maintained allowed Dean Bakovic to complete the review process with only minor delay, and none of the faculty members thought the review process had treated them unfairly.

Illustrative Case 2: Proper Organization of Personnel Information
Analysis

The unexpected illness of the person responsible for personnel decisions did not result in a substantial loss of time or accuracy in the evaluations completed. The dean had clearly outlined the procedures used and had maintained the integrity of the data throughout the evaluation process. This included secure storage, information backup, accuracy checks, and clear instructions regarding data interpretation and use. The accurate record keeping and documentation made it possible for others to complete the evaluation task and ensured that the decisions made by Dean Bakovic were defensible and based on quality information.

Supporting Documentation

Guthrie, J. W., & Reed, R. J. (1991). *Educational administration and policy: Effective leadership for American schools.* Boston: Allyn & Bacon.

Rebore, R. W. (1997). *Personnel administration in education.* Englewood Cliffs, NJ: Prentice Hall.

Wexley, K. N., & Yuki, G. A. (1984). *Organizational behavior and personnel psychology* (Rev. ed.). Homewood, IL: Irwin.

A8   Bias Identification and Management

> **STANDARD**   **The evaluation process should provide safeguards against bias.**

Explanation.   The potential always exists for the intrusion of bias in personnel evaluations. Bias is any perception or belief held by the evaluator that is unrelated to the job performance of an individual, but systematically influences the evaluator's judgment. Bias can be based on any number of widely held stereotypes including regional accents, age, language differences, race, gender, ethnicity, sexual orientation, disabilities, and manner of dress.

Bias also may occur if an evaluator's judgment is influenced by a close personal relationship with the evaluatee. This is not to be confused with conflict of interest, in that the evaluator may not stand to gain or lose financially or otherwise by the outcome of the evaluation. This type of bias occurs more often when an evaluator's judgment is skewed due to personal feelings toward the evaluatee such as a close friendship or personal conflict.

An unbiased evaluation is one that is based solely on criteria and information relevant to the evaluatee's job. It is difficult to eliminate all bias from personnel evaluation; however, safeguards can be put in place by the organization or district. The first is to establish a system for monitoring documentation and evaluation reports for signs of bias. Such signs would include judgments that are not defensible based on data from multiple sources or judgments from an individual evaluator that conflict with those of other evaluators (see A1, Valid Judgments; A5, Defensible Information; A6, Reliable Information; A11, Metaevaluation).

No one is completely free of personal biases, and often individuals may not be aware that a bias exists. Therefore, safeguards include bias training for evaluators. Such training should address the various sources of bias. Within this training, organizations also should provide remedies for bias when simple awareness by the evaluator is not sufficient. Suggested remedies may include such steps as changing or adding evaluators. It is important, however, that such remedies not include steps that would place an undue burden on the evaluatee, such as requiring additional documentation or data beyond the scope of the adopted policies and procedures of the system in place.

The organization can select or develop instruments and procedures that decrease subjectivity and potential bias by aligning with the criteria for satisfactory job performance (see U4, Explicit Criteria). Evaluation systems that require input from the evaluatee (e.g., work samples, artifacts, interviews, etc.) along with rating scales or rubrics that are not vague or open to misinterpretation are far more likely to control bias than simple rating scales of four or fewer levels (unsatisfactory, satisfactory, at standard, above standard) based solely on observations using a checklist-type instrument.

Organizations should have a policy in place that allows an individual to file a grievance if he or she suspects that bias played a role in an evaluation. This offers a remedy that protects both the organization and the individual from unwarranted personnel actions that may result in decisions that are not only detrimental to the career of the individual but, in some cases, to the organization, if a valuable employee is lost due to bias on the part of an evaluator.

Rationale.   Bias can undermine the fairness of a personnel evaluation. Bias can distort the information-gathering process and corrupt decisions, actions, and recommendations to the detriment of an evaluatee. Bias also can lead to expensive and damaging court cases.

An unbiased personnel evaluation is one based solely on defensible criteria such as specific job performance expectations and sound supporting information (see A5, Defensible Information; U4, Explicit Criteria). Evaluators must recognize that bias is an ever-present threat to personnel evaluation, develop a plan for identifying and addressing bias, and be vigilant and resistant to the sources of bias.

GUIDELINES

A. Acknowledge for the evaluation record any personal relationships resulting either from friendship or conflict that may influence the judgment of the evaluator.

B. Include necessary steps for remediation in the evaluation process, such as removing an evaluator from the process where the potential for bias exists.

C. Ensure that training of evaluators includes bias control (see U3, Evaluator Qualifications).

D. Provide a system for monitoring the evaluation system in terms of bias control (see A11, Metaevaluation).

E. Exclude factors from the process that disadvantage some evaluatees despite their actual performance level and ability to perform their assigned duties (e.g., age, style of dress, accent, etc.).

F. Develop a written policy advising all stakeholders of the grievance process to address suspected influences of bias (see P7, Legal Viability).

G. Obtain data and judgments from multiple sources to ensure validity and consistent indications of performance (see A1, Valid Judgments; A6, Reliable Information).

   H. Ensure that both observations and scoring of performance are not influenced by factors that are irrelevant to the purpose of the evaluation and the use of the results.

   I. Ensure that evaluation reports are complete in their descriptions of strengths and areas for growth, promoting a balanced report (see P5, Comprehensive Evaluations).

   J. Allow evaluatees and other relevant personnel the opportunity to review data and participate in interpreting it where appropriate (see U5, Functional Reporting; P4, Interactions With Evaluatees).

   K. Be particularly alert to the potential for bias in those parts of the evaluation system that are more subjective than objective (see A1, Valid Judgments; A6, Reliable Information).

COMMON ERRORS

   A. Continuing to use evaluators whose biases have become evident without providing additional training and oversight concerning bias (see U3, Evaluator Qualifications).

   B. Implementing a system with a narrow scope of data sources such as relying on brief classroom observations and using vague rating scales with limited descriptors.

   C. Judging qualifications or performance on the basis of irrelevant characteristics such as race, age, sex, religion, or other characteristics that are not job related (see A1, Valid Judgments).

   D. Ignoring or distorting certain relevant information because it conflicts with the general conclusion or recommendation (see A10, Justified Conclusions).

   E. Employing an inflexible approach to obtaining and interpreting information irrespective of differing language and cultural backgrounds.

   F. Assuming that an evaluator's observations are not affected by the evaluator's perspective, training, previous experience, or personal bias.

Illustrative Case 1: The Buddy Evaluation
Description

Mr. Stoner, a high school principal, began his rounds of teacher evaluations in the fall. That summer, he had hired several new teachers. Three of these teachers had graduated from his alma mater and shared his enthusiasm for that university's athletic program. He enjoyed lively discussions with them concerning the university's athletic teams. One of these three teachers, Mr. van Balen, was particularly disorganized and lacked appropriate planning skills. This resulted in lost instructional time for his students. The assistant principal, Ms. McMillan, had noted these discrepancies in performance during the first round of observations. She shared the observation data with Mr. van Balen, made recommendations for improvement, and arranged for him to work with the department chair to improve his lesson planning and use of instructional time. Mr. van Balen, however, failed to follow up on any of these recommendations and often missed scheduled meetings with the department chair to review lesson plans and curriculum.

This district's evaluation procedures required administrators in the same building to rotate through classroom observations of teachers. In this case, the principal, Mr. Stoner, conducted the second formal classroom observation for Mr. van Balen. Although he had made little or no progress in planning lessons that maximized use of instructional time, Mr. Stoner focused more on Mr. van Balen's positive relationship with students during his write-up and consequent conference. Although Mr. Stoner suggested during the postobservation conference that Mr. van Balen might want to "continue working on planning as noted by the assistant principal," he did not include this remark in the formal write-up. His write-up contained a glowing report of Mr. van Balen's strong relationship with his students and made only vague reference to wasted instructional time and lack of alignment with the curriculum. These remarks became part of the evaluation record for the overall summative performance rating at the end of the year.

Mr. Stoner continued his friendly chats with Mr. van Balen concerning the athletic program at their alma mater as well as discovering additional common interests. When the assistant principal noted Mr. van Balen's continued lack of organization and planning, Mr. Stoner assured her that Mr. van Balen had excellent training in his teacher education program and would improve with time. He also assured the department chair that his students would do well on the state test.

At the end of the year, primarily due to the lack of focus on curriculum and low quality instruction, Mr. van Balen's students scored well below the district and state average on the standardized test for the course. This affected the overall standing of the school on accountability measures. Mr. Stoner reassigned Mr. van Balen to a nontested course for the next school year.

Illustrative Case 1: The Buddy Evaluation
Analysis

Bias entered this evaluation process at several points and persisted unchecked. This is a case of the halo effect caused by strong positive and personal feelings on the part of the principal due to his friendship and shared interests with the evaluatee. Even when faced with the judgment of another evaluator, the principal did not adjust his judgment (see P5, Comprehensive Evaluation). This source of bias is far more subtle and therefore common in many school settings because of the close working conditions and interactions of evaluators and evaluatees outside of the evaluation process. In allowing his personal feelings to mask the true performance level of the teacher, the principal actually prevented Mr. van Balen from improving by not holding him accountable for the follow-up recommended by the assistant principal and department chair (see U6, Follow-Up and Professional Development).

While unintentional, masking Mr. van Balen's deficiencies through Mr. Stoner's bias resulted in an unfortunate chain of consequences. The students in this teacher's course did not receive the level of instruction they deserved, resulting in their poor performance on a criterion-referenced test. The lower performance of these students then held consequences on the state accountability model for both the school and district. A final consequence was the lack of development of a teacher who may have benefited from more direct professional development. Mr. Stoner's ratings provided Mr. van Balen with a false sense of accomplishment, preventing him from seeking additional help in improving his skills. Unfortunately, reassigning Mr. van Balen to another course without addressing the deficits in his teaching will not further the overall instructional goals of the school, which should go beyond test score results.

Illustrative Case 2: Avoiding Bias in Difficult Personnel Decisions
Description

A college of education needed to lay off some nontenured faculty due to a drop in enrollment and budget cuts for the next fiscal year. It would have been simpler for department chairs to make recommendations based on their own preferences of who should be retained and who would be let go. The dean, Dean Long, feared that this approach might lower morale among the remaining faculty members. It could have the possibly lasting effect of making it difficult to recruit high quality candidates for future positions should the college acquire a reputation for treating faculty members in an unfair manner.

Dean Long, with input from the department chairs, determined a set of criteria for selecting those faculty members who would be retained based on previously determined expectations for promotion and tenure as stated publicly on the department's Web site and in its policy manual. The performance evaluations of the past year would play a key role in making this determination. These performance evaluations consisted of teaching observations by at least one peer, the department chair or the dean, student surveys, and a review of current academic publications and presentations.

In addition to the performance evaluation, Dean Long and the department chair considered such factors as the person's willingness to contribute to the overall health of the college of education and his or her department through service on committees and advising graduate students. The department chairs and Dean Long met to develop guidelines for determining the expectations for contributing to the growth and climate of the department and college in general, such as commitment to institutional goals, service beyond teaching, collaboration with colleagues, and student advisory activities. While these were not explicit expectations in the performance evaluations, such participation in departmental functions was implicitly understood by all faculty members; and the department chairs invited review of the guidelines by the faculty.

Based on these criteria, several nontenured faculty members were laid off before the start of the new semester. In each case, the results of these multiple data sources were shared with the person, who was given the opportunity to provide data and artifacts in support of his or her progress on the tenure track. The decisions were made by committee and based on clear criteria.

Illustrative Case 2: Avoiding Bias in Difficult Personnel Decisions
Analysis

The necessity to reduce faculty numbers based on funding created urgency in evaluating faculty members to determine those with the greatest ability to contribute to the overall health of the department. In this case, the dean faced a challenging task that could have been fraught with bias had the department chairs been allowed to select those faculty members for nonrenewal of contract. The potential of subjectivity and personal bias resulting from perceptions concerning race, gender, age, national origin, regional accent, and so forth, was a real threat in this process. The guidelines for making the decisions for layoffs were based on clearly defined criteria established for tenure and promotion. The performance evaluations allowed multiple sources of data, further reducing the possible effects of bias. By developing guidelines for behaviors and skills not formally addressed in the performance evaluations but included in expectations for promotion and tenure, additional safeguards were established. Dean Long also encouraged input from the department chairs in applying the criteria and the faculty in reviewing the process. The result of this process was that the college of education was strengthened by a review of all nontenured faculty based on multiple sources of data.

Supporting Documentation

American Educational Research Association, American Psychological Association, & National Council on Measurement in Education. (1999). *Standards for educational and psychological testing.* Washington, DC: American Educational Research Association.

Clift, R. T., Veal, M. L., Holland, P., Johnson, M., & McCarthy, J. (1995). *Collaborative leadership and shared decision making.* New York: Teachers College Press.

Guion, R. M. (1998). *Assessment, measurement, and prediction for personnel decisions.* Mahwah, NJ: Lawrence Erlbaum.

Guthrie, J. W., & Reed, R. J. (1991). *Educational administration and policy: Effective leadership for American schools.* Boston: Allyn & Bacon.

Hoffman, C. C., Nathan, B. R., & Holden, L. M. (1991). A comparison of validation criteria: Objective versus subjective performance measures and self versus supervisor ratings. *Personnel Psychology, 44,* 601–619.

Hoy, W. K., & Tarter, C. J. (1995). *Administrators solving the problems of practice.* Boston: Allyn & Bacon.

Imundo, L. V. (1980). *The effective supervisor's handbook.* New York: AMACOM-American Management Association.

Malos, S. B. (1998). Current legal issues in performance appraisal. In J. W. Smither (Ed.), *Performance appraisal: State of the art in practice* (pp. 49–94). San Francisco: Jossey-Bass.

Manasse, A. L. (1984). *A policymaker's guide to improving conditions for principals' effectiveness.* Alexandria, VA: National Association of State Boards of Education.

Rebore, R. W. (1997). *Personnel administration in education.* Englewood Cliffs, NJ: Prentice Hall.

A9   Analysis of Information

> **STANDARD**   The information collected for personnel evaluations should be analyzed systematically and accurately.

Explanation.   Systematic and accurate analyses of the data resulting from an evaluation help ensure that the resulting judgments are fair, valid, and justified (see A1, Valid Judgments; A10, Justified Conclusions). The analyses of data collected during an evaluation period are as important as the collection process itself. In most personnel evaluation systems, the evaluator collects data using required sources and analyzes it using a rating scale or scoring guide. It is quite possible for an evaluator to adhere to procedures by using the correct forms, meeting all deadlines, and collecting data from all required sources, yet still make errors when analyzing the data and reach an invalid judgment. Such errors in judgment are likely to occur when the evaluator does not understand or misinterprets the scale or scoring guide used in analyses. This is much more likely to occur when the rating scale or scoring guide allows the evaluator to interpret the difference between points on the scale without specifically defining the criteria that would determine where a performance would rate. That is, the more specific and discrete the measures, the more accurate the analysis.

Personnel evaluators often will need to use both quantitative and qualitative analyses. The key distinguishing feature between quantitative and qualitative information resides in the use of numbers and when the numbers are obtained. The numbers used for analysis of quantitative information are set and standardized before collecting the information. In contrast, use of numbers to summarize the analyses of qualitative information takes place after the information is collected and is determined by the evaluator or others responsible for analyzing this qualitative information.

Quantitative analyses involve summarizing numerical data to form summary measures (e.g., total scores on an observation checklist, student achievement gains, number of publications in refereed journals, etc.) that can be interpreted. The numerical data may come from data collection instruments that yield numerical data directly, or they may be derived, as explained later, from a qualitative analysis of nonnumerical information. The quantitative analytic methods chosen should be appropriate for the evaluation question(s) being addressed and the characteristics of the information being analyzed.

Qualitative analyses involve systematically compiling and synthesizing nonnumerical information (written responses, descriptive observations, portfolios, oral presentations). Typically, this involves categorizing the data and then arranging the categories into interpretable themes. The categories can be assigned numerical scores and then analyzed using quantitative analytic procedures, or the interpretation may be carried out descriptively and directly on the categories and themes that have been developed.

The reliability or the consistency of the set of items or tasks used to measure personnel performance needs to be addressed for both quantitative and qualitative analyses (see A6, Reliable Information). For qualitative analyses, attention typically focuses on the consistency of categorization and interpretation by a single rater (intrarater consistency) or by two or more raters who observe or categorize the same performance (interrater consistency).

Just as analyses must meet prescribed guidelines, interpretations and judgments based on analysis results must be made within an accepted frame of reference. Typical frames of reference include the following:

- Performance in relation to prespecified performance standards.
- Performance in relation to amount of improvement or skills learned (see U6, Follow-Up and Professional Development).
- Performance in relation to any contextual variables that must be included in the analysis (see A3, Analysis of Context).

The plan for qualitative and quantitative analyses should be prepared at the time the evaluation plan or process is created. When specific evaluation instruments and procedures are created, adapted, or adopted, the purposes and evaluative judgments to be made are identified. The information to be collected is determined; the rules for scoring, categorizing, and summarizing the information are prescribed; and the range of decisions arising from the evaluation is identified and clearly described.

In addition to being used for constructive evaluations, analyses serve as the basis for important personnel decisions. These decisions require the information that has been gathered over time and across expectations to be summarized for a formative or summative decision, with the type of decision dependent on the purpose of the evaluation. This process calls for weighting individual results and combining them in a way that ensures that each result receives its intended emphasis and impact in the decision to be made. Since these decisions are high stakes for the evaluatee, quantitative and qualitative summaries of the evaluation information should be in accord with each other and not tell a different story.

Rationale.   When performed correctly, qualitative and quantitative analyses of information can provide accurate and valid insights into evaluatee performance over time and meaningfully guide the follow-up professional development, in-service education, and training. Similarly, sound analyses can provide insights into how well data collection procedures are working and how they might be improved. Improper or inadequate analyses lead to distorted interpretations and incorrect decisions about evaluatee performance, resulting in a disservice to these individuals, their students, and the organizations for which the evaluators work.

GUIDELINES

A. Choose analyses that are relevant to the purposes and uses of the evaluation (see P1, Service Orientation; U1, Constructive Orientation; U2, Defined Uses) and to the nature of the data and information to be analyzed.

B. Ensure that the evaluation procedure is both comprehensive (i.e., properly samples the full range of performance expectations) and well balanced (i.e., gives appropriate weight to all of the identified performance expectations; see U4, Explicit Criteria; P5, Comprehensive Evaluation).

C. Prepare a scoring guide that limits subjectivity of the evaluator by defining specific performance indicators for each point in the scale (see A1, Valid Judgments).

D. Before collecting information, explain to the persons being evaluated the criteria and performance standard(s) to be used to judge or categorize their performance (see U4, Explicit Criteria).

E. Combine numerical and descriptive information to produce summaries that provide a comprehensive and comprehensible evaluation of each individual being evaluated.

F. Explain to those with legitimate rights to see and use the results of personnel evaluations the way in which summaries are formulated and interpreted.

G. Do not include the results of nonrelevant constructs in the analysis of personnel information. In situations where attitude, for example, is not a performance expectation, measurements of attitude should not be part of the personnel information collected.

H. Establish procedures to monitor and corroborate results of the analyses such as comparing judgments across evaluators.

I. Communicate to personnel the emphasis (weighting) placed on each aspect of the evaluation and the manner in which this information is combined to produce the final evaluation and resulting decisions.

J. Require concise and clear language for written comments and summaries directly related to the evaluation criteria (see U3, Evaluator Qualifications).

K. Maintain records across time periods and personnel that show the performance characteristics of the evaluation items, tasks, and methods (e.g., standard error of measurement, reliability, dependability, rubrics, intrarater and interrater reliability, revisions made).

L. Ensure that those responsible for analyzing the data have received the appropriate training (see U3, Evaluator Qualifications).

COMMON ERRORS

A. Choosing qualitative or quantitative analysis techniques based only on past approaches, convenience, tradition, or evaluator comfort.

B. Conducting analyses intuitively or based on preconceptions of such factors as race, gender, national origin, regional accent, or age (see A8, Bias Identification and Management).

C. Failing to link the results obtained from the analyses of information to the final evaluative decisions and summaries.

D. Failing to recognize and consider the tendency to overemphasize dramatic or unusual performance when developing summative reports (see A3, Analysis of Context).

Illustrative Case 1: Unequal Weighting of Information
Description

Dr. Siddiqi, an assistant professor of political science, was being considered for promotion and tenure in his department at a large university. In addition to his substantive interests in political science, Dr. Siddiqi had developed some computer applications that were useful in public administration.

This university's primary bases for promotion and tenure were research and publication, although aspects of university service and teaching also were considered. In line with department requirements, Dr. Siddiqi submitted for evaluation his list of publications, teaching appraisals, and service contributions. He included a small number of articles published in established journals in political science, but the majority of the papers were in two journals specializing in computer applications. One of these journals dealt with various fields including public administration. The other was focused on computer applications and did not apply to any specific field. Dr. Siddiqi's teaching reviews from public administration were quite strong, but they were somewhat lower for courses taught in political science. In particular, the scoring of one set of teaching reviews for a large second-year political science class was very low. In addition, Dr. Siddiqi did not have a strong service record within the university, having participated on only two small committees. He had, however, worked extensively on trying to change the manner in which computers were being used by the faculty, but with little to show for his efforts.

The senior faculty members responsible for conducting the evaluation struggled with this case. In particular, the unique nature of Dr. Siddiqi's research interests had resulted in teaching, service, and research that were outside the scope of the department. Given their unfamiliarity with the quality of the journals and unable to comment on the articles themselves, the committee focused on the poor service record and inconsistent teaching in the departmental courses. Based on the analysis of this information, the committee decided not to grant tenure or promotion to Dr. Siddiqi.

Illustrative Case 1: Unequal Weighting of Information
Analysis

The senior faculty members in this case were required to analyze information with which they had little expertise. Given their lack of familiarity with the research and publication record, they gave extra weight to the more familiar teaching and service components of the evaluation. In particular, the committee focused on the negative teaching reviews and the inability of Dr. Siddiqi to enact changes with respect to faculty computer usage.

This unequal weighting of evaluation components occurred unbeknown to Dr. Siddiqi, who could then do nothing to mitigate it. The lack of clear guidelines for rating atypical research such as his had resulted in overreliance on other factors, in particular, negative information that stood out. In the case of work that is unexpectedly beyond the scope of previous evaluations, the evaluators should have informed themselves thoroughly about the quality of Dr. Siddiqi's publications before reaching a conclusion about their merit and worth. Further, they should have investigated factors that may have contributed to the poor teaching review and the lack of success of the computer adoption program (see A3, Analysis of Context).

The data were analyzed only once to address two distinct decisions, resulting in the likelihood that both decisions were poor. Tenure and promotion typically have different criteria and performance expectations. Evaluation information should be analyzed as it specifically relates to each decision. In this case, the committee did not separate the two.

Illustrative Case 2: Analysis Versus Perception
Description

Dr. O'Neil, the superintendent of a small rural school district, became concerned with the lack of consistency among the results of teacher evaluations. In some schools, the results indicated that all teachers were superior in performance, while in others teachers tended to cluster just below the superior level. This tendency for teachers to cluster around certain levels within a school remained steadfast, even when teachers transferred from one school to another. The transferring teacher's evaluation rating appeared to take on the group characteristic. This posed a serious question concerning the reliability of the evaluation reports across schools. It also raised the question of how the principals were using the rating scale to analyze the data.

In conferencing with the director of human resources, Dr. O'Neil found that procedures were being followed in terms of number and dates of classroom observations, postobservation conferences, review of submitted artifacts, and completion of reviews. The issue to Dr. O'Neil seemed to be one of analyses of data collected rather than the data itself.

Dr. O'Neil called a meeting of all principals to discuss their interpretations of the data collected for teacher evaluations. She first asked each principal to identify his or her most marginal teacher. Then she asked the principals to name their most outstanding teacher. She then asked the director of human resources to retrieve those personnel files. When examined, each principal found no significant difference in the rating of either the marginal teacher or the superior teacher. The evaluation reports for each school indicated that the two teachers representing these extreme performance levels were virtually the same.

Dr. O'Neil asked each principal to look deeper in the files to compare the recorded data from observations, artifact reviews, and other sources. On closer examination, each principal realized that the data for the two teachers did not indicate similar ratings and that the ratings tended to be skewed toward a central tendency. In some schools, the principal admitted that it was just easier to assign superior ratings to all teachers than to endure criticism and low morale. Another principal indicated that he really did not analyze the data against the scoring matrix. He simply based his rating on his "overall impression" of the teacher. Still another principal indicated that "no one in my building will ever deserve a superior rating, as everyone needs room for improvement." The director of staff development, who would have liked to have used the teacher evaluation reports to guide his efforts, threw up his hands and began developing a training session for the principals in how to apply the scoring matrix to analyze data accurately.

Illustrative Case 2: Analysis Versus Perception
Analysis

In this case, the superintendent, Dr. O'Neil, was correct in investigating the clustering of scores among the evaluation reports in the district. While this case raises many issues, including bias control (see A8, Bias Identification and Management), most, if not all, of these issues could be addressed through a more reliable process of systematically and accurately analyzing the data collected. The principals basically were ignoring the data and the need to analyze them against a scoring guide. This resulted in evaluation reports based on their own interpretations and perceptions of the teachers. In the absence of analysis, the scores tended to cluster regardless of the actual performance level of the teachers. This created many problems related to the use of invalid judgments. The director of staff development could not use these reports to create appropriate activities. Teachers who received inflated scores were not motivated to seek additional support to improve their practice, thus diminishing their effectiveness in the classroom (see U6, Follow-Up and Professional Development). Additionally, the data analysis shortcomings compromised the school's ability to address staff accountability matters. The director of staff development was correct, however, in trying to remedy this issue with additional training of the principals in the analysis of the data (U3, Evaluator Qualifications).

Supporting Documentation

Elmore, R. F. (2005). Accountable leadership. *The Educational Forum, 69*(2), 134–142.

Frechtling, J., & Sharp, L. (Eds.). (1997, August). *User-friendly handbook for mixed method evaluations.* Washington, DC: Division of Research, Evaluation, and Communication, Directorate for Education and Human Resources, National Science Foundation.

Halverson, R. (2004). Accessing, documenting, and communicating practical wisdom: The phronesis of school leadership practice. *American Journal of Education, 111*(1), 90–121.

Reeves, D. R. (2004). Evaluating administrators. *Educational Leadership, 61*(7), 52–58.

Smith, M. L., & Glass, G. V. (1987). *Research and evaluation in education and the social sciences.* Englewood Cliffs, NJ: Prentice Hall.

A10   Justified Conclusions

> **STANDARD   Conclusions about an evaluatee's performance should be justified explicitly to ensure that evaluatees and others with a legitimate right to know can have confidence in them.**

Explanation.   Evaluators should plan, conduct, and present evaluations in ways that lead to justifiable and understandable conclusions. They should work from clear evaluation purposes, questions, and pertinent information. Their methods should be logically and technically sound. Evaluators should be prepared to share their procedures, findings, and rationale with the evaluatee and others (e.g., supervisors) as relevant and appropriate per confidentiality agreements and regulations. If it becomes necessary to deviate from publicly stated procedures, evaluators should document the deviations and inform evaluatees of the deviation and explain and justify the action. Where possible, conclusions should be accompanied by a discussion of plausible alternative explanations of the findings and why these alternatives were rejected.

Rationale.   The important consequences of personnel evaluations argue strongly for ensuring that decisions are justified appropriately. This justification is important in ensuring the acceptability of evaluation conclusions and the consequences of these conclusions. The acceptability of resulting actions or personnel decisions is heavily dependent on the adequacy of the data and information collected, the procedures employed to collect and analyze data and information, and the persuasiveness of the logical, theoretical, and empirical rationales supporting the conclusions.

GUIDELINES

A. Develop and make available to each employee a written document regarding the individual's evaluation, including purposes, areas covered, sources of information, guides for analyzing data, and guides for making interpretations and drawing conclusions (see A4, Documented Purposes and Procedures).

B. Ensure that evaluators are conducting personnel evaluations in ways consistent with the organization's overall evaluation policies, and periodically remind the evaluators of the policies.

C. Limit conclusions to those situations, periods, contexts, and purposes for which the evaluation findings are applicable.

D. Maintain evaluation materials for review by appropriate individuals (e.g., personnel and human resources department officials, supervisors, administrators; see A7, Systematic Data Control).

COMMON ERRORS

A. Failing to recognize and take into account limitations in the evaluation methods used (see A1, Valid Judgments).

B. Encountering problems when collecting or judging information and interpreting evaluation information (see A5, Defensible Information).

C. Citing an evaluation report as justification for a recommendation or decision when the evaluation lacked sufficient information or was too narrow in scope to support those conclusions.

D. Using an authority base to justify conclusions rather than providing reasons for evaluative judgments.

E. Presenting new reasons for a prior judgment as a means to quell an evaluatee's questions or objections.

Illustrative Case 1: Stakeholders Receive Insufficient Information
Description

Miss Borges, an elementary school teacher, was in her first year of teaching. She had completed her student teaching experience, and this was the first class that was fully hers without the support of a supervising teacher or university supervisor. While some parents had discussed among themselves that Miss Borges was a bit stern and assigned more homework than her predecessor, the parents recognized that their children liked their teacher and were learning what was expected.

Consequently, it came as a great surprise to parents to find at the beginning of the following school year that Miss Borges' contract had not been renewed. No announcement had been made at the end of the previous year that Miss Borges would be leaving. When the parents dropped off their children for the first day of school in the fall, they discovered that a different teacher had been hired, that she had three years of teaching experience, and that she was the daughter of a key benefactor of the school. The principal, when asked why the change in personnel had been made, simply stated, "She was let go as per the terms that her contract allowed."

As the year progressed, parents became suspicious about why the replacement teacher was hired. Their children were not as positive about the replacement teacher as they had been about Miss Borges. Parents became convinced that the teacher replaced Miss Borges simply because of her relationship to the school benefactor and not her qualifications, of which they were not informed. Parents again approached the principal, who refused to provide any additional insight into the issue, citing confidentiality of personnel issues.

Illustrative Case 1: Stakeholders Receive Insufficient Information
Analysis

The principal's vague justification raised more questions than it answered and led to a considerable amount of rumor trading among parents regarding the reasons for Miss Borges's dismissal. As stakeholders in the education of their children, parents had a legitimate need to be informed about teacher evaluations. However, governing union contracts and state laws regarding confidentiality of personnel files may have limited the nature and amount of information the principal could reveal regarding the reasons for dismissal. Nevertheless, hiring the daughter of a key patron of the school as the replacement teacher led to suspicions that the nonrenewal of Miss Borges's contract was not justified.

Although the data and specific findings of personnel evaluations are routinely kept confidential, the evaluation procedures employed and resulting contractual decisions are not confidential. In Miss Borges's case, the contractual decision was made public without corresponding public knowledge of the personnel evaluation processes. In this case, the public's perception was determined not just by the determination to not renew the first contract but by the following decision to hire a person related to a key patron. An explanation of the evaluation process along with assurances of the independence of the process might well have quieted community concerns about patronage rather than evaluative data driving firing and hiring decisions.

Because stakeholder groups (parents, clients, subordinates) often raise questions about the evaluations of employees, the organization should take steps a priori to inform these groups about the evaluation processes for all school employees and any limits on the nature of information that might be revealed. As part of this, the principal should ensure that parents understand their role in teacher evaluations (e.g., how and when their input might be sought) as well as their rights to information about teacher performance.

Illustrative Case 2: Good Intentions Skew Evaluation Results
Description

Ms. Freedman, an administrative specialist working in a support role within a large university, was terminated after numerous complaints from high-level administrators in various departments about the quality of her work. In each instance, the complaint was clearly documented by a letter from the complaining administrator to Ms. Freedman's immediate supervisor. Ms. Freedman, who was past the age of retirement, alleged age discrimination as the primary reason for her dismissal. She noted that her immediate supervisor had reported that she was doing fine work and had awarded her a merit raise. Repeated efforts were made to help Ms. Freedman establish better working habits including attention to accuracy of reports, filing, and communication; however, letters of complaint continued from other administrators. The supervisor had noted these areas for improvement on each evaluation form, had worked with Ms. Freedman to set specific goals for improvement, and had conducted monthly follow-up meetings to discuss these performance areas. Before making the termination decision, the senior administrator in the area asked the immediate supervisor to justify his positive evaluations and found that the major motivation for providing satisfactory ratings in spite of the documented problems and failure of remedial efforts was attributable to the immediate supervisor's desire to be kind and encouraging to Ms. Freedman.

Illustrative Case 2: Good Intentions Skew Evaluation Results
Analysis

In this case, the age discrimination complaint did not prevail, because the organization had documented evidence of poor performance with efforts to remediate unrelated to issues of age. Nevertheless, problems arose because the immediate supervisor told Ms. Freedman that her performance was fine and even rewarded her with a merit raise based on conclusions that could not be justified by the documentation. In this instance, the immediate supervisor was biased in awarding higher evaluation rates and merit pay based on positive personal feelings, which resulted in substandard performance. Better training of supervisors in how to weigh information in an evaluation might have prevented this problem. Further, raises for good performance should be based on specified criteria that are clearly listed in an employee handbook. While the organization prevailed in the lawsuit brought by Ms. Freedman, the university's legal defense may have been less costly or avoided altogether if the overall evaluation had been in line with documented performance problems (see P7, Legal Viability).

Supporting Documentation

Byrd v. Ronayne, 68 FEP Cases 769 (1st Cir. 1995).

Malos, S. B. (1998). Current legal issues in performance appraisal. In J. W. Smither (Ed.), *Performance appraisal: State of the art in practice* (pp. 49–94). San Francisco: Jossey-Bass.

Millman, J., & Darling-Hammond, L. (Eds.). (1990). *The new handbook of teacher evaluation: Assessing elementary and secondary teachers.* Newbury Park, CA: Sage.

A11 Metaevaluation

STANDARD Personnel evaluation systems should be examined systematically at timely intervals using these and other appropriate standards to make necessary revisions.

Explanation. Sound personnel evaluations can guide decisions and future actions designed to further the development of evaluatees, the students they serve, and the institutions in which they are employed. In contrast, flawed personnel evaluations can lead to incorrect decisions and actions that impede or harm the evaluatees and their students. Over time, even the best system of evaluation can become outdated by changed standards of performance or the addition of new evaluators and administrators to the system. Consequently, a regular, systematic review of a personnel evaluation system should be part of the process of maintaining a sound system.

A metaevaluation is an evaluation of an evaluation. Metaevaluation can be expected to facilitate early identification and correction of fatal flaws in a personnel evaluation system, increase the likelihood that the conclusions drawn and the decisions made about individual evaluatees are valid, and enhance the acceptance by evaluatees and their employers. It can support fair treatment of personnel evaluators when evaluatees or others (e.g., parents, other teachers or instructors) affected by the evaluation want to discredit unfavorable results.

Personnel evaluators should create and sustain the expectation that their personnel evaluations and personnel evaluation systems will be evaluated against the standards presented in this book and other professional standards. Reviews should be based on the extent to which the evaluations and systems are (a) designed to meet the institution's needs, (b) being implemented as planned, (c) achieving their purposes, and (d) accepted by evaluatees and users of the evaluation results.

The results of the reviews should be used to increase the effectiveness and fairness of personnel evaluations. If an evaluation is not being implemented as planned, appropriate staff development activities or personnel adjustments must be enacted. If the evaluation or evaluation system is not achieving the purposes for which it was designed, the evaluation or system should be examined and modified appropriately or the initial expectations concerning those purposes should be revised. If a review indicates that changes are necessary, the same concerns for propriety, utility, feasibility, and accuracy will apply to the revised evaluation.

Rationale.   Personnel evaluation is difficult to do well and is subject to mistakes and complaints. Personnel evaluation procedures and systems must be scrutinized regularly to ensure that they yield fair and accurate information that is useful for the specified purposes. Failure to evaluate and ensure the quality of personnel evaluations may lead to incorrect follow-up actions that may be harmful to the person evaluated, the employer, or both. Complaints need to be investigated to ensure fairness, avoid expensive appeals and litigation, and identify components of the evaluation that need to be revised.

Metaevaluations of personnel evaluation procedures are also necessary to keep pace with developments in the personnel evaluation field, changes in working conditions, such as those brought about by technological advances, and changes to the law and other related aspects, such as affirmative action. Accordingly, even when personnel evaluation procedures and systems seem to be working satisfactorily, they should be kept in a state of review, evolution, and improvement.

GUIDELINES

A. Budget sufficient resources and personnel time to review the evaluation process at least annually (see F3, Fiscal Viability).

B. Involve evaluatees, managers, union representatives, and other appropriate stakeholders to review and revise the personnel evaluation system as needed. When feasible, engage an external person to assist in the metaevaluation.

C. Ensure that individuals who conduct a metaevaluation are knowledgeable and skilled in using the standards in this document to evaluate the evaluation system (see U3, Evaluator Qualifications).

D. Investigate whether the evaluation system is having a positive effect on the quantity and quality of instruction and the students served (see U1, Constructive Orientation).

E. Compare the way the evaluation was conducted with the way in which it was planned.

F. Judge the extent to which the evaluation purposes, plans, and procedures meet the standards in this document and other relevant standards.

G. Identify the parts of the evaluation system that require more frequent review or closer monitoring.

H. Periodically survey the staff to obtain their criticisms of and recommendations for revising the evaluation system.

I. Expect that a metaevaluation may be subject to rebuttal and evaluation and, consequently, document the metaevaluation procedures, results, and findings (see A4, Documented Purposes and Procedures).

COMMON ERRORS

A. Assuming that a well-developed and carefully implemented personnel evaluation system will continue to operate as well in succeeding years as it does in the first year.

B. Ignoring metaevaluation findings or otherwise failing to make needed revisions.

C. Waiting to review and examine an evaluation system until complaints are received.

D. Failing to record the full range of information that is pertinent to the evaluation being conducted.

E. Failing to monitor and record the extent to which evaluations fulfill due process requirements.

F. Allowing a poorly performed or politically motivated metaevaluation to destroy a fundamentally sound personnel evaluation system.

G. Revising the evaluation system without first conducting a metaevaluation of the existing system.

Illustrative Case 1: Maintaining a Functional Evaluation System
Description

A school system developed a comprehensive performance-based teacher evaluation system with help from an outside consultant. A steering committee of teachers, administrators, and teacher organization representatives was formed to oversee the development of the system. Considerable time and effort were devoted to planning the system and determining the criteria to be used for evaluation. Each component was pilot tested and then refined. In-service training was provided for teachers and administrators during the year preceding its implementation. When the evaluation system was put into effect, school principals assumed responsibility for the process.

No complaints were filed during the first two years. However, during the third year the teachers' association began receiving an unusual number of complaints from teachers in five schools. The basic concern was that principals in these schools were making fewer and fewer classroom observation visits, and there were cases in which evaluations were based on a single visit. The teachers' professional portfolios, sample lesson materials, and supporting documents were void of comments or any other indication of careful analysis. After several unsatisfactory sessions with the superintendent, the teachers' association complained strongly to the school board. Now, five years after being implemented, the superintendent was instructed to review the evaluation system.

Illustrative Case 1: Maintaining a Functional Evaluation System
Analysis

This well-planned teacher evaluation system initially was implemented quite well. As often occurs, however, over time some of those responsible for conducting evaluations became lax and began taking shortcuts. Although principals were responsible for evaluating their professional staff, evaluation was only one of their many duties, and their evaluations were not monitored. The principals were able to depart significantly from the prescribed procedures, and some of them did so.

Instead of waiting until complaints were received, the superintendent should have instituted a strictly enforced policy of checking at regular intervals (e.g., twice a year) that each principal was making at least the specified minimum number of classroom observation visits and was using the professional portfolios and other materials to support the evaluations. He could have instituted a formative metaevaluation at the time the system was implemented. If this frequent, but relatively easy to accomplish monitoring indicated consistent patterns of noncompliance, the superintendent would have been in a position to take immediate steps to correct the problem. These might have included a comprehensive review of the entire evaluation system, periodic retraining of principals in the use of the system, and the usual appropriate corrective actions directed at the noncomplying principals.

Illustrative Case 2: Establishing a New Evaluation System
Description

Dean Bockstiegel, the dean of the college of education at a large, state-supported university, appointed a faculty committee to make recommendations for a procedure for admission into the undergraduate teacher education program. The faculty appointed to the committee represented each department in the college.

The dean charged the committee to recommend a basic skills test for inclusion in the admissions process and to propose a procedure for validating its use in the program. The committee concentrated on developing content specifications for a basic skills test that would yield reliable information that could be interpreted validly to indicate whether candidates possessed the appropriate entry-level skills. After spending considerable time, the committee found that no commercial tests satisfied their specifications for the basic skills test. Time was running short in the semester and a decision had to be made, so the committee recommended an available off-the-shelf test. They reported that it covered the three required areas of reading, math, and writing, was reasonably priced, and that the price included an administration and scoring service. The test, however, did not fully meet the committee's content specifications. Also, as a result of concentrating on developing the content specifications and looking for a suitable test, they had talked little about other techniques and procedures for making admissions decisions.

The committee recommended to Dean Bockstiegel that students who applied for admittance to the teacher education program should be required to submit the following items before the end of their sophomore year in the university:

- Application form.
- Essay on why they wanted to become a teacher.
- Transcript of their college courses.
- Scores on the basic skills test.
- Three letters of recommendation.

The committee also recommended a pilot year of using the basic skills test, so that student performance could be examined and realistic cut scores could be set. The committee also was concerned about the potential for gender and racial bias inherent in the use of the test and recommended that scores be examined for gender and race bias as a safeguard against it.

Illustrative Case 2: Establishing a New Evaluation System
Analysis

This evaluation system for entry into the teaching profession was sketchy in its design and thus a good candidate for careful monitoring and further development. It needed to be reviewed and pilot tested. The committee was wise to recommend a pilot year because the evaluation design left many decisions to be made. A careful analysis of the design using *The Personnel Evaluation Standards* before and during the pilot year would guide the committee toward a more complete and defensible plan.

The committee also could have used the *Standards for Educational and Psychological Testing* (American Educational Research Association, American Psychological Association, & National Council on Measurement in Education, 1999) to guide its choice of tests and to assess its selection during the pilot year. If the selected basic skills test proved to have serious flaws, the committee should consider alternatives. At the same time, the current evaluation criteria and rubrics for assessing the essay and letters of recommendation should be reexamined.

Once an admissions procedure was fully designed, the committee should involve stakeholders in a review of the system and the results of the pilot test. By opening the system to public review, the committee would demonstrate its openness to revising the procedure before implementation. If major issues emerged, the committee might want to delay implementation another year until the flaws were corrected and agreement achieved.

Once the system was implemented, Dean Bockstiegel should have assigned an individual or a committee to conduct annual reviews. This person or committee could examine the quality and demographics of candidates admitted and those denied admission with the system in effect. The reviewers might give special attention to contextual analysis that could require revision of the system with regard to costs and benefits, fairness in providing minorities access to teacher education, validity and reliability of measurements, administrative complexity, uniformity of use, and ease of central control. In succeeding years, they could look at relationships between the achievement of the students in their university courses and student teaching and the program's admission criteria, thereby collecting further evidence of the validity of the entrance procedure.

Supporting Documentation

Airasian, P. W., & Gullickson, A. (1997). Teacher self-evaluation. In J. H. Stronge (Ed.), *Evaluating teaching: A guide to current thinking and best practice* (pp. 215–247). Thousand Oaks, CA: Corwin Press.

American Educational Research Association, American Psychological Association, & National Council on Measurement in Education. (1999). *Standards for educational and psychological testing.* Washington, DC: American Educational Research Association.

Clift, R. T., Veal, M. L., Holland, P., Johnson, M., & McCarthy, J. (1995). *Collaborative leadership and shared decision making.* New York: Teachers College Press.

Davis, A., Wolf, K., & Borko, H. (1999–2000). Examinee's perceptions of feedback in applied performance testing: The case of the National Board for Professional Teaching Standards. *Educational Assessment, 6,* 97–128.

Guthrie, J. W., & Reed, R. J. (1991). *Educational administration and policy: Effective leadership for American schools.* Boston: Allyn & Bacon.

Howard, B. B., & Harman, S. S. (2007, Spring). An application of the personnel evaluation standards to determine the effectiveness of a system of teacher evaluation. *ERS Spectrum: Journal of Research and Information, 25*(2), 45–55.

Hoy, W. K., & Tarter, C. J. (1995). *Administrators solving the problems of practice.* Boston: Allyn & Bacon.

Iwanicki, E. F. (1990). Teacher evaluation for school improvement. In J. Millman & L. Darling-Hammond (Eds.), *The new handbook of teacher evaluation: Assessing elementary and secondary school teachers* (pp. 158–171). Newbury Park, CA: Sage.

Rebore, R. W. (1997). *Personnel administration in education.* Englewood Cliffs, NJ: Prentice Hall.

Sergiovanni, T. J. (1984). Expanding conceptions of inquiry and practice in supervision and evaluation. *Educational Evaluation and Policy Analysis, 6,* 355–365.

Society for Industrial and Organizational Psychology. (2003). *Principles for the validation and use of personnel selection procedures* (4th ed.). Bowling Green, OH: Author.

Stufflebeam, D. L. (1999a). *Evaluation plans and operations checklist.* Retrieved April 15, 2005, from http://www.wmich.edu/evalctr/checklists/plans_operations.htm

Resource A

JCSEE Statement of Diversity

The Joint Committee on Standards for Educational Evaluation (JCSEE) sets evaluation standards and promotes their use. The mission of the Joint Committee is . . . "to promote concern for evaluations of high quality based on sound evaluation practice and procedures, and to meet existing and emerging needs in the field of evaluation . . ."[3] There is a need to conduct periodic and systematic updates of the standards, to give attention to issues in interpretation and specific applications, to train in the use of standards, and to inform practitioners and users about future developments.[4] The Diversity Committee of the JCSEE attends to the role of diversity in all phases of committee work, with an emphasis on standards development and use.

The Joint Committee recognizes that its evaluation standards are used in many diverse contexts, by national and international organizations and individuals to define, implement, and assess the evaluation process. This statement presents the Joint Committee's views on the role of diversity in the creation, revision, and use of the Standards documents to perform these activities. The purpose of the Diversity Statement is to promote equity and fairness in the development and application of the Standards to the evaluation process.

Diversity is defined by the Joint Committee to include, but is not limited to:

- Culture, race, ethnicity, language, social class, and religion
- Age, experience, gender, sexual orientation
- Abilities of all types, e.g., physical, mental, emotional
- Academic disciplines or areas of study
- Philosophical and epistemological orientation toward evaluation, methodologies, types, and approaches
- The type, focus, and activities of member organization (e.g. schools, governments, public organizations, private sector companies)
- Geography, including all regions of the world[5]

The Joint Committee not only seeks to address diversity in the standards it has developed, but also to achieve diversity in its membership, which is composed of supporting organizations with a focus on evaluation, and in its audiences of users. Within this framework, the Joint Committee acts to:

- Establish a representative community in the development of standards;
- Increase the awareness, understanding, and valuing of diversity by incorporating attention to the cultural competence[6] of evaluators in the Standards documents;
- Increase awareness of the standards' relevance and expand the use of the standards documents among diverse communities; and
- Raise the level and richness of discourse about diversity in the process of educational evaluation through discussions with relevant professional organizations, e.g., ACA, NEA, AEA, AERA, NCME, and other user and participant groups.

In addition to defining the concept of diversity as used by the Joint Committee, the JCSEE will conduct the following activities to ensure that it establishes and maintains diversity in all areas of its work:

- Continuously monitor issues of diversity as they relate to all phases of standards development, review, revision, and use.
- Analyze diversity issues represented in JCSEE standards documents during all scheduled reviews and revisions of such documents.
- Offer training and orientation activities to users of the standards documents to facilitate the recognition and application of principles of equity and fairness in the use of the standards.
- Solicit additional sponsoring organization based, in part, on their ability to broaden the diversity of the Committee in philosophy, theory and methods, use, and membership characteristics.

This statement will be revised as part of the scheduled review and subsequent revision of all standards documents, to maintain a current perspective on diversity within the standards and in the work of the Joint Committee.

Accepted by Joint Committee on Standards
for Educational Evaluation 9/27/07

Resource B

Personnel Evaluations to Which the Standards Apply

Table 1 depicts the general evaluative context within which the standards apply. The table portrays personnel evaluation as an integral part of societal and institutional efforts to prepare, engage, and develop education personnel. The main horizontal dimension includes three systems called Preparation (e.g., teacher education), Practice (e.g., school teaching), and Continuing Education (e.g., study leaves and in-service education). The vertical dimension divides each system into Entry activities (e.g., selection of students for a principalship program), Participation (e.g., tenure reviews), and Exit (e.g., reduction in force decisions). The second horizontal dimension denotes Evaluations and Decisions that are involved in the Entry, Participation, and Exit stages of each personnel system.

The entries in the cells of the matrix reveal that a wide range of evaluations and decisions is involved in education personnel work. Moreover, the evaluations are of three different types. Some of them are program evaluations, for example, evaluations of recruitment programs. Others, such as evaluations of students' mastery of college courses, are student evaluations. Finally, the great majority of the evaluations identified in the matrix fit the common view of personnel evaluation, that is, assessments of the qualifications and performance of individual educators for certification, selection, tenure, staff development, and promotion.

The full range of evaluations depicted in the matrix are important to the effective staffing of education institutions, and all such evaluations should adhere to appropriate professional standards. Professional standards for program evaluations have existed for at least three decades, but the 1988 personnel evaluation standards were the first to be focused specifically on education personnel evaluations.

This document is aimed at providing the standards needed to judge and improve the education personnel evaluations denoted in the matrix. Those evaluations and decisions on which these standards are primarily focused are provided in bold type. It is interesting and important that given categories of evaluation often provide information useful in making different decisions. This is especially the case for performance reviews that generate information for decisions about tenure, merit pay, promotion, and awards, as well as counseling for staff development. The standards require all parties to an evaluation to enter into the process with a clear idea of how the information to be collected will be used.

In the area of Preparation, the evaluations and decisions of most interest in these standards are those associated with selection of members of the profession. First, there are evaluations of applicants for particular preparation programs, such as teacher, counselor, and administrator education programs. A prime example is the system of assessment centers operated by the National Association of Secondary School Principals to assist in choosing and recruiting persons to enter graduate programs leading to employment as a high school principal. The second type of evaluation serving Preparation is done in the Exit stage to determine certification or licensing to practice. Evaluations of qualifications to practice are the evaluative bridge from the Preparations system to the Practice system.

As denoted by the bold entries under the Practice column, these standards apply most heavily to an institution's various evaluations of its staff members. Within the Entry stage, the standards apply most to evaluations of applicants for positions in teaching, administration, and other related roles. In the Participation stage of Practice, the standards concentrate on evaluations of job assignments and on performance reviews. The performance reviews are the most complex type of evaluation being addressed, since they provide information for such uses as deciding whether or not to continue probation; deciding about tenure, promotion, merit pay, honors, or recertification; and guidance on counseling for staff development. In the Exit stage of the Practice system, the standards are addressed to evaluations used to help decide on reduction in force, termination for cause, or withdrawal of licenses or certificates.

As seen under the third column, these standards are not addressed directly to evaluations in Continuing Education; the ones receiving primary attention in this realm are assessments of an individual staff member's needs or special qualifications to engage in some type of continuing education.

The evaluations and decisions identified in Table 1 are generic, and the Joint Committee intends that the standards be applied broadly. Education institutions of all types share a need for sound evaluations for entering professional training, certifying competence, defining roles within the institution, selecting from job applicants, monitoring and providing feedback about performance, counseling for staff development, determining merit awards, and making decisions about tenure, promotion, and termination.

Table 1 Types of Evaluations and Decisions Involved in Preparing, Deploying, and Developing Professional Educators

Stages of Involvement	Educational Personnel Systems					
	PREPARATION		PRACTICE		CONTINUING EDUCATION	
	Evaluations	*Decisions*	*Evaluations*	*Decisions*	*Evaluations*	*Decisions*
ENTRY	Evaluations of supply and demand	Assigning priorities and allocating funds to specialized training programs	Evaluations of staffing needs	Definitions of jobs / Decisions to fill certain job vacancies	Correlated assessments of institutional and staff needs	Deciding on continuing education offerings/ opportunities
	Evaluations of recruitment programs	Determining how the programs should be changed or strengthened	Evaluations of recruitment programs	Determining how the programs should be changed or strengthened	***Assessments of the needs and achievements of individual staff members**	***Deciding whether to approve applications for study leaves, sabbatical leaves, and for special grants**
	*Assessments of applicants	***Selection of students**	***Evaluations of applicants**	***Selection of staff members**		
PARTICIPATION	Intake evaluations	Determining student programs	***Correlated evaluations of jobs and incumbents' qualifications**	***Updating of job definitions**	Intake evaluations	Designing individualized continuing education programs

(Continued)

Table 1 (Continued)

	Educational Personnel Systems					
	PREPARATION		PRACTICE		CONTINUING EDUCATION	
Stages of Involvement	Evaluations	Decisions	Evaluations	Decisions	Evaluations	Decisions
	Evaluations of students' mastery of course requirements	Assigning course grades	**Reviews of job performance and special achievements**	***Deciding whether to remove or continue probationary status or to terminate *Tenure *Promotion *Merit Pay *Counseling for staff development *Honors (awards) *Recertification**	Progress reviews	Providing feedback to guide the learning process
	Cumulative progress reviews	Counseling for remediation Revising program plans Referrals to a termination review	Grievance hearings	Rulings on the grievances		

Educational Personnel Systems

Stages of Involvement	PREPARATION		PRACTICE		CONTINUING EDUCATION	
	Evaluations	*Decisions*	*Evaluations*	*Decisions*	*Evaluations*	*Decisions*
EXIT	Final evaluations of students' fulfillment of their programs	Graduation decisions	***Correlated evaluations of finances, staffing needs, seniority of present staff, and options for downsizing**	***Reduction in force decisions**	Evaluations of participants' achievements in continuing education experiences	Deciding whether given applicants should be rewarded with future grants and/or leaves
	*Evaluations of qualifications to practice given educational roles	***Certification *Licensing**	***Evaluations of performance and/or investigations of charges**	***Deciding whether to terminate *Deciding whether to withdraw licenses or certificates**	Evaluations of qualifications to practice given educational roles	Certification Licensing New assignments

*These are evaluations and associated decisions that are of most concern in the evaluation of standards.

Resource C

The Support Groups

The Joint Committee on Standards for Educational Evaluation (Joint Committee) is a self-standing, nonprofit organization dedicated to the development and dissemination of evaluation standards to serve education. Initially created in 1975 as a joint committee of three organizations (American Educational Research Association, National Council on Measurement in Education, and American Psychological Association), the founders quickly recognized the need to include a much larger group of researchers and practitioners. Today 17 organizations sponsor the work of the Joint Committee.

Developing standards follows a rigorous multistep process that involves members of these sponsoring organizations and professional educators, researchers, and practitioners around the globe. This process includes an initial review of literature, drafting of standards, review of the draft standards by national and international panels of reviewers, revision of the draft based on the panel reviews, field trials of the draft standards, and national hearings to both inform individuals and organizations about the standards and gain feedback to improve the draft materials. At the end of the process, the standards are "published" on the Web for final review and feedback. At this time a validation panel, independent of the Joint Committee, completes its review of the development process and the standards and presents its findings to the Joint Committee. The Joint Committee can choose to approve the standards based on the work to that point or can require additional steps to be taken. In the case of these personnel evaluation standards, the Joint Committee extended the review time by several months to obtain more input, and several standards were revised based on the analysis provided by the validation panel. In September 2007, these standards were approved by the Joint Committee. Following that approval the standards were submitted to the American National Standards Institute for certification as an American National Standard. American National Standard approval was received in February 2008.

THE SPONSORING ORGANIZATIONS

American Association of School Administrators
American Counseling Association
American Educational Research Association
American Evaluation Association
American Indian Higher Education Consortium
American Psychological Association
Canadian Evaluation Society
Canadian Society for the Study of Education
Consortium for Research and Accountability on Teacher Evaluation
Council of Chief State School Officers
National Association of Elementary School Principals
National Association of Secondary School Principals
National Association of School Psychologists
National Council on Measurement in Education
National Education Association
National Legislative Program Evaluation Society

NATIONAL REVIEW PANEL

R. J. Alfonso, East Tennessee State University
Stefanie Anderson, Centers for Disease Control and Prevention
Richard Antes, Indiana State University
Jan Beatty, West Des Moines (IA) Community Schools
Yvonne Belanger, Duke University
Barbara Bichelmeyer, Indiana University
Katrina Bledsoe, Claremont Graduate University
Ron Bonnstetter, University of Nebraska
Walter Borman, University of South Florida
Teresa Boyd, University of Connecticut
Tony Brads, Indiana State University
E. P. Braverman, AT&T
Debbie Breaux, Raleigh, NC
Peter Bresciani, Regina, SK, Canada, Catholic Schools
William Byham, Development Dimensions International
Marianne Cinaglia, Rowan University, Glassboro, NJ
Susan Colby, Appalachian State University
Virginia Collier, Texas A&M
A. C. Conley, University of California, Santa Barbara
Margaret Curtis, National Science Foundation
D. R. Davis, Georgia State University
Patti Davis-Tussey, Cave Creek (AZ) Unified School District
Marguerita DeSander, Lincoln County School, North Carolina

Emily Dickinson University of South Florida
Sandra Enger, University of Alabama, Huntsville
R. Joel Farrell II, Faulkner University, Montgomery, AL
Paul Favaro, Peel Catholic District School Board, Mississauga, Ontario, Canada
Richard Fossey, University of Houston
Russell French, University of Tennessee, Knoxville
Amy Germuth, Compass Consulting Group, Durham, NC
Kate Goddard, ORC Macro, Calverton, MD
Jacqueline Graham, Data Recognition Corporation, Maple Grove, MN
Donald Haefele, Ohio State University
Carine Strebel Halpern, University of Central Florida
Dean Halverson, Western Illinois University
Elaine Hampton, University of Texas at El Paso
Fenna Hanes, New England Board of Higher Education
Kelly Hannum, Center for Creative Leadership, Greensboro, NC
Benjamin Harris, University of Texas, Austin
Cheryl Harris, SEDL, Austin, TX
Micki Harris, Spokane (MO) R-7 Public Schools
Sarah Heinemeier, Compass Consulting Group, Durham, NC
Guy Hermann, Stuart R. Paddock School, Palatine, IL
James Horn, Monmouth University, West Long Beach, NJ
Sarah Hough, University of California, Santa Barbara
Marthe Hurteau, Piedmont, Quebec, Canada
Melanie Hwalek, SPEC Associates, Detroit, MI
James Impara, University of Nebraska
Edward Iwanicki, University of Connecticut
Trav Johnson, Brigham Young University
Ivan Katz, Eldred (NY) Central School District
Zach Kelehear, University of Alabama
Jacqueline Kelleher, University of Connecticut
James King (contact information not available)
Nicki King (contact information not available)
Natalie Kishchuk, Kirkland, Quebec, Canada
Karen Korabik, University of Guelph
Brett Kramer, Mariana (AZ) Unified School District
Amy Kruppe, Morton Grove, IL
Frank Landy, Landy Litigation Support Group, New York
Carol Langdon, Phi Delta Kappa International
Kenneth Leithwood, University of Toronto
Jim Longin, Sekiu, WA
Goldie MacDonald, Centers for Disease Control and Prevention
Peter Madonia, Southern Connecticut State University
Tim Markley, White Mountains (NH) Regional School District
Thomas McGreal, University of Illinois
Larry McKenzie, York, SC
Tom McKlin, Georgia Tech

Daphne Minner, Education Development Center, Inc., Newton, MA
Charles Mitsakos, Rivier College, Nashua, NH
Allan Mohrman, University of Southern California
Lynn Montoya, Portland (OR) Community College
Diane Murphy, Connecticut State Department of Education
Joseph Murphy, The Ohio State University
Howard Mzumara, Indiana University-Purdue University at Indianapolis
Rena Faye Norby, Mercer University, GA
George Olson, Appalachian State University
Geoffrey Palmer, University of Virginia
Linde Paule, Portland, OR
Raymond Pecheone, Stanford University
Kenneth Peterson, Portland State University
Nancy Petersen, ACT, Inc., Iowa City, IA
Barbara Plake, University of Nebraska
W. James Popham, UCLA
Susan Ragan, Maryland Virtual High School
Kathy Rhoades, North Carolina Department of Health and Human Services
Pete Rubba, Penn State University
Joseph Rudnicki, Sunnyvale (CA) School District
Iris Saltiel, Troy State University, Phenix City, AL
Barbara Sandall, Western Illinois University
David Sawyer, Tulsa (OK) Public Schools
Maria Schefter, University of Guam
Regina Schoenfeld-Tacher, Colorado State University
Michael Scriven, Claremont Graduate School
T. J. Sergiovanni, Trinity University
Neil Shipman, Germantown, MD
E. Marie Steichen, Kansas State University
Steven Stemler, Yale University
Jennifer Stepanek, Northwest Regional Educational Laboratory
K. D. Strike, Cornell University
Ginger Studebaker, North Spencer County School Corporation, IN
Regina Tacher, Ft. Collins, CO
Nancy Tippins, GTE Service Corporation, Irving, TX
William Trost, Shaker Heights (OH) City School District
Pamela Tucker, University of Virginia
Pattie Tucker, Centers for Disease Control and Prevention
Barbara Turnbull, Rutgers University
James P. Van Haneghan, University of South Alabama
Norma Velasquez-Bryant, University of Nevada, Reno
Marcia Weinhold, Purdue University-Calumet
Karen Wetherill, University of North Carolina, Wilmington
Jennifer Williams, J. E. Williams & Associates, Cincinnati, OH
Bert Wiser, Worthington, OH, City Schools
Cynthia Zengler, Ohio Department of Education

VALIDATION PANEL

Chair

> Robert Rodosky, Jefferson County (KY) Public Schools

Members

> Jeff Berger, Iowa Department of Education
> Cynthia Carver, Michigan State University
> Robert Joyce, University of North Carolina, Chapel Hill
> Deniz Ones, University of Minnesota
> Pamela Tucker, University of Virginia

FIELD-TEST PARTICIPANTS

> Ginger Studebaker, Indiana
> Arlen R. Gullickson, Western Michigan University
> Jefferson County (KY) Schools, Louisville
> Kalamazoo (MI) Public Schools
> Mary Ramlow, Western Michigan University
> Sally Veeder, Western Michigan University
> Worthington (OH) City Schools
> Barbara Wygant, Western Michigan University
> Pamela Zeller, Western Michigan University

NATIONAL HEARINGS PARTICIPANTS

> North Carolina Association of Researchers in Education Annual Meeting,
>   Chapel Hill, April 2005
> Seven participants (central office administrators, university professors, K–12
>   administrators, researchers, consultants)
> CREATE National Evaluation Institute, Memphis, July 2005
> Ten participants representing higher education and K–12
> American Evaluation Association/Canadian Evaluation Society Joint
>   Conference, Toronto, 2005
> Katrina Bledsoe, Claremont Graduate University
> Martha Forero-Wayne (contact information not available)
> Chuck Fuller, Atlanta, GA
> Trav Johnson, Brigham Young University
> Gwen Keith, Regina, SK, Canada, Catholic Schools
> Joan Kruger, Canadian Evaluation Society
> Emiel Owens, Texas Southern University
> Darlene Thurston, Jackson (MS) State University
> Donald Yarbrough, University of Iowa
> SERVE Regional Forum, Savannah, GA, November 2005
> Twelve participants representing K–12 teachers and administrators

EDITORIAL ASSISTANCE

Tish Davidson, Corwin Press
Sally Veeder, Western Michigan University Evaluation Center

WORD PROCESSING AND FORMATTING

Christine Hummel, Western Michigan University Evaluation Center

Notes

1. The first edition of *The Personnel Evaluation Standards* contained 21 standards.

2. Dr. McGinnis appealed her decision and subsequently was granted tenure and promotion on the basis that while the department chair used what was now considered the norm for tenure and promotion, the faculty member had indeed met the criteria as set out in the faculty handbook.

3. Joint Committee on Standards for Educational Evaluation, *Governing Principles* (1980), p. 4 [Electronic Version]. Retrieved February 21, 2007, from Western Michigan University, The Evaluation Center Web site: http://www.wmich.edu/evalctr/jc/

4. Joint Committee on Standards for Educational Evaluation, *Governing Principles* (1980), p. 2 [Electronic Version]. Retrieved February 21, 2007, from Western Michigan University, The Evaluation Center Web site: http://www.wmich.edu/evalctr/jc/

5. While the Standards are utilized worldwide, membership is concentrated in the United States and Canada.

6. "To ensure recognition, accurate interpretation and respect for diversity, evaluators should ensure that the members of the evaluation team collectively demonstrate cultural competence. Cultural competence would be reflected in evaluators seeking awareness of their own culturally-based assumptions, their understanding of the worldviews of culturally-different participants and stakeholders in the evaluation, and the use of appropriate evaluation strategies and skills in working with culturally different groups. Diversity may be in terms of race, ethnicity, gender, religion, socio-economics, or other factors pertinent to the evaluation context" (American Evaluation Association, *Guiding Principles for Evaluators*, n.d. [Electronic Version]. Retrieved February 21, 2007, from http://www.eval.org/Publications/GuidingPrinciples.asp).

Glossary

The terms in this glossary are defined as they are used in this volume, in the context of evaluation. In other settings, a number of them may have different or less specialized definitions.

Accuracy   The extent to which an evaluation conveys technically adequate information about the performance and qualifications of an evaluatee.

Administration   Management of an organization through such actions as planning, staffing, motivating, directing, controlling, communicating, and evaluating.

Assessment   The act of rating or describing an evaluatee on some variable of interest.

Assessment procedure   Any method used to rate or describe some characteristic of an evaluatee.

Attribute   A characteristic or quality seen as possessed by a person.

Audiences   Those persons to be guided by the results of an evaluation in making decisions and all others with a legitimate stake in evaluation results and findings.

Audit (of an evaluation)   An independent examination and verification of the quality of an evaluation plan, the adequacy of its implementation, the accuracy of results, and the validity of conclusions (see metaevaluation).

Behavior   An individual's specific, observable actions in response to internal and external stimuli.

Benefit   An advantageous consequence of a program or action.

Bias   A particular tendency or inclination, prejudice, preformed judgment. Any systematic influence on measures or on statistical results irrelevant to the purpose of measurement (compare with random error).

Client   The individual, group, or organization that employs the evaluator; persons who receive or benefit from education services, such as students and parents.

Competency   A skill, knowledge, or experience that is suitable or sufficient for some purpose.

Conclusions (of an evaluation)   Final judgments and recommendations resulting from the assessment information collected about an evaluatee.

Conflict of interest   A situation in which an evaluator's private interests affect his or her evaluative actions or in which the evaluative actions might affect private interests.

Contamination   Any systematic influence on measures or on statistical results irrelevant to the purpose of measurement; any bias or error.

Context   The set of circumstances or acts that surround and may affect a particular job situation or person's performance.

Contextual variables   Indicators or dimensions that are useful in describing the facts or circumstances that surround a particular job situation and influence an evaluatee's performance in that situation.

Contract   A written or oral agreement between any two parties that describes a mutual understanding of expectations and responsibilities to both parties.

Correlation   The degree to which two or more sets of measurements vary together; a positive correlation exists when high values on one scale are associated with high values on another; a negative correlation exists when high values on one scale are associated with low values on another.

Cost-effectiveness   The extent to which a program, project, or instructional material or procedure produces equal or better results than competitors in time, effort, and resources; or the extent to which a program, project, or instructional method produces the same results as competitors but is less costly.

Credibility   Believability or confidence by virtue of being trustworthy and possessing pertinent knowledge, skills, and experience.

Criterion   A measure of job performance, such as productivity, accident rate, absenteeism, reject rate, or training score. It also includes subjective measures such as supervisory ratings.

Cross-validation   A process by which a finding obtained by a process for one sample of a population is confirmed by findings obtained by applying the same process to another sample from the same population.

Cultural competence   The knowledge, skill, or experience with culturally diverse populations. It is demonstrated in evaluators seeking awareness of their own culturally based assumptions, their understanding of the worldviews of culturally different participants and stakeholders in an evaluation, and the use of appropriate evaluation strategies and skills in working with culturally different groups.

Cultural diversity   Various or different cultural characteristics such as race, ethnicity, gender, religion, socioeconomics, or other factors pertinent to the evaluation context.

Data   Evidence, in either numerical or narrative form, gathered during the course of an evaluation that serves as the basis for information, discussion, and inference.

Data access   The extent and conditions under which an evaluator and other specified individuals will be permitted to obtain or view data during or from an evaluation.

Data analysis   The process of organizing, summarizing, and interpreting numerical, narrative, or artifact data, so that the results can be interpreted validly and used to arrive at answers to questions.

Data collection procedures   The steps used to obtain quantitative or qualitative information about the qualifications or performance of an individual.

Dependability   A measure of how consistent the results obtained in an assessment are in a criterion-referenced evaluation; consistency of decisions in relation to prespecified standards (compare with reliability).

Design (evaluation)   A representation of the set of decisions that determine how an evaluation is to be conducted. These decisions may involve any one or more of the following: identifying the purposes and uses of the information, developing or selecting assessment methods, collecting evaluative information, judging and scoring evaluatee performance, summarizing and interpreting results, reporting evaluation findings, and following up.

Evaluatee   The person whose qualifications or performance is evaluated.

Evaluation   Systematic investigation of the worth or merit of an evaluatee's qualifications or performance in a given role in relation to a set of expectations or standards of performance.

Evaluation system   A structure and set of procedures by which an institution initiates, designs, implements, and uses evaluations of its personnel.

Evaluator   Anyone who accepts and executes responsibility for planning, conducting, and reporting evaluations.

External evaluation   Evaluation conducted by an evaluator from outside the organization employing the persons to be evaluated (compare with internal evaluation).

Extrapolate   A prediction or estimate based on past experience or known data. The statistical definition is to estimate the value of a variable outside the observed range.

Feasibility   The extent to which an evaluation is appropriate and practical for implementation.

Field test   The study of a program, project, procedure, or instructional material under various conditions of intended use. Field tests may range from preliminary primitive investigations to full-scale summative studies.

Fiscal viability   The requirement that adequate time and resources be provided for evaluation activities.

Formative evaluation   Evaluation conducted while an evaluatee is performing; designed and used to promote growth and improvement in the evaluatee's performance or in a program's development (compare with summative evaluation).

Generalizability   The extent to which evaluative information collected in one setting can be used to reach a valid prediction of its utility and reliability in other settings.

Incentive pay   Compensation paid to employees for doing different *kinds* or *amounts* of work. Incentive pay plans may open new opportunities for professional development, or they may increase the volume of work tasks. Although some such plans require that employees be judged meritorious to participate, incentive pay differs from merit pay.

Instrument   An assessment device adopted, adapted, or constructed for the purposes of an evaluation.

Internal evaluation   Evaluation conducted by a person from within the organization in which the evaluation is occurring (compare with external evaluation).

Internal referent   A body of persons within an evaluatee's work group environment with whom he or she interacts because of similar interests, complementary skills, common professional allegiances, collaborative assignments, and so forth.

Job analysis   A method of analyzing jobs in terms of the tasks performed, the performance standards and training content, and the required knowledge, skills, and abilities.

Legal viability   The requirement that evaluation activities should take into account the legal provisions pertaining to local, state, and federal laws and in reference to the context in which the evaluation takes place.

Longevity pay   Pay increases based solely on accrued length of service.

Master teacher   A teacher recognized for superior ability and performance. Master teacher plans generally enable career advancement and development through the assignment of new duties, such as curriculum development, supervision and coaching of new faculty members, teaching special classes for gifted students, or other leadership roles.

Merit   Excellence as assessed by intrinsic qualities or performance.

Merit pay   Monetary compensation in the form of higher wages or salaries awarded to deserving employees—who may have the same job descriptions and responsibilities as other employees not receiving merit pay—on the basis of verifiable superiority in the *quality* of the work performance. The differences in compensation, which may be one-time bonuses or permanent pay increases, are usually based on annual systematic evaluations of employee performance.

Metaevaluation   An evaluation of an evaluation.

Objective evaluation   Evaluation carried out in a way that minimizes random error or bias due to the predilections of the evaluator.

Performance standard   A formal specification of the expected level of achievement in fulfilling employment requirements (e.g., teacher duties).

Personnel evaluation   The systematic assessment of a person's performance or qualifications in relation to a professional role and some specified, defensible institutional purpose.

Personnel evaluation system   All of the rules, procedures, assignments, and other elements that an institution uses to evaluate its personnel.

Pilot test   A brief, simplified preliminary trial study designed to learn whether a proposed project or program seems likely to yield valuable results.

Political viability   The requirement that evaluation activities should be planned, conducted, reported, and followed up in ways that are responsive to stakeholders' expectations, questions, and concerns.

Propriety   The extent to which an evaluation will be conducted legally, ethically, and with due regard for the welfare of those involved in an evaluation and those affected by its results.

Qualitative information   Information presented or summarized in narrative form.

Quantitative information   Information presented or summarized in numerical form.

Random error   Error that occurs by chance; nonsystematic or unpredictable influence on measures irrelevant to the purpose of measurement (compare with bias).

Reliability   A measure of how consistent the results obtained in an assessment are in a norm-referenced evaluation situation; consistency of an evaluatee's ranking within a group of evaluatees against which the evaluatee is being compared (compare with dependability).

Replication   Repetition of a study intended to investigate the generalizability or stability of the results.

Role definition   Specification of the behavior that is characteristic and expected of the occupant of a defined position in a group.

Sample   A representative part of a larger whole (e.g., observing a teacher during instruction on a few occasions during the school year as a sample of the teacher's classroom practices)

School district   A legally constituted collection of institutions within defined geographic or philosophical boundaries that collaborate in teaching persons under college age.

Score   Any specific value in a range of possible values describing the assessment of an individual.

Self-report instrument   A device in which persons make and report judgments about their own performance.

Standard   A principle commonly agreed to by those who conduct and use evaluation to measure the value or quality of something.

Standardized test   Assessment methods, either criterion- or norm-referenced, designed to be administered, scored, and interpreted in the same way regardless of when, where, or by whom they are administered.

Summative evaluation   An evaluation designed to present conclusions about the merit or worth of a person's performance (compare with formative evaluation).

Utility   The extent to which an evaluation serves the relevant information needs of evaluatees and other users.

Validity   The degree to which inferences drawn about an evaluatee's qualifications or performance from the results of the evaluation methods used are correct, trustworthy, and appropriate for making decisions about the evaluatee.

References

Abadiano, H. R., & Turner, J. (2004). Professional development: What works? *The New England Reading Association Journal, 40*(2), 87–91.

Airasian, P. W., & Gullickson, A. (1994). Teacher self-assessment: Potential and barriers. *Kappa Delta Pi Record, 31*(1), 6–9.

Airasian, P. W., & Gullickson, A. (1997). Teacher self-evaluation. In J. H. Stronge (Ed.), *Evaluating teaching: A guide to current thinking and best practice* (pp. 215–247). Thousand Oaks, CA: Corwin Press.

American Association of School Administrators. (1978). *Standards for school personnel administration* (3rd ed.). Seven Hills, OH: Author.

American Educational Research Association, American Psychological Association, & National Council on Measurement in Education. (1999). *Standards for educational and psychological testing.* Washington, DC: American Educational Research Association.

American Evaluation Association. (2004). *Guiding principles.* Retrieved January 14, 2005, from http://www.eval.org/Publications/GuidingPrinciples.asp

American Federation of Teachers. (2003). *Where we stand: Teacher quality.* Washington, DC: Author.

American National Standards Institute. (2008, January). *Essential requirements: Due process requirements for American National Standards.* New York: Author.

American Psychological Association, Division 14. (1980). *Principles for the validation and use of personnel selection procedures.* Washington, DC: Author.

Anderson, L., & Wilson, S. (1997). Critical incident technique. In D. L. Whetzel & G. R. Wheaton (Eds.), *Applied measurement methods in industrial psychology* (pp. 89–112). Palo Alto, CA: Davies-Black Publishing.

Andrews, H. A. (1985). *Evaluating for excellence.* Stillwater, OK: New Forums Press.

Andrews, H. A. (1995). *Teachers can be fired.* Peru, IL: Catfeet Press.

Athanases, S. (1994). Teachers' reports of the effects of preparing portfolios of literacy instruction. *The Elementary School Journal, 94,* 421-439.

Atwater, L. E. (1998). The advantages and pitfalls of self-assessment in organizations. In J. W. Smither (Ed.), *Performance appraisal: State of the art in practice* (pp. 331–369). San Francisco: Jossey-Bass.

Avraamidou, L. (2003). Exploring the influence of web-based portfolio development on learning to teach elementary science. *Journal of Technology and Teacher Education, 11*(3), 415–442.

Bennett, D. E. (2000/2001). Electronic educational data security; system analysis and teacher training. *Journal of Educational Technology Systems, 29*(1), 3–20.

Bernardin, H. J., & Beatty, R. W. (1984). *Performance appraisal: Assessing human behavior at work.* Boston: Kent.

Bernardin, H. J., Hagan, C. M., Kane, J. S., & Villanova, P. (1998). Effective performance management: A focus on precision, customers, and situational constraints. In J. W. Smither (Ed.), *Performance appraisal: State of the art in practice* (pp. 3–48). San Francisco: Jossey-Bass.

Bernstein, E. (2004). What teacher evaluation should know and be able to do. *NASSP Bulletin, 88,* 80–88.

Brennan, R. L. (2001). *Generalizability theory.* New York: Springer-Verlag.

Brennan, R. L., & Johnson, E. G. (1995). Generalizability of performance assessments. *Educational Measurement: Issues and Practice, 14*(4), 9–12.

Bridges, E. M. (1985). *The incompetent teacher: The challenge and the response.* Philadelphia: Falmer Press.

Bridges, E. M. (1992). *The incompetent teacher: Managerial responses.* Washington, DC: Falmer Press.

Bunting, C. E. (1998). Self-directed teacher growth: Helping it happen in schools. *Schools in the Middle, 8*(1), 21–23.

Burmeister, L., & Hensley, P. A. (2004). It's all about relationships. *Leadership, 34*(1), 30–31.

Byrd v. Ronayne, 68 FEP Cases 769 (1st Cir. 1995).

Cizek, G. J. (Ed.). (2001). *Setting performance standards: Concepts, methods, and perspectives.* Mahwah, NJ: Lawrence Erlbaum.

Clift, R. T., Veal, M. L., Holland, P., Johnson, M., & McCarthy, J. (1995). *Collaborative leadership and shared decision making.* New York: Teachers College Press.

Coker, H., Medley, D., & Soar, R. (1980). How valid are expert opinions about effective teaching? *Phi Delta Kappan, 62,* 131–134.

Cooper, B. S., Ehrensal, P. A., & Bromme, M. (2005). School-level politics and professional development: Traps in evaluating the quality of practicing teachers. *Educational Policy, 19*(1), 112–125.

Costa, E. W., II. (2004). Performance-based evaluation for superintendents. *School Administrator, 61*(9), 14–16, 18.

Council of Chief State School Officers. (1996). *Interstate school leaders licensure consortium: Standards for school leaders.* Washington, DC: Author.

Dalessio, A. T. (1998). Using multisource feedback for employee development and personnel decisions. In J. W. Smither (Ed.), *Performance appraisal: State of the art in practice* (pp. 278–330). San Francisco: Jossey-Bass.

Darling-Hammond, L. (2003). Keeping good teachers. *Educational Leadership, 60*(8), 76–77.

Darling-Hammond, L., & Youngs, P. (2002). Defining "high qualified teachers": What does "scientifically-based research" actually tell us? *Educational Researcher, 31*(9), 13–25.

Davis, A., Wolf, K., & Borko, H. (1999-2000). Examinee's perceptions of feedback in applied performance testing: The case of the National Board for Professional Teaching Standards. *Educational Assessment, 6,* 97–128.

Deojay, T. R., & Novak, D. S. (2004). Blended data. *Journal of Staff Development, 25*(1), 32–36.

Dufour, R. (2000). School leaders as staff developers: The key to sustained school improvement. *Catalyst for Change, 29*(3), 13–15.

Duke, D. L. (1990). Developing teacher evaluation systems that promote professional growth. *Journal of Personnel Evaluation in Education, 4,* 131–144.

Educational Testing Service. (1998). *The Praxis series.* Princeton, NJ: Author.

Elmore, R. F. (2005). Accountable leadership. *The Educational Forum, 69*(2), 134–142.

Feldt, L. S., & Brennan, R. L. (1989). Reliability. In R. L. Linn (Ed.), *Educational measurement* (3rd ed., pp. 105–146). New York: American Council on Education.

Fenstermacher, G. D., & Richardson, V. (2005). On making determinations of quality in teaching. *Teachers College Record, 107*(1), 186–212.

Frechtling, J., & Sharp, L. (Eds.). (1997, August). *User-friendly handbook for mixed method evaluations.* Washington, DC: Division of Research, Evaluation, and Communication, Directorate for Education and Human Resources, National Science Foundation.

Fredricks, J. G. (2001). Why teachers leave. *The Education Digest, 66*(8), 46–48.

French-Lazovik, G. (Ed.). (1982). *Practices that improve teaching evaluation.* San Francisco: Jossey-Bass.

Gilliland, S. W., & Langdon, J. C. (1998). Creating performance management systems that promote perceptions of fairness. In J. W. Smither (Ed.), *Performance appraisal: State of the art in practice* (pp. 209–243). San Francisco: Jossey-Bass.

Glasman, N. S., & Heck, R. H. (2003). Principal evaluation in the United States. In T. E. Kellaghan & D. L. Stufflebeam (Eds.), *International handbook of educational evaluation* (pp. 643–670). Dordrecht, The Netherlands: Kluwer.

Grantham, T. C., & Ford, D. Y. (1998). Principal instructional leadership can reverse the under-representation of black students in gifted education. *NASSP Bulletin, 82,* 100–109.

Grossman, P., & Thompson, C. (2004). District policy and beginning teachers: A lens on teacher learning. *Educational Evaluation and Policy Analysis, 26*(4), 281–301.

Guion, R. M. (1998). *Assessment, measurement, and prediction for personnel decisions.* Mahwah, NJ: Lawrence Erlbaum.

Guthrie, J. W., & Reed, R. J. (1991). *Educational administration and policy: Effective leadership for American schools.* Boston: Allyn & Bacon.

Haertel, E. (1991). New forms of teacher assessment. *Review of Research in Education, 17,* 3–29.

Haertel, G. D. (1994). *Qualification, roles, and responsibilities of assessors, evaluators, and mentors in teacher evaluation.* Livermore, CA: EREAPA Associates.

Haertel, G. D., & Wheeler, P. H. (1994). *Rater effects when judging performance.* Livermore, CA: EREAPA Associates.

Halverson, R. (2004). Accessing, documenting, and communicating practical wisdom: The phronesis of school leadership practice. *American Journal of Education, 111*(1), 90–121.

Harrison, M. I. (1994). *Diagnosing organizations: Methods, models, and processes* (2nd ed.). Thousand Oaks, CA: Sage.

Heller, D. A. (2002). The power of gentleness. *Educational Leadership, 59*(8), 76–79.

Helm, V. M. (1997). Conducting a successful evaluation conference. In J. H. Stronge (Ed.), *Evaluating teaching: A guide to current thinking and best practice* (pp. 251–269). Thousand Oaks, CA: Corwin Press.

Hoerr, T. R. (1998). A case for merit pay. *Phi Delta Kappan, 80*(4), 326–327.

Hoffman, C. C., Nathan, B. R., & Holden, L. M. (1991). A comparison of validation criteria: Objective versus subjective performance measures and self versus supervisor ratings. *Personnel Psychology, 44,* 601–619.

Honaker, C. J. (2004). How leaders can enrich the school environment. *Kappa Delta Pi Record, 40*(3), 116–118.

Horn, J. (2001). *A checklist for developing and evaluating evaluation budgets.* Retrieved April 22, 2005, from http://www.wmich.edu/evalctr/checklists/evaluationbudgets.htm

Howard, B. B., & Harman, S. S. (2007, Spring). An application of the personnel evaluation standards to determine the effectiveness of a system of teacher evaluation. *ERS Spectrum: Journal of Research and Information, 25*(2), 45–55.

Howard, B. B., & McColsky, W. H. (2001). Evaluating experienced teachers. *Educational Leadership, 58*(5), 48–51.

Howard, B. B., & Sanders, J. R. (2006). Applying the personnel evaluation standards to evaluatee evaluation. In J. H. Stronge (Ed.), *Evaluating teaching: A guide to current thinking and best practice.* Thousand Oaks, CA: Corwin Press.

Howe, K., & Eisenhart, M. (1990). Standards for qualitative (and quantitative) research: A prolegomenon. *Educational Researcher, 19*(4), 2–9.

Hoy, W. K., & Tarter, C. J. (1995). *Administrators solving the problems of practice.* Boston: Allyn & Bacon.

Imundo, L. V. (1980). *The effective supervisor's handbook.* New York: AMACOM-American Management Association.

Interstate New Teacher Assessment and Support Consortium. (1995). *Next steps: Moving toward performance-based licensing in teaching.* Washington, DC: Council of Chief State School Officers.

Iwanicki, E. F. (1990). Teacher evaluation for school improvement. In J. Millman & L. Darling-Hammond (Eds.), *The new handbook of teacher evaluation: Assessing elementary and secondary school teachers* (pp. 158–171). Newbury Park, CA: Sage.

Joint Committee on Standards for Educational Evaluation. (1988). *The personnel evaluation standards. Thousand Oaks,* CA: Corwin Press.

Joint Committee on Standards for Educational Evaluation. (1994). *The program evaluation standards* (2nd ed.). Thousand Oaks, CA: Sage.

Joint Committee on Standards for Educational Evaluation. (2003). *The student evaluation standards.* Thousand Oaks, CA: Corwin Press.

Keig, L. (2000). Formative peer review of teaching: Attitude of faculty of liberal arts colleges toward colleague assessment. *Journal of Personnel Evaluation in Education, 14*(1), 67–87.

Kimball, S. M., White, B., Milanowski, A. T., & Borman, G. (2004). Examining the relationship between teacher evaluation and student assessment results in Washoe County. *Peabody Journal of Education, 79*(4), 54–78.

Kirk, J., & Miller, M. L. (1986). *Reliability and validity in qualitative research* (Qualitative Research Methods Series, No. 1). Beverley Hills, CA: Sage.

Kleinfeld, J., & McDiarmid, G. W. (1986). Living to tell the tale: Researching politically controversial topics and communicating the findings. *Educational Evaluation and Policy Analysis, 8*(4), 393–401.

Koppich, J. (2005). Addressing teacher quality through induction, professional compensation, and evaluation: The effects of labor-management relations. *Educational Policy, 19*(1), 90–111.

Kozlowski, S. W. J., Chao, G. T., & Morrison, R. F. (1998). Games raters play: Politics, strategies, and impression management in performance appraisal. In J. W. Smither (Ed.), *Performance appraisal: State of the art in practice* (pp. 163–208). San Francisco: Jossey-Bass.

Landy, F. J., Barnes, J. L., & Murphy, K. R. (1978). Correlates of perceived fairness and accuracy of performance evaluation. *Journal of Applied Psychology, 63,* 751–754.

Landy, F. J., & Farr, J. L. (1983). *The measurement of work performance: Methods, theory, and applications.* New York: Academic Press.

Lingenfelter, P. E. (2003). Educational accountability: Setting standards, improving performance. *Change, 35*(2), 18–23.

Linn, R. L., Baker, E. L., & Dunbar, S. B. (1991). Complex, performance-based assessment: Expectations and validation criteria. *Educational Researcher, 20*(8), 5–21.

Malos, S. B. (1998). Current legal issues in performance appraisal. In J. W. Smither (Ed.), *Performance appraisal: State of the art in practice* (pp. 49–94). San Francisco: Jossey-Bass.

Manasse, A. L. (1984). *A policymaker's guide to improving conditions for principals' effectiveness.* Alexandria, VA: National Association of State Boards of Education.

Manatt, R. P. (1988). Teacher performance evaluation: A total systems approach. In S. J. Stanley & W. J. Popham (Eds.), *Teacher evaluation: Six prescriptions for success* (pp. 79–108). Alexandria, VA: Association for Supervision and Curriculum Development.

Marshall, M. (1998). Using teacher evaluation to change school culture. *NASSP Bulletin, 82*(600), 117–119.

McConney, A., Wheeler, P. H., Wiersma, W., Millman, J., Stufflebeam, D., Gullickson, A., et al. (1996). *Teacher evaluation kit and data base of CREATE products* [CD-ROM]. Kalamazoo: Western Michigan University, Center for Research on Educational Accountability and Teacher Evaluation.

McGrath, M. J. (2000). The human dynamics of personnel evaluation. *School Administrator, 57*(9), 34–38.

Messick, S. (1989). Validity. In R. L. Linn (Ed.), *Educational measurement* (3rd ed., pp. 13–103). Washington, DC: American Council on Education.

Messick, S. (1994). The interplay of evidence and consequences in the validation of performance assessments. *Educational Researcher, 23*(20), 13–23.

Millman, J. (Ed.). (1981). *Handbook of teacher evaluation.* Beverly Hills, CA: Sage.

Millman, J., & Darling-Hammond, L. (Eds.). (1990). *The new handbook of teacher evaluation: Assessing elementary and secondary teachers.* Newbury Park, CA: Sage.

Monteau, P. (1987). Establishing corporate evaluation policy: Cost versus benefit. In L. S. May, C. A. Moore, & S. J. Zammit (Eds.), *Evaluating business and industry training.* Boston: Kluwer.

National Association of Elementary School Principals. (2001). *Leading learning communities: Standards for what principals should know and be able to do.* Alexandria, VA: Author.

National Board for Professional Teaching Standards. (1997). *What teachers should know and be able to do.* San Antonio: The Psychological Corporation.

National Commission on Teaching and America's Future. (1996). *What matters most: Teaching for America's future.* New York: Author.

National Staff Development Council, in cooperation with the National Association of Elementary School Principals. (1995a). *Standards for staff development (elementary school ed.).* Oxford, OH: Author.

National Staff Development Council, in cooperation with the National Association of Secondary School Principals. (1995b). *Standards for staff development (high school ed.).* Oxford, OH: Author.

National Staff Development Council. (1995c). *Standards for staff development (middle school ed.).* Oxford, OH: Author.

National Staff Development Council. (2001). *Standards for staff development* (Rev. ed.). Oxford, OH: Author.

Oldham, A. (2004). Lessons learned about standards-based teacher evaluation systems. *Peabody Journal of Education, 79*(4), 126–137.

Olsen, F. (2001, July 6). Hacker attack strikes Indiana U. for second time in 4 months. *The Chronicle of Higher Education,* p. A30.

Pearlman, M., & Tannenbaum, R. (2003). Teacher evaluation practices in the accountability era. In T. E. Kellaghan & D. L. Stufflebeam (Eds.), *International handbook of educational evaluation* (pp. 609–642). Dordrecht, The Netherlands: Kluwer.

Peters, L. H., & DeNisi, A. S. (1990). An information processing role for appraisal purpose and job type in the development of appraisal systems. *Journal of Managerial Issues, 2*(2), 160–175.

Peterson, K. (2004). Research on teacher evaluation. *NASSP Bulletin, 88,* 60–79.

Pigford, A. B. (1987). Teacher evaluation: More than a game that principals play. *Phi Delta Kappan, 69,* 141–142.

Ponticell, J. A., & Zepeda, S. J. (2004). Confronting well-learned lessons in supervision and evaluation. *NASSP Bulletin, 88,* 43–59.

Rebell, M. A. (1990). Legal issues concerning teacher evaluation. In J. Millman & L. Darling-Hammond (Eds.), *The new handbook of teacher evaluation: Assessing elementary and secondary school teachers* (pp. 337–355). Newbury Park, CA: Sage.

Rebore, R. W. (1997). *Personnel administration in education.* Englewood Cliffs, NJ: Prentice Hall.

Reeves, D. R. (2004). Evaluating administrators. *Educational Leadership, 61*(7), 52–58.

Regan, S. D. (1998). Becoming a dean: The impact of humanistic counselor training on a career in academic administration. *Journal of Humanistic Education and Development, 37*(1), 21–26.

Remington, L. R. (2002). School internal investigations of employees, open records law, and the prying press. *Journal of Law & Education, 31*(4), 459–468.

Rettig, P. R. (1999). Differentiated supervision: A new approach. *Principal, 78*(3), 36–39.

Revell, P. (2004). Why big brother must be right. *The Times Educational Supplement, 4576*, 9.

Rossow, L. F., & Parkinson, J. (1991). *The law of teacher evaluation.* Dayton, OH: Education Law Association (formerly National Organization for Legal Problems in Education, Topeka, KS).

Rowan, B., Chiang, F., & Miller, R. J. (1997). Using research on employee's performance to study the effects of teachers on students' achievement. *Sociology of Education, 70*, 256–284.

Sanders, W. L., & Rivers, S. P. (1994). The Tennessee value-added assessment system (TVAAS): Mixed-model methodology in educational assessment. *Journal of Personnel Evaluation in Education, 8*, 299–311.

Sawyer, L. (2001). Revamping a teacher evaluation system. *Educational Leadership, 58*(5), 44–47.

Scriven, M. (1988a). Duty-based teacher evaluation. *Journal of Personnel Evaluation in Education, 1*, 319–334.

Scriven, M. (1988b). Evaluating teachers as professionals: The duties-based approach. In S. J. Stanley & W. J. Popham (Eds.), *Teacher evaluation: Six prescriptions for success* (pp. 110–142). Alexandria, VA: Association for Supervision and Curriculum Development.

Scriven, M. (1990). Can research-based teacher evaluation be saved? *Journal of Personnel Evaluation in Education, 4*(1), 19–32.

Scriven, M. (1997). Due process in adverse personnel action. *Journal of Personnel Evaluation in Education, 11*(2), 127–137.

Sergiovanni, T. J. (1984). Expanding conceptions of inquiry and practice in supervision and evaluation. *Educational Evaluation and Policy Analysis, 6*, 355–365.

Shavelson, R. J., & Webb, N. M. (1991). *Generalizability theory: A primer.* Newbury Park, CA: Sage.

Shinkfield, A. J., & Stufflebeam, D. L. (1995). *Teacher evaluation: Guide to effective practice.* Boston: Kluwer.

Shulman, L. (1988). A union of insufficiencies. Strategies for teacher assessment in a period of reform. *Educational Leadership, 46*, 36–41.

Smith, M. L., & Glass, G. V. (1987). *Research and evaluation in education and the social sciences.* Englewood Cliffs, NJ: Prentice Hall.

Smith, P. L. (2001). Using multimedia portfolios to assess preservice teacher and P–12 student learning. *Action in Teacher Education, 22*(4), 28–39.

Sobel, D. M., Taylor, S. V., & Anderson, R. E. (2003). Teacher evaluation standards in practice: A standards-based assessment tool for diversity-responsive teaching. *The Teacher Educator, 38*(4), 285–302.

Society for Industrial and Organizational Psychology. (2003). *Principles for the validation and use of personnel selection procedures* (4th ed.). Bowling Green, OH. Author.

Stanley, S. J., & Popham, J. W. (Eds.). (1988). *Teacher evaluation: Six prescriptions for success.* Alexandria, VA: Association for Supervision and Curriculum Development.

Steele, B. (1997). Coaching teachers in assessment. *Scholastic Early Childhood Today, 11*, 11.

Strike, K. A. (1990). The ethics of educational evaluation. In J. Millman & L. Darling-Hammond (Eds.), *The new handbook of teacher evaluation: Assessing elementary and secondary school teachers* (pp. 356–373). Newbury Park, CA: Sage.

Stronge, J. H. (1995). Balancing individual and institutional goals in educational personnel evaluation: A conceptual framework. *Studies in Educational Evaluation, 21*, 131–151.

Stronge, J. H. (Ed.). (1997a). *Evaluating teaching: A guide to current thinking and best practice.* Thousand Oaks, CA: Corwin Press.

Stronge, J. H. (1997b). Improving schools through teacher evaluation. In J. H. Stronge (Ed.), *Evaluating teaching: A guide to current thinking and best practice* (pp. 1–23). Thousand Oaks, CA: Corwin Press.

Stronge, J. H. (2003). Evaluating educational specialists. In T. E. Kellaghan & D. L. Stufflebeam (Eds.), *International handbook of educational evaluation* (pp. 671–694). Dordrecht, The Netherlands: Kluwer.

Stronge, J. H., & Helm, V. M. (1991). *Evaluating professional support personnel in education.* Newbury Park, CA: Sage.

Stronge, J. H., Helm, V. M., & Tucker, P. D. (1995). *Evaluation handbook for professional support personnel.* Kalamazoo: Western Michigan University, Center for Research on Educational Accountability and Teacher Evaluation.

Stronge, J. H., & Tucker, P. D. (1999). The politics of teacher evaluation: A case study of new design and implementation. *Journal of Personnel Evaluation in Education, 13*(4), 339–360.

Stufflebeam, D. L. (1999a). *Evaluation plans and operations checklist.* Retrieved April 15, 2005, from http://www.wmich.edu/evalctr/checklists/plans_operations.htm

Stufflebeam, D. L. (1999b). Using professional standards to legally and ethically release evaluation findings. *Studies in Educational Evaluation, 25*, 325–334.

Stufflebeam, D. L., & Pullin, D. (1998). Achieving legal viability in personnel evaluations. *Journal of Personnel Evaluation in Education, 11*(3), 215–230.

Stufflebeam, D. L., & Pullin, D. (2001). *Legal viability checklist for personnel evaluations and personnel evaluation systems.* Retrieved September 23, 2005, from http://www.wmich.edu/evalctr/checklists/legal_viability.htm

Sullivan, K. A., & Zirkel, P. A. (1998). The law of teacher evaluation: Case law update. *Journal of Personnel Evaluation in Education, 11*(4), 367–380.

Sweeney, J. (1992). The effects of evaluator training on teacher evaluation. *Journal of Personnel Evaluation in Education, 6*(1), 7–14.

Taylor, L. K., & Shawn, J. (2003). The long and winding road to accountability. *Leadership, 32*(3), 32–33.

Thomas, G. (1999). The core work of school leaders. *Thrust for Educational Leadership, 28*(5), 24–26.

Tucker, P. D., & Kindred, K. P. (1997). Legal considerations in designing teacher evaluation systems. In J. H. Stronge (Ed.), *Evaluating teaching: A guide to current thinking and best practice* (pp. 59–90). Thousand Oaks, CA: Corwin Press.

Valente, W. D. (1985). *Education law: Public and private.* St. Paul, MN: West.

Valentine, J. W. (1992). *Principles and practices for effective teacher evaluation.* Boston: Allyn & Bacon.

Van der Linde, C. H. (1998). Clinical supervision in teacher evaluation: A pivotal factor in the quality management of education. *Education, 119*(2), 328–334.

Vanscriver, J. H. (1999). Developing rubrics to improve teacher evaluation. *High School Magazine, 7*(2), 32–34.

Weber, M. R. (2003). Coping with malcontents. *School Administrator, 60*(2), 6–10.

Wexley, K. N., & Yuki, G. A. (1984). *Organizational behavior and personnel psychology* (Rev. ed.). Homewood, IL: Irwin.

Wheeler, P. H., & Scriven, M. (1997). Building the foundation: Teacher roles and responsibilities. In J. H. Stronge (Ed.), *Evaluating teaching: A guide to current thinking and best practice* (pp. 27–58). Thousand Oaks, CA: Corwin Press.

Whitaker, T. (2003). Power plays of difficult employees. *School Administrator, 60*(2), 12–14, 16.

Wolf, K. (1996). Developing an effective teaching portfolio. *Educational Leadership, 53,* 34–37.

Wright, S. P., Horn, S. P., & Sanders, W. L. (1997). Teacher and classroom context effects on student achievement: Implications for teacher evaluation. *Journal of Personnel Evaluation, 11,* 57–67.

Zembal-Saul, C. (2002). Web-based portfolios: A vehicle for examining prospective elementary teachers' developing understandings of teaching science. *Journal of Science Teacher Education, 13*(4), 283–302.

Zimmerman, S., & Deckert-Pelton, M. (2003). Evaluating the evaluators: Teachers' perceptions of the principal's role in professional evaluation. *NASSP Bulletin, 87,* 28–37.

Zirkel, P. A. (1996). *The law of teacher evaluation: A self-assessment handbook.* Bloomington, IN: Phi Delta Kappa Educational Foundation in cooperation with the National Organization on Legal Problems in Education.

Zirkel, P. A. (2004, March/April). Evaluating teachers. *Principal, 83*(4), 10–12.

Index